INGMAR BERGMAN

FILM AND STAGE

INGMAR BERGMAN

FILM AND STAGE

ROBERT EMMET LONG

HARRY N. ABRAMS, INC., PUBLISHERS

To John and Peggy Cleveland

Project Manager: Mark Greenberg

Editor: Joanne Greenspun

Designer: Dirk Luykx

Photo Editor: John K. Crowley

Frontispiece: Ingmar Bergman talking to Bengt Ekerot, in the costume of Death, on the set of *The Seventh Seal*.

Library of Congress Cataloging-in-Publication Data
Long, Robert Emmet.
   Ingmar Bergman: film and stage / by Robert Emmet Long
      p.   cm.
   Includes filmography, bibliographical references, and index.
   ISBN 0–8109–3322–5
   1. Bergman, Ingmar, 1918–   —Criticism and interpretation.
1. Title.
PN1988.3.B47L66   1994
791.43′0233′092—dc20   93–26853

CONTENTS

Preface

FILMS OF INGMAR BERGMAN that I saw years ago, many when they first appeared in American movie houses, made a strong and lasting impression, and it has been a great pleasure in undertaking this book to return to Bergman's world. It has given me the opportunity to see his films in full—to revisit some and to discover others—and to acquaint myself with his stage work. I remember many particular moments of discovering Bergman. One night in June 1991, I was in the audience at the BAM Majestic Theater in Brooklyn, attending a performance of Eugene O'Neill's *Long Day's Journey into Night* that Bergman sent to New York for the city's International Festival of the Arts. The production was in Swedish, but through the use of headphones members of the audience were able to have a simultaneous translation into English. Bibi Andersson, who first appeared in Bergman's films playing fresh young girls, was the Tyrone mother, an older woman whose dreams of youth were in tatters; and Jarl Kulle, cast as a young lover in an early Bergman film, was her aging actor-husband whose outward success was checked by inner failure. They belonged to O'Neill's conception totally, and the spell that they and the others in the production wove over the audience was complete. Although four hours long, the play passed quickly, and at the end the audience gave it a tumultuous ovation, demanding curtain call after curtain call.

I did not know then that exactly a year later I would be in Stockholm, entering far more closely into the theater of Ingmar Bergman. At the Royal Dramatic Theater I met the members of the company, then about to leave for an engagement of *Peer Gynt* in Seville, and talked to the staff and management. I also interviewed Gunilla Palmstierna-Weiss, widow of author-playwright Peter Weiss and longtime set designer for Bergman's stage productions. Others I interviewed included Harriet Andersson, whose doomed, schizophrenic girl in *Through a Glass Darkly* was still sharply etched in my memory, and Harry Schein, a close friend and counselor of Bergman's who founded the Swedish Film Institute in 1963 and was its director for fifteen years. Bergman, who had just left for his summer seclusion on the island of Fårö, authorized this book, and I thus enjoyed the full cooperation of Svensk Filmindustri, the film-production company for which Bergman made most of his movies, and the Swedish Film Institute. A number of early Bergman films were screened for me, and I had complete access to the extensive Bergman photo archives at the Institute and at theater museums in Sweden.

In preparing this work, I also read all of the books and many of the articles published on Bergman in English. I became particularly interested in his comments on his films in interviews, including the extensive ones in the book *Bergman on Bergman*. They made me curious to find televised interviews with Bergman, which record not only what he said but also how he looked and spoke. The search took me to the Library of Congress in Washington, D.C., the Museum of Television and Radio in New York, the British Film Institute in London, and the Arkivet för ljud och bild in Stockholm.

Clearly the most strenuous was a four-hour interview (in one-hour segments) in 1981 at the Meadows School for the Arts at Southern Methodist University in Dallas, on the occasion of their honoring him with the Meadows Award for Excellence in the Arts. In these interviews, Bergman is shown seated before a group of students, whose questions he answers in fluent if slightly accented English. One is struck by his magnetic, nervously edged voice and by his restless, gesturing hands that accompany and illustrate his comments. The students obviously like him and enjoy the openness of his manner and his sense of humor. There is no formality about him: his dress is casual and at one point, indeed, he removes his shoes for the comfort of being in his stocking feet. A shy man, Bergman gives interviews only rarely, but when he does he is thoughtful, engaging, and in possession of his audience.

In a lively interview with Melvyn Bragg on the BBC's "South Bank Show," Bergman is also cordial and candid about himself, often dwelling on his shortcomings. "I am extremely pedantic," he remarks, "and torture my collaborators. When I was younger and was scared, I thought life was cruel to me. I made many walls around me to protect myself. Now I have taken those walls away." At the end of the program, as if to emphasize his point, he leaps from his seat exclaiming, "So!" and embraces his host. In a TV interview with Dick Cavett in Stockholm in 1972, Bergman is again disarmingly candid. "Until I was twelve," he remarks, "I was very happy because I lived with dreams, lived far away from the world with puppets and dolls, afraid of all animals. A scared little child, I liked to be alone." A humorous moment occurs when, joined by Bibi Andersson in the second half, Bergman tells of a problem he once had with "restless legs," which kept him from sleeping. He went to a psychiatrist seeking a cure, and after several sessions the psychiatrist told him that he was a "healthy man." "But Ingmar," Bibi Andersson interjects, "don't you remember: he told you that you were a 'neurotic man.'"

The best interview-profile appears in the documentary "Ingmar Bergman—The Director," presented on British television's Channel 4 in 1988 and narrated by the film director Lindsay Anderson. Max von Sydow, Bibi Andersson, Harriet Andersson, Erland Josephson, Liv Ullmann, Birger Malmsten, and Sven Nykvist all comment on Bergman, and clips from his films are shown, concluding with one from *Fanny and Alexander* in which the members of the Ekdahl family and household, holding hands and singing a festive song, dance

The Christmas dinner. Bergman among the diners, orchestrating the scene in *Fanny and Alexander*.

through the house at Christmastime. In a closing, held image, an elated Bergman is shown laughing. In all of these interviews what emerges is a Bergman quite different from the conception of him held by many people as simply a distant and gloomy figure. I study the interviews with close attention, acquiring some sense of the man who is so much on my mind in my research. Later it will be time to write about his films, in which Bergman is more fully revealed.

Robert Emmet Long
May 1993

Acknowledgments

I WOULD LIKE to express my grateful appreciation to Ingmar Bergman; to the Swedish Information Service in New York; the Swedish Embassy in Washington, D.C.; and the Royal Dramatic Theater, Svensk Filmindustri, and the Swedish Film Institute in Stockholm. I am also greatly and pleasurably indebted to Herman and Christina Orth, who provided me with a home to live in in the Stockholm archipelago and made many things possible for me in Sweden. Others in Stockholm to whom I owe thanks include Harriet Andersson, Ster Åke Hedstrom, Elisabet Helge, Ann-Christine Jernberg, Arne Lindahl, Rolf Lindfors, Gunilla Palmstierna-Weiss, Harry Schein, Katarina Stackelberg, and Birgitta Steene. I have especially enjoyed and benefited from many hours of conversation with Frank Gado, the most informed and searching of Bergman scholars, and from discussions with Gerhard Zeller. Nor should I forget to mention Bill Barry, Ingmar Björnsten, Harry Carlson, Mary Corliss, John Crowley (the editor), John Crowley (the scholar), Terry Geeskin, Mark Greenberg, Joanne Greenspun, Cyrus Harvey, Ron Harvey, Annette Insdorf, Barry Jacobs, Carolyn Long, Dirk Luykx, Howard and Ron Mandelbaum, Radley Metzger, Ruth Nathan, the late Bill O'Connell, Egil Tornqvist, Donald and Mary Vanouse, and Rochelle Wright. My search for photographs included the cooperation, among others, of the Museum of Modern Art, Photofest, the Everett Collection, the New York Public Library for the Performing Arts at Lincoln Center, the Library of Congress, the British Film Institute, the Drottningholms Theater Museum, the Royal Dramatic Theater, and the Swedish Film Institute. I thank them all.

Background

The veteran team of Ingmar Bergman, right, and Sven Nykvist, at camera, while shooting *Autumn Sonata*.

THE CENTERPIECE OF Bergman's personal myth is contained in his childhood in Sweden between the two World Wars.[1] Born Ernst Ingmar Bergman on July 14, 1918, at the Academic Hospital in Uppsala, he was the second son of Erik Bergman, a Lutheran clergyman, and Karin Åkerblom. His parents were, in fact, cousins, but the Åkerbloms stood higher socially than the Bergmans. Karin's mother, Anna Calwagen, who had intellectual interests and taught French at a school in Uppsala, had married Johan Åkerblom, a man twenty years older than herself who built the Southern Dalarna Railroad. By contrast, Erik's father was a middle-class pharmacist who could offer no exceptional advantages to his family and, moreover, died while Erik was still a boy. Erik's decision early in life to enter the ministry was, at least from an economic point of view, unpromising.

Among the obstacles that lay in the path of Erik's courtship of his second cousin Karin Åkerblom was that their children would be at risk of contracting a rare disease, involving progressive muscular degeneration, that ran in their families. Johan Åkerblom suffered from this condition, but it was in Erik's family as well. Later in life, Erik would be affected by the ailment, and Dag, the Bergmans' first-born son, would also fall victim to it. As Bergman relates chillingly in his autobiography, *The Magic Lantern*, Dag was totally paralyzed for twenty years before his death in 1985. Yet soon after Erik's ordination, and despite the opposition of Anna Åkerblom, the Bergmans were married.

At first Erik served as chaplain of the small mining community of Forsbacka, where he had spent most of his childhood; then a few years later he was appointed curate at the prestigious Hedvig Eleonora Church in the well-to-do Östermalm district of Stockholm. The Bergmans' circumstances were straitened, since Erik's salary was modest, and their expenses increased with the birth of their three children—Dag in 1914, Ingmar in 1918, and Margareta in 1922. But what more seriously clouded their marriage was that the parents were temperamentally at odds. Karin, who had the Åkerblom "nerves" and suffered chronically from insomnia, drew away emotionally from her husband. Tension between them, felt by all the children, became enormous. By 1925 the strains in the marriage reached an explosive point when Karin fell in love with another minister, Torsten Bohlen. Karin and Bohlen may have been tempted to run off together, but had they done so the scandal would have destroyed Bohlen's promising career. She stayed with her husband, and the couple kept up all the correct appearances required of a clergyman and his wife. But beneath the surface, the marriage continued to be troubled. Erik suffered a nervous breakdown after the Bohlen affair, and Karin spent periods of time in nursing homes.

Despite the difficulties of the marriage, Erik's situation in the church improved. In 1924, a year before the Bohlen affair, he attracted the attention of the queen by a sermon she heard him preach, and she used her influence to have him appointed chaplain to the Royal Hospital, Sophiahemmet. The appointment meant that the Bergmans would now have an attractive vicarage, a villa in the parkland adjoining the hospital. Ingmar, who was six years old at the time and was to spend much of his childhood at the vicarage, would remember as one of the pleasures of that time the bicycle trips ("festive journeys") he took with his father to churches in the Uppland district north of Stockholm. But what he recalled chiefly was the sense of his difference from other children, a profound inner isolation that had its pleasures but was often accompanied by terrifying fear.

His relationship with his mother was singular and curious. "As a child," Bergman relates, "I was in love with my mother: I found her beautiful, desirable, and unattainable. I did almost anything to purchase her tenderness."[2] But this was no easy matter: "My expressions of tenderness and my violent outbursts worried her. She often sent me away with cool ironic words and I wept with rage and disappointment."[3] Later in life, his mother told him that a famous pediatrician had warned her solemnly to reject his appeals to be caressed and enveloped with tenderness, which would damage him seriously. As it was, the beautiful, unattainable mother would have much to do with Ingmar's creative life as an adult, involving an intense preoccupation with women, perceived with a ripe sensuousness and almost always stronger and more dimensional than the men who are drawn to them.

But if the hypersensitive boy tended to exalt his mother, he cast his father in the role of a tyrant. From all accounts Erik Bergman was a popular, even beloved, minister who shone in the pulpit and particularly attracted the admiration of women. But in his domestic life he was a weaker figure than his wife, and he unwisely enjoined a system of intimidating discipline upon his sons. Dag, the mother's favorite, was treated with particular harshness that, according to Bergman, included canings. "Mother often used to sit by his bed," he comments, "bathing his back where the carpet beater had loosened the skin and streaked his back with bloody weals."[4] The father's disciplining of the boys was virtually theological in nature, with the commission of "sin" followed by confession, punishment, forgiveness, and grace. After being punished, Ingmar had to kiss his father's hand and was then formally forgiven.

But there were terrors other than corporal punishment. Chief among them was being locked in a wardrobe beside the stairs to the attic, which contained, he had been told, a tiny dwarf with razor-sharp teeth who gnawed off the feet of offending children. The experience of being locked in the wardrobe occurs or is alluded to repeatedly in Bergman's films as the epitome of childhood phobia. Whether the father had actually shut Ingmar in the wardrobe is another matter. Bergman's sister Margareta has expressed the strongest doubts that he was actually the victim of the experience he has recalled so vividly; and one of his earliest childhood friends has commented that "Ingmar never could distinguish between lie and truth, fantasy and reality."[5] At school he solemnly confided to another boy that his parents had sold him to a circus and that he would soon be taken out of school to be trained as an acrobat—a story that he had convinced himself was true. But whether real or intensely imagined, the system of punishment under which Ingmar lived at the vicarage resulted in a lasting trauma of guilt and dread of humiliation.

As important as the vicarage was, however, another household was to play a crucial role in Bergman's early years—the fourteen-room apartment of his grandmother Åkerblom in Uppsala, where he spent his summers. The apartment was arranged exactly as it had been when the grandmother came there as a bride in the 1890s. It contained "lots of big rooms with ticking clocks," Bergman recalls, "enormous carpets and massive furniture . . . the combined furniture of two upper middle-class families."[6] Ingmar enjoyed a special relationship with his grandmother, who made him feel important, and in her large, quiet apartment that seemed to him to have an air of enchantment he knew his happiest moments. "We read aloud to each other," Bergman remarks, "we invented stories, especially ghost stories or other horrors, and we also drew 'people', a kind of serial. One of us started by drawing a picture, then the other continued with the next picture and thus the action developed."[7]

The matriarchal influence on Ingmar, drawing him toward the arts, was very strong, since his mother would read aloud as part of their Sunday entertainment from such writers as Hans Christian Andersen and Selma Lagerlöf; she also introduced him to the theater. When he was twelve, he was taken to see Alf Sjöberg's production of the fairy tale "Big Klas and Little Klas" at the Royal Dramatic Theater, an experience that inspired him to build his own puppet theater in the children's room at the vicarage. His sister Margareta sewed the costumes for the toy figures, and Ingmar painted the sets, while their mother, who provided an embroidered velvet curtain for the makeshift revolving stage, looked on. As time passed, Ingmar's theatrical programs became more elaborate and were accompanied by phonograph music.

Movies also seized Ingmar's interest at an early age. In 1927 he was given a magic lantern, enabling him to project an image onto a screen, a first small step in the direction of moviemaking. A bigger one came the following year when he acquired a more sophisticated projector. The projector had been a Christmas gift to his brother Dag, but Ingmar, who coveted it desperately, arranged an exchange of most of his army of tin soldiers for this marvel. With snippets of film that he collected and glued together, he was able to project moving images onto the screen, little dramas for which he acted as narrator. His fascination with film was especially aroused when in 1930 he was taken to the film studios at Råsunda in the Stockholm suburbs. The experience, Bergman remarks, "was just like entering heaven."[8]

In 1934 the Bergmans moved up in the world when Erik was appointed pastor of Hedvig Eleonora Church and soon after made Royal Chaplain. The family moved to the Östermalm neighborhood, and Ingmar was placed in the district's Palmgren School. Following his next-to-final year, he spent a summer month in Germany at the home of a pastor and his family as part of a European exchange program. As it happened, the pastor was a committed Nazi; his son Hannes, who would later stay reciprocally with the Bergmans in Sweden, was a member of the Hitler Youth. The experience was part of an awkward episode in Bergman's life since it led to an impressionable, adolescent admiration of Hitler. The Bergman family itself, like many others in Sweden, were impressed by him, too, in the prewar years; Bergman's brother Dag was a founder and an ideologist of the National Socialist party. Only at the end of the war, when newsreels of the concentration camps were shown, did Bergman understand the enormity of the Fascist experience in Germany, and only thirty-five years after that did he acknowledge his teenage beguilement.

In 1937 Bergman passed his student examinations, which qualified him to enter Stockholm University, where he was to study literature and art history. Actually, however, little of his time was spent studying, since he devoted himself almost entirely to working with actors. The university period was particularly stressful for Bergman in relation to his father, now a prominent figure in the Lutheran church in Sweden, who expected him to prepare for one of the professions, while he himself insisted on pursuing a career in the theater ("I *will* be a great director, I *want* to be!").[9]

While at the university, Bergman was involved with an amateur dramatic group at the Mäster Olofsgården youth mission in the "Old Town" area of Stockholm, where he staged puppet shows. He also applied for a job at the Royal Dramatic Theater, and after being turned down was accepted as a production assistant at the Royal Opera House. "I was assistant to everybody," Bergman comments, "and paid nothing . . . but it helped me to learn my craft."[10] When he left the university in 1940 to devote himself entirely to the theater, his relations with his family reached a point of crisis. One day, while still living with his parents, Bergman entered into a violent argument with his father, who struck him. Bergman struck his father back, pushed his mother aside when she attempted to intercede, and moved out of the house. He did not see his parents again for four years.

Bergman moved in with Sven Hansson, the manager of Mäster Olofsgården, and plunged into further theatrical work, staging Shakespeare's *Macbeth* (a production in which he himself played Duncan) at Mäster Olofsgården and August Strindberg's *The Pelican* at Stockholm University's Student Theater. The following year, 1941, fired with ambition, he directed productions of *A Midsummer Night's Dream* and Strindberg's *The Ghost Sonata* at the Stockholm Civic Center. A turning point in Bergman's early career came in 1942, for it was then that he staged his own two-act play *The Death of Punch* at the Student Theater, which drew an unforeseen and remarkable review by Sten Selander in *Svenska Dagbladet*. "No debut in Swedish," Selander wrote, "has given such unambiguous promise for the future."[11]

Accounts differ as to how the review came to the attention of Sweden's leading film-production company, Svensk Filmindustri. According to one, Stina Bergman, widow of one of Sweden's greatest writers, Hjalmar Bergman, and head of the script department, came upon it while reading her morning newspaper. She then rang the Student Theater, obtained Bergman's telephone number, and called him. When they talked, she invited him to come to the studio to see her. He appeared at her office, shabby and unshaven, later that day. "He seemed," she recounted, "to emerge with a scornful laugh from the darkest corner of Hell," yet had a "charm so deadly that after a couple of hours' conversation, I had to have three cups of coffee to get back to normal."[12] She asked him that afternoon to come to work at Svensk Filmindustri as an assistant in the script department, an offer he gladly accepted. Thereafter he was given a desk in an office with a number of others who "washed" or polished screenplays.

Bergman's apprenticeship at Svensk Filmindustri would prove difficult at times, but circumstances favored him in some respects at the beginning. He attracted the interest of Carl-Anders Dymling, former head of Swedish Radio, who took charge of the company in 1942 and guided its renewal after a period of decline in the 1930s. He was favored, too, by the fact that Victor Sjöström, one of the great Swedish actor-directors in the silent-film era and recently appointed by Dymling as artistic director at Svensk Filmindustri, befriended him and became a kind of counselor to him. Success came early for Bergman, for in 1944 *Torment*, the first of his screenplays to be accepted by Svensk Filmindustri, was filmed by the prestigious director Alf Sjöberg. It scored not only a commercial but also a critical success, winning the Swedish Film Society's awards for Best Screenplay, Best Direction, Best Photography, and Best Actor; it later received the Grand Prix National at the Cannes Film Festival. In 1945 the production company gave Bergman his first opportunity to direct a film; and although *Crisis* did not remotely have the success of *Torment*, it did at least give him a directing credential.

While employed at the film studio, Bergman also continued to be active in the theater, and it was in the theater that he then attracted the most attention. In April 1944, when he was twenty-six, he was appointed director of the Hälsingborg City Theater, making him the youngest director of a major theater in northern Europe. The theater had a proud history but had recently been eclipsed by the opening of a new theater at nearby Malmö, which had superb facilities that included multiple stages. It was Bergman's assignment to restore the Hälsingborg theater's luster. Despite its minimal subsidy and modest facilities and salaries, Bergman acquitted himself well, directing ten stimulating productions within two seasons.

In 1946, following his success at Hälsingborg, Bergman accepted an appointment as a director at the Gothenburg City Theater, headed by Torsten Hammarén, where he would remain until 1952. It was a trying period since Bergman's and Hammarén's temperaments clashed. But Hammarén also proved a great teacher and was a lasting influence, sharpening Bergman's professionalism and making him more responsive to the suggestions of his actors. Then in 1952 he was appointed director of the City Theater in Malmö, Sweden's largest city after Stockholm and Gothenburg. The assignment was particularly attractive because it gave him the freedom to stage many different kinds of works—musicals and operettas on its large stage, and modern drama and ballet on its smaller one. Bergman was director at Malmö for six years, during which time he presented seventeen plays while at the same time directing eight films. It was one of the richest periods of his life, a time of adventurous stagings in the theaters and of his international breakthrough as a film director.

Bergman's life in this earlier phase of his career was crowded with events of both a professional and personal nature. An early love affair with a young woman with a troubled past, when he bolted from home for a bohemian life, was followed by his marriage in spring 1943 to Else Fisher, a dancer and choreographer. They had met a year earlier when she accepted his offer to supervise a pantomime program called "Beppo the Clown" at the Civic Center. Bergman's first child, Lena, was born in December 1943. The marriage ended two years later, however, when Bergman fell in love with another dancer, Ellen Lundström.

By Ellen Lundström Bergman had four more children—Eva (1945), Jan (1946), and the twins, Anna and Mats (1948). But in 1950 strife in the marriage led to divorce, and in the following year Bergman married again, this time to Gun Hagberg, a well-regarded journalist specializing in Serbo-Croatian history and current affairs, by whom he had his third son, Ingmar. But this marriage, too, soon foundered and was followed by Bergman's relationships first with Harriet Andersson and then with Bibi Andersson in the 1950s. Later in his career Bergman embarked on other marriages and had other lovers, but the early period affected his films profoundly, in their concern with the fragile nature of marital relationships and the desperation of his characters. The child support Bergman was obliged to pay to his former wives also kept him working at a hectic pace, and it was fortunate for him that he possessed the astonishing energy and willpower he did.

The one early ambition of Bergman's that did not come to term was his desire to become a playwright—the inheritor of the mantle, in fact, of Sweden's great national playwright August Strindberg. While he "washed" scripts during the day at Svensk Filmindustri and rehearsed stage productions at night, he did, somehow, find time to write plays. According to him, he wrote twenty in one year, but of these only a small number are still extant. *The Death of Punch*,[13] one of the earliest of the plays, concerns a character named Kasper (the Swedish word for Punch), who escapes a stultifying marriage by consorting with rogues in a tavern. They soon turn on him, however, forcing him to dance on a table until he drops dead from exhaustion. Brought before the Council of the Lord, he is offered an afterlife in heaven, but he prefers the torments of hell to heaven's suffocating morality, an infinite extension of what he has known in his marriage. All avenues of escape are closed for Bergman's hero, a fate that threatens the protagonists of his early films.

Tivoli,[14] presented in 1943 at the Student Theater, is set at Stockholm's Gröna Lund amusement park, where four separate stories contribute to the theme of life's futility. On the journey from childhood to adulthood, the various characters become the victims of their own failed dreams. Central to the work are the distorting prisms of the funhouse mirrors; in time they have blinded the funhouse custodian with their brilliant reflections, but they have a blinding effect, too, on those who go to the amusement park in search of gaiety and find only illusion. In a sense, they are puppets, like Kasper in *The Death of Punch*. The puppet theme is explored more elaborately in another early play, *Jack Among the Actors*.[15] In this work Jack Kasperson, a soldier, meets an aging actor named Michael Bro, preparing nervously for opening night in a provincial town. Both men take orders from those above them and lack control over their own lives. An almost surreal dimension, however, is felt in the case of the actor, since his director, strangely, has never shown himself. Near the end the director at last appears, an ugly, malignant being who has played with his actors (worthless "half-alive puppets") merely to divert himself. Tired of the tawdry game, and himself a puppet in a Godless universe, the director vanishes, and the play ends with Jack calling out piteously to God, "who must be somewhere."

In 1946 at Malmö, Bergman directed his play *Rakel and the Cinema Doorman*, in which a writer is brought to a recognition of his futility; and in the following year at Gothenburg he staged two of his other plays, *The Day Ends Early* and *To My Terror*, dealing with psychic disintegration. The three were collected under the title *Moraliteter* (*Morality Plays*) and published in book form in Sweden in 1948. Several other Bergman plays also went into production. *Draw Blank* was staged at the Hälsingborg City Theater in 1948; *The City*, which evolved from an earlier play, *Joachim Naked*, was presented on Swedish radio in 1951; and *The Murder in Barjärna* was mounted by Bergman at the Malmö City Theater in 1952. Although Bergman's plays attracted attention, he himself came to doubt his future as a playwright and increasingly devoted his time to

making films. Later in life, he spoke dismissively of the plays as "unreadable."

Bergman was right in recognizing that he had a future in films, where the powerfully focused visual image was his expressive instrument. But the plays were not merely a false start. Bergman, after all, has been a writer as well as a director. Of the forty-two feature films he directed between 1946 and 1982, he wrote original screenplays for thirty-one (in addition to two documentaries), was co-author of five others, and contributed screenplays for six films by other directors. Moreover, his background in the theater is often relevant to his film work, and his stage productions at times reflect his experience in cinema. The large body of his work in the two media makes him unique among modern filmmakers, a figure of brilliant virtuosity.

Bergman at camera, with Sven Nykvist beside him, preparing to shoot a scene in *Fanny and Alexander.*

Beginnings

Torment
(1944)

BERGMAN HAD NOT been with Svensk Filmindustri long when he made his debut as a screenwriter with *Torment* (British title: *Frenzy*). Asked by the film-production company to submit an original synopsis, Bergman fleshed out a conception that first occurred to him in the summer after he had passed his university entrance examination. The story deals with a triangular conflict involving Jan-Erik Widgren (Alf Kjellin), a student in his final year at a Stockholm Latin school; a tyrannical Latin teacher named Caligula (Stig Järrel); and a shopgirl, Bertha Olsson (Mai Zetterling), who seems born to be victimized. In the classroom Jan-Erik is harassed by Caligula, ostensibly for inattention to his work but more deeply because Caligula envies his youth and sensitivity. In scene after scene Caligula mercilessly taunts Jan-Erik, who finds consolation in a relationship that develops with Bertha, whose garret room certifies her place as an outcast. Strangely, the long shadow of Caligula falls over Bertha, too. An unnamed figure stalks her and fills her with fear, and in the end she dies under mysterious circumstances. When Jan-Erik discovers her body in her room and then comes upon Caligula lurking in the shadows of the hallway, he reports him to the police. An autopsy, however, reveals that Bertha died of a heart attack, and the schoolmaster is cleared of any blame.

right: Stig Järrel as Caligula directing his long pointer at his chief classroom victim, Jan-Erik (Alf Kjellin). Järrel's performance as the tormented Latin teacher deservedly won him the Swedish Film Society's award for Best Actor.

overleaf: Night scene between Jan-Erik (Alf Kjellin) and Bertha (Mai Zetterling), lighted expressionistically by Martin Bodin. Stairways filmed with sinister chiaroscuro effect recur throughout the film.

At the school Caligula continues his persecution of Jan-Erik and is instrumental in having him expelled only days before graduation. The two meet again when Jan-Erik goes to live in the room Bertha had occupied. But by the end of the film, his fortunes begin to take a turn for the better. He is visited by the school's sympathetic headmaster, who gives him money and steers him in a direction that will enable him to take his place in the adult world. As he leaves the room (the final shot, significantly, shows Jan-Erik outdoors in a shower of sunlight), he again encounters Caligula in the shadows of a stairwell, where the Latin master pleads piteously for understanding. "I didn't want things to be like this," he cries. "I've been ill. I didn't do it purposely! I have nobody. Four walls, bookshelves, bed, writing desk—charwoman, schoolboys, waitresses. No one cares for me. . . . They're afraid of me—but always I'm afraid of myself. . . . Turn on the light—don't leave me alone. Turn on the light! Widgren—turn on the light!" Caligula is a stunning projection of torment, a neurotic prisoner of his own distorted nature.

The impact of *Torment* comes in large part from the expressionist direction of Alf Sjöberg, who has filmed the scenes in the school and in Bertha's room with striking juxtapositions of light and dark; in a number of scenes his camera tilts at odd angles to capture steep, menacingly shadowed stairways. A particularly effective opening scene, shot from a spire of the school, looks down over a large, vacant courtyard where a small boy, late for chapel, hurries into the building in a panic. He steals up a steep staircase and along a corridor until he is discovered by a schoolmaster, who pursues him through a maze of high-ceilinged hallways. The cringing schoolboy's capture is not seen at first but heard in his shrill squeal of pain. The opening immediately establishes the school as a place of imprisonment where innocence is violated. The film's frequent shock effects belong to the genre of the horror film. When Bertha is in her garret at night and believes, although uneasily, that she is alone, the presence of the nameless intruder who haunts her is announced by the fantastically large shadow his figure casts on the ceiling.

At the same time, *Torment* depicts a world that is socially believable. The translation exercises in the Latin class have an air of absolute reality. Jan-Erik is provided with at least one school friend, a cynical fellow named Sandman (Stig Olin), who reads Nietzsche. Among the teachers at the school, a man named Pippi has a common decency lacking in Caligula, and at one point he denounces the Latin teacher to his face as a petty tyrant who can only torture other people. Jan-Erik's homelife in the well-to-do Östermalm district (a stab by Bergman at his own family home) is presided over by his civil servant father, who is a stickler for rules that govern the house and has little insight into his son. When Jan-Erik attempts to give his explanation of Caligula's charge that he has been guilty of cheating, the father does not question the Latin master's story and is concerned chiefly with the consequences for the family's standing. All of these

characters are plausible, yet, curiously, the character with the strongest reality is the fantastically perverse Caligula. His eyes, behind his spectacles, are those of a disturbed and haunted man; although Jan-Erik comes to feel alone and excluded, Caligula exists within a solitude fearful to contemplate. He attempts to make contact with others in an inhuman way, by instilling fear of him in them. Stig Järrel's is a great performance: his enclosure within himself becomes the sharpest pang felt in the picture.

The sense of oppression Jan-Erik feels at school and at home, and his attempt to escape from these constrictions, belong to Bergman's own adolescent experience. The film is filled with father figures against whom the hero rebels: Jan-Erik's father and Caligula are versions of authoritarianism, with the father a social version of Erik Bergman and Caligula a fantasized projection of the fear he inspires. Uncharacteristically for Bergman, the film's conflicts deal most directly with male characters, and the work ends with a male fantasy of the youthful hero's besting the elder man. Although *Torment* has a romantic interest in Jan-Erik's relationship with Bertha, she is so passive and easily destroyed as to be merely a pawn. The film is weakest of all in its depiction of Bertha in her relationship to Caligula, since it is never made clear why he has the hold over her that he does. It is a shadowy affair between them, spun with Gothic spookiness, and like Bertha's heart attack it is unconvincing. On its release *Torment* made a strong impression, exceeding Svensk Filmindustri's hopes for it at the box office, and winning a number of awards, including Best Screenplay for Bergman and Best Actor for Stig Järrel. It also made stars of its principal performers, Alf Kjellin and Mai Zetterling. Of incidental interest are the fleeting presence of two actors, Gunnar Björnstrand as a teacher and Birger Malmsten as a student, who will appear frequently in prominent roles in Bergman's later films. The camera passes over Malmsten's face twice. He is the handsomest of the young men who are about to graduate, but he has no lines.

left: Alf Kjellin as Jan-Erik Widgren and Mai Zetterling as Bertha. *Torment* launched them as stars in Swedish film.

right: Jan-Erik and Bertha in her room, lost in their own solitude. They are Bergman's first pair of lovers.

opposite: Jan-Erik discovers Bertha's dead body in her cramped, prisonlike quarters. This shot of Bertha looking toward her feet rather than her head, reversing a normal frontal view, reveals the hand of director Alf Sjöberg, but it will later be a signature shot, too, for Bergman.

20

Crisis

(1946)

WITH THE SUCCESS of *Torment*, Bergman hoped to be given a chance to direct a film, but no offers were forthcoming until one day in 1945, when Carl-Anders Dymling came to see him at Hälsingborg, where Bergman was installed as the bright young director of the municipal theater. Dymling had just bought a play by Leck Fischer called *Moderhjertet* (*The Mother Animal*), which had been presented on Danish radio a year earlier. He believed that this simple morality about a young woman who leaves her small town for the city, is seduced and disillusioned, and returns to the wholesome setting of the town would play well in the provinces. After none of the directors at Svensk Filmindustri would touch it, he turned to Bergman. "It was an out-and-out bit of whoredom for the public," Bergman later told an interviewer, "and no one could have called it anything else,"[1] but it was an opportunity to direct. Bergman asked only that he be allowed to write in a part for Stig Olin, one of the resident actors with his company, to which Dymling agreed.

The part that Bergman wrote in, a character named Jack, drawn from one of his own plays, altered the film considerably. Bergman is supposed to have sent a revised script to Dymling shortly before shooting, but apparently Dymling did not read it. Although the most dramatic character in the work, Jack is out of key with the rest of the story, creating a sense of two competing dramas at once. Dymling had considered *Crisis* a safe investment inasmuch as it was very modestly budgeted and would be marketed for a well-defined audience. But Bergman's conception of Jack was too sophisticated for provincial audiences.

Crisis begins in a quiet, small town where an eighteen-year-old girl, Nelly (Inga Landgré), lives with her foster mother, Ingeborg (Dagny Lind). One day they are visited by Nelly's real mother, Jenny (Marianne Löfgren), who now wants Nelly to return with her to the city to work in her beauty salon. The foster and actual mothers are a study in contrasts: Ingeborg, who has a mild, serious face, is shown teaching a small boy how to play the piano; Jenny is a woman who dresses fashionably and has a lover, Jack, who appears later in the day. That evening a ball is held in the town, which Nelly attends with an unsophisticated but sturdy young admirer named Ulf. At the ball, in a lively scene, Jack attracts Nelly's attention by his antics, interrupting a program of traditional dance music by improvising a jazz entertainment in an adjoining room.

The incident shocks the townspeople and fills Ingeborg and Ulf with a distrust of Jack. Nevertheless, Nelly goes to the city with Jenny. The country and urban settings are counterpointed as the film progresses, and at one point Ingeborg travels to the city by train and returns to her town more concerned about her foster child than ever. She has good reason. Jack is a fantasist who makes up stories about his experiences and is totally self-involved. He is convinced that life is merely a dream and that people are its marionettes. Things come to a climax one night at the beauty salon when Jack seduces Nelly, and they are discovered by Jenny. The scene ends with Jack's going out into the street and shooting himself, after which Nelly returns, sobered, to Ulf and her small town.

Crisis is burdened by its homiletic story and the melodrama of the seduction and suicide, but it has some interest for the glimpses it reveals of Bergman becoming a filmmaker. It contains the first use of mirrors in Bergman, as Jenny stares at herself in the glass near the end to confront the reality of her life, and a first dream episode when Ingeborg is aboard a train bound for the city. In the lowest of a tier of berths, she lies staring into the darkness, until her anxious thoughts become a nightmare from which she awakens badly shaken. Bergman has also modeled the scene at the beauty parlor near the end expressionistically. Neon light from the marquee of a theater flashes periodically in the window, casting an eerie illumination over a row of dummy heads on which wigs are modeled. As the scene is played out with Jack, the ex-actor, one hears a roar of laughter rising and falling from the theater. The word "Theater" flashes in the darkness outside, where Jack will blow out his brains. Oddly, the death scene appears to end with a joke. Jack's body lies in the street by the theater, his face covered with a newspaper showing a photograph of Ingmar Bergman and a caption announcing the death of the local theater director. The image was to prove prophetic insofar as Bergman "died" with his first directed film, which was savaged by reviewers and ignored by the public.

A scene from *Crisis*, Bergman's first directing assignment. Nelly (Inga Landgré), the heroine, is at the right, next to her natural mother, Jenny (Marianne Löfgren), and across from her foster mother, Ingeborg (Dagny Lind). The two older women make an interesting contrast. Jenny's plunging neckline is obviously at odds with Ingeborg's demure dress, which is fastened close to the neck with a brooch.

It Rains on Our Love

(1946)

AFTER the disappointing reception of *Crisis*, Dymling put Bergman on a back shelf as a director at Svensk Filmindustri. But rather than accept his fate stoically, Bergman approached Lorens Marmstedt, head of the smaller studio Sveriges Folkbiografer, later renamed Terrafilm, and persuaded him to give him a directing assignment. Marmstedt, who would continue to gamble on Bergman in the future, had acquired the rights to a Norwegian play called *Bra Mennesker* (*Decent People*) by Oskar Braathen. Its film adaptation as *It Rains on Our Love* is credited to Herbert Grevenius, a theater critic and playwright, and Bergman; but as Bergman acknowledges, the screenplay was almost entirely Grevenius's work.[2] The movie was shot in and around Stockholm on a lean budget in the spring and summer of 1946.

It Rains on Our Love is a realistic fairy tale that begins with a narrator (the man with the umbrella), who sets the stage and becomes one of the characters. Its principal characters are Maggi (Barbro Kollberg), a would-be actress who has become a prostitute, and David (Birger Malmsten), who has recently been released from prison. They meet on a rainy day in Stockholm's Central Station and before long decide to form an alliance that will be tested by the hard realities of the world around them. David finds a job at a garden nursery but has trouble at work, and when Maggi reveals that she is pregnant he goes off on a drunken spree before returning and offering to marry her. A minister with the soul of a bureaucrat impedes the marriage for a time, and the tiny cottage the couple buy is claimed by the town council. When David strikes the civil servant who harasses them about leaving, he is hauled into court. By the logic of events, David should be returned to prison, but instead is saved by the man with the umbrella (a *deus ex machina* figure), who acts as his attorney and gets an acquittal. At the end Maggi and David part company with the man with the umbrella at a crossroad near the edge of town. Signposts pointing in opposite directions read "Country" and "City," and they take the road to the city—to be battered by life further, no doubt, but with the pluck to survive. Another good angel may yet help them through their difficulties.

David and Maggi are stylized in such a way as to give a sense of life that borders on the tragic but is lightened by humor and whimsy. The feel of the film is French, which is to say that the style Bergman brings to it is borrowed.[3] Yet the picture has charm in its almost total lack of pretensions. Among the cast, one notices actors who will figure in Bergman's later films—Erland Josephson as the vicar's clerk, and Gunnar Björnstrand as the pestiferous bureaucrat Mr. Purman, who insists that the couple must vacate their cottage. The film won a Charlie, the Swedish Oscar, but audiences thought it slight and stayed away. *It Rains on Our Love* never recovered the cost of its production.

Woman Without a Face
(1947)

OF THE FOUR or five synopses Bergman wrote for Svensk Filmindustri at this time, two were turned into movies, but they were assigned to other directors. *Woman Without a Face* (1947) was drawn from a story Bergman wrote a year earlier called "The Puzzle Represents Eros," suggested by his entanglement with a young woman in Stockholm before his marriage in 1943 to Else Fisher. It was directed by Gustaf Molander, who had been making movies since the days of silent films and had directed *Intermezzo* (1936), which made Ingrid Bergman an international star. The story deals with a young man, recently married and a student at Stockholm University, who becomes involved with a demimonde, a kind of cousin of Somerset Maugham's Miriam in *Of Human Bondage*. Its contrast between the safe bourgeois world of Martin Grandé's wife and parents and the hazards of youthful rebellion gives it a certain resemblance to *Torment*. The resemblance is heightened by the casting of Alf Kjellin, who played Jan-Erik Widgren in the earlier film, as Martin; and of Stig Olin, Jan-Erik's school friend Sandman, as Martin's friend Ragnar Ekberg.

Martin's emotional turmoil is dramatized in the opening sequence when Ragnar arrives at his hotel room in time to save him from a suicide attempt. Ragnar then goes to see the young woman, Rut Köhler (Gunn Wållgren), with whom Martin has been involved, and as they talk the film moves into a long flashback, beginning with the time that she and Martin first met. Abandoning his wife and children, Martin enters into an affair with Rut, but before long (the time is 1944) he is drafted into the army. Unable to stay away from her, he deserts and returns to Stockholm. The two hide out together in a series of dismal quarters, including an empty warehouse loft (one of a number of isolated retreats to which Bergman's young lovers escape). Recognizing that Martin must leave Sweden, Rut goes to see her mother and coerces money from her mother's lover, Victor, who had sexually abused her as a child. But when Rut produces the money that can buy his passage out of the country, Martin believes she has come by it through tawdry sexual transactions and, disgusted by the depths to which he has fallen, leaves her. He returns to his wife and manages to avoid a court-martial on the grounds of having suffered a nervous breakdown. But Rut retaliates for his having left her in a terrible scene at the hotel in the opening of the film, following which Martin attempts suicide by slashing his wrists. At the end, Martin leaves Sweden for a period of recuperation in America, and at the station his wife, Frida, and Rut meet and talk. Rut has had a change of

25

heart, and Frida is civil to her; what she feels toward her rival now is chiefly pity. Like the forced happy ending, the film is burdened by clichés, and the characters lack dimension. Although reviews were harsh, the public went to see the movie. Its story of a handsome, ingenuous young man of good family who is brought down by a *femme fatale* seemed a steamy situation.

Ship to India

(1947)

ALTHOUGH MARMSTEDT gambled and lost on Bergman in *It Rains on Our Love*, he took a chance on him again with *Ship to India*, based on Martin Söderhjelm's play *Skepp till Indialand*, recently produced at the Swedish Theater in Helsinki. Bergman wrote the screen adaptation with Marmstedt while the two

opposite: Sally (Gertrud Fridh) and Johannes (Birger Malmsten) begin a romance that will wreck the captain's unrealistic dreams.

below: Much of *Ship to India,* Bergman's second directing assignment, is set aboard the salvage vessel of Captain Alexander Blom (Holger Löwenadler), shown here as he dreams of sailing to foreign ports of call. In his review of the film, French critic André Bazin declared that Bergman had created "a world of blinding cinematic purity."

bottom: Birger Malmsten, in the first of many leading roles in Bergman's early films, is shown here as Johannes Blom, the captain's thwarted son. The shot captures the sense of Johannes's spiritual imprisonment.

were together in Nice, and the film was shot by Bergman on a tiny budget in Stockholm in the summer of 1947.[4] *Ship to India* is unlike Bergman's previous movies in that it deals with socially marginal people inhabiting the Stockholm waterfront—the captain of a salvage vessel who is going blind and is obsessed with sailing to exotic lands of his dreams before his vision fails; his hunchbacked, ineffectual son, whom the captain oppresses and against whom he rebels; the captain's wife, who has been emotionally broken in her marriage; and a girl from a music-hall revue with whom the captain hopes to sail away to distant ports—before she and his son fall in love. A story of frustrated desire involving intense emotional conflicts, it is reminiscent of O'Neill and Strindberg.

Ship to India opens in the present, when Johannes Blom (Birger Malmsten), in the merchant-marine service, returns to the Stockholm waterfront, and then fades into a long flashback in which the events of seven years earlier are shown. Johannes was then a youth broken in morale as the "crippled" son his father despises. In a startling early image, as Captain Blom (Holger Löwenadler) makes a disdainful reference to his son, the viewer sees a pair of eyes belonging to the maimed Johannes peering over a pile of the ship's rope. A confrontation follows in which Johannes draws a knife on the captain, only to reveal himself as a weakling when, after his father strikes him across the face, he drops the knife and slinks away beaten. All of the characters, however, are stymied. The dance-hall girl Sally (Gertrud Fridh) has been used by men and denied a sense of identity; when she is picked up by Captain Blom, she merely becomes an adjunct to his obsessions. His obsessions, growing out of his thwarted life, are destructive to himself and others. The most his wife, Alice (Anna Lindahl), has to look forward to vindictively is the day her husband becomes blind and will be totally dependent upon her.

Things go awry for Blom when Johannes and Sally fall in love. In a scene typical of the early Bergman, they go out in a rowboat to a deserted windmill, where they make love. On their return, Captain Blom, who has quickly grasped the situation, whips Johannes across the face with his gloves; but this time Johannes strikes him back, and Sally denounces Blom as a "miserable, frustrated old man." Before long Blom attempts to do away with his son, cutting the cord to his oxygen supply after sending him down to dive for salvage. When Johannes is rescued, Blom flees to a room in the city where he keeps ship models associated with his dreams of escape. After the police come to take him away, he hurls himself through a window, and although he does not die he will be a thoroughly broken man. The ending of the film returns to the present, as Johannes looks up Sally and the two leave together on a ship.

The atmosphere of *Ship to India* appears to have been influenced by Marcel Carné,[5] one of Bergman's favorite directors in the 1940s. Like Carné's characters on the Parisian waterfront, Bergman's inhabit an urban proletarian twilight in which not much hope exists—

27

The waterfront cabaret where Captain Blom meets Sally, with whom he plans to begin a new life.

although Bergman supplies a happy ending. A number of structural problems hamper the film. Captain Blom is too important a character to disappear from the movie after his suicide attempt. It is also odd that Johannes takes seven years to return. And I had trouble with the hump on Johannes's back that goes away once he achieves his manhood. In France at least the movie drew favorable reviews, but it was little noticed in Sweden and failed commercially.

Night is My Future
(1948)

DESPITE THE FACT that Bergman had yet to make a film that made money, Marmstedt gave him another opportunity to direct. The new film, *Night is My Future* (British title: *Music in Darkness*), was drawn from Dagmar Edqvist's popular 1946 novel (Edqvist herself did the screenplay) about a young man who comes to accept a woman's love after going blind. Bergman recalls that as they initiated the venture Marmstedt told him: "Ingmar, you are a flop. Here's a very sentimental story that will appeal to the public. You need a box-office success now."[6] Marmstedt kept watch over Bergman this time with an eagle eye to see that he did not deviate from the story. He appeared on the set on a daily basis to supervise the shooting of the movie and later had an active role in its editing. Marmstedt's instincts about the appeal of the story proved to be well founded; the picture attracted an audience and managed to turn a profit.

Its plot is uncomplicated. Bengt Vyldeke (Birger Malmsten), while attempting to rescue a puppy that has wandered into the firing range of his army training unit, is gravely wounded. Waking from a stunningly photographed hallucinatory dream following an eye operation, he finds that he is blind. At his family's home in the country, he begins an adjustment to his new life by playing the organ in the local church. Ingrid Olofsdotter (Mai Zetterling), a poor girl from the

Birger Malmsten as Bengt Vyldeke, who will awake from his operation to find that he is blind.

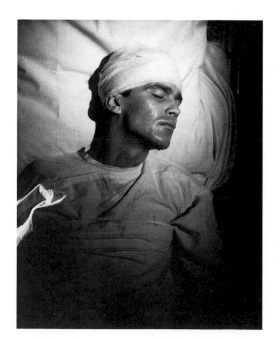

Mai Zetterling as Ingrid Olofsdotter, the poor girl who will prove Bengt's salvation. Lorens Marmstedt, who produced the sentimental film, told Bergman: "You need a box-office success now."

area, becomes a servant in the house and not only looks after Bengt but also begins to fall in love with him. But when she overhears a slighting remark he makes about her lower-class origins, in response to a relative's suggestion that he might consider marrying her, she leaves to study at a teachers' college. Bengt goes out to face the world alone and has many disillusioning experiences in a series of jobs, including a period as a café pianist in which people take ferocious advantage of him. By the end, after surmounting many difficulties, Bengt and Ingrid are united again and begin a new life teaching at a school. By its very nature *Night is My Future* is sentimental, but Bergman handled his assignment with tact and professionalism, and the film is memorable for a fine performance by Mai Zetterling that combines modesty and radiance.

Port of Call

(1948)

IN 1948 Svensk Filmindustri approached Bergman, asking if he would make a screen adaptation of a manuscript called *The Gold and the Walls*, which had been submitted to them by the Gothenburg writer Olle Länsberg. He would not only write the film but also direct it. After Bergman agreed, he and Länsberg worked together on the screenplay, and Bergman shot the film on location in Gothenburg in the summer of 1948. Concerned as it is with the social conditions of working-class people, *Port of Call* is an unusual film for Bergman. An important influence, readily acknowledged by Bergman, was Italian neorealism, particularly of Roberto Rossellini, in whose *Open City* (1946) he heard "the melody of postwar thought."[7] The semi-documentary style of Rossellini, he told an interviewer, was a "revelation—all that extreme simplicity and poverty, that greyness."[8] He added that the many different styles of his films thus far were the result of his having no style of his own: "I still had nothing of my own to offer. . . . I had no independence at all. . . . I just grabbed helplessly at any form that might save me."[9]

The film opens on the Gothenburg docks, where Gösta (Bengt Eklund), a twenty-nine-year-old sailor who has just returned from eight years at sea, witnesses a commotion caused by the drowning attempt of a young girl named Berit (Nine-Christine Jönsson). Following her rescue, Gösta meets her at a dance hall in the waterfront district. The two return to her house and sleep together, but the following morning, after the seaman leaves, Berit's mother appears and it becomes apparent that their relationship is filled with conflict. The mother's spitefulness that has driven away her husband is concentrated now on Berit, whom she berates for her misconduct in the past.

Flashbacks that follow reveal how Berit has attempted to escape from her quarrelsome home, been locked out by her mother, and been sent to a girls' reformatory. She is even now on probation while working in a ball-bearing factory near the waterfront. Things worsen for Berit when the mother reports her evening with the seaman to the probation authorities and when she reveals her past to Gösta on a second date. A cut above the average seaman and rather naïve, Gösta is disillusioned and gets drunk with a whore. After these and other complications, the two plan to go away together on a boat in the harbor, but in the end they decide to stay and make the best of it, and the film closes on a note of qualified hope.

Authority figures in the film are treated unsympathetically. Berit's mother, a sanctimonious hypocrite, seems determined to punish others for any happiness they might have in their lives, and the probation officers, male and female, are faceless bureaucratic functionaries. The workplace, furthermore, with its routinized drudgery

The lives of Gösta (Bengt Eklund) and Berit (Nine-Christine Jönsson) in *Port of Call* are marginal and unpromising. Neither has a trace of glamour.

and leering male co-workers, provides Berit with no source of fulfillment; the fate that threatens her is one of emotional starvation. *Port of Call* begins well with its views of the city's hive of industrial works, accompanied by the driving musical score of Erland von Koch, and it offers a number of effective realistic scenes in which, for example, Gösta and Berit are shown at work, in a dance hall, and at an amusement park. Berta Hall as Berit's mother is real enough to get on one's nerves, and both Gösta and Berit are carefully deprived of any glamour. Significantly, the cinematographer for the film was a relative newcomer named Gunnar Fischer, who would soon begin a steady, longtime collaboration with Bergman.

But if *Port of Call* is influenced by Italian neorealism, it never fully captures its naturalness. When Berit's friend Gertrud dies of a bungled abortion attempt, it seems contrived to call attention to the disparity in the medical treatment available to the rich and the disadvantaged. Bergman attempts as far as possible to enter into Länsberg's concern with the problems of proletarian characters, but his direction lacks a sense of passionate commitment. In the early 1950s, he will use elements from *Port of Call* in *Summer with Monika*, in which a young couple who work at drab jobs in the city attempt to escape together. But in that film there is no interest in social issues, and the young lovers, by contrast with the ones in *Port of Call*, are imagined poetically and possess the resonance of life.

31

Eva
(1948)

BERGMAN as screenwriter and Gustaf Molander as director collaborated a second time, for the film *Eva*, which concerns a young man's (and Bergman's own) attempt to come to terms with death. Drawn from Bergman's first unstaged play, *The Station*, the picture begins with the return home on leave of Bo Fredriksson (Birger Malmsten), a trumpeter in the navy. His arrival at the local train station quickly dissolves into a flashback of Bo as a twelve-year-old boy, who runs away from home and meets an improbable but charming little band of touring performers (a yodeling trio), together with their blind ten-year-old daughter Marthe. The film then returns to Bo's reception at home in the present, and his visit to a neighboring family, the Berglunds. There Bo meets and later makes love to their niece Eva (Eva Stiberg)—an episode that occurs as Mr. Berglund lies dying, tended by his devoted wife, and prompts another flashback in which Bo, as a boy, with little Marthe, climbs aboard an untended switch engine standing on the tracks and sets it in motion. The adventure soon turns to horror as the locomotive derails and little Marthe is killed. Bo is savagely beaten by his father, and thereafter the trauma of death and guilt will haunt him into his adult life.

Bo's adult life is shown in another flashback. After he leaves the navy, he becomes a jazz trumpeter in Stockholm, sharing digs with another musician, Göran (Stig Olin), and his wife, Susanne (Eva Dahlbeck), who is sexually attracted to Bo. In what seems to be actually happening but is really a dream, Susanne goads Bo to do away with Göran. While Göran lies unconscious in a closed room, Bo cuts the gas hose—only to awaken from his dream on a bright sunlit morning to find Eva, who has come to Stockholm, beside him in the room. A year after this second incident in which death and guilt are linked, Bo and Eva are married and living in the Stockholm archipelago, a private preserve of sunlight and spiritual health. Eva is pregnant, and they are expecting the birth of their first child. Then one day (World War II is in progress), the body of a German soldier washes up on shore, and Bo is again assailed by the presence of death. The shock of their discovery of the dead man also precipitates Eva's labor pains, and Bo rows his wife in a boat to a medical station, where the baby is born. At the end Bo holds the infant in his arms, against the expansive background of the sea, and declares the lifting of his dread of death in the presence of the miracle of life. *Eva* suffers from melodramatic plotting and an over-urged release from dread, but contains some fine moments. The elderly Berglund couple and the husband's death are so sensitively handled that they would not be out of place in one of Bergman's later films.

Prison

(1949)

*P*rison (British title: *The Devil's Wanton*) has special relevance to Bergman's emergence as a director in the 1940s, since it is the first film he made that was wholly under his own control. He was the sole author of the screenplay, which he directed in a bold new style. In preparing the script, Bergman drew from his earlier seventy-page tale called "True Story." When he showed it to Carl-Anders Dymling at Svensk Filmindustri, it was turned down and Bergman applied once again to Lorens Marmstedt at Terrafilm. Although Marmstedt suspected, correctly, that it would be a commercial failure, he nevertheless agreed to produce it. He did, however, impose the strictest austerities on the project, which was budgeted at a mere $30,000, half the usual cost of the production company's films. To contain expenses it was shot in only eighteen days, and the actors worked for half their normal salaries.

With a bow to the German expressionists, whose films Bergman had been collecting, the picture opens with a mysterious figure wrapped in a dark overcoat hurrying across a lot to a building in the distance, which houses the studio of the film director Martin Grandé (Hasse Ekman). Once inside, the visitor is revealed as Martin's former mathematics professor, Paul (Anders Hendrikson), who has recently been released from a mental institution. He tells Martin of his idea for a film in which life is hell, with evil triumphant. Martin and his colleagues are skeptical of the idea, but later Martin's friend Tomas (Birger Malmsten), a writer, recalls an interview he had with a prostitute that bears out the professor's thesis. This story-within-the-story is then "visualized" by Bergman.

Birgitta-Carolina Söderberg (Doris Svedlund) is a prostitute living in Stockholm's Gamla Stan district with her fiancé and pimp Peter (Stig Olin) and his sister Linnéa (Irma Christensson). In her first appearance, she has been severely beaten in the course of her prostitution, but when she is shown next she is in bed in Peter's apartment with the infant to whom she has given birth. Peter and Linnéa persuade her to give them the child, despite her fears that they will kill it—as they do. Birgitta's life then touches that of Tomas, whose relationship with his wife, Sofi (Eva Henning), has also reached a point of desperation. When his talk of their committing suicide becomes serious, Sofi strikes him on the head with a bottle, and when he comes to he believes that he has murdered her. He goes to the police to confess, but after he leads them to the apartment they can find no body. On the street outside the police station, Tomas meets Birgitta, whom he had interviewed for his article six months earlier and who has just been interrogated by the police in connection with the baby's death. Before long Tomas and Birgitta do what a series of Bergman's

Birgitta-Carolina Söderberg (Doris Svedlund), a girl much abused by life. Is the world ruled by Satan?

Birger Malmsten as the writer Tomas and Doris Svedlund as Birgitta-Carolina watch a comic sequence from a silent film in which Death pursues a frightened man in a nightshirt around his room.

couples have done earlier—escape to a private sanctuary, in this case the attic of a boardinghouse.

Here they find an old movie projector and some strips of film, and with the delight of children they view a silent-film farce. In the comedy a man in a nightshirt is awakened by the appearance of a burglar, who chases him around the room. A large, hideous spider is suddenly seen suspended by a filament from the ceiling, and when the man in the nightshirt attempts to hide in a chest, the skeletal figure of Death pops out. Then a policeman arrives and the three characters pursue each other in antic confusion until Death chases all three out of the window. The farce forms a concise summary of the film's story of psychic fear, flight, and extinction.

Tomas and Birgitta make love and find a momentary sense of release. But when she falls asleep, Birgitta has a disturbing, luminously photographed dream that evokes her guilty anguish over the death of her baby. As she wanders in a misty terrain strewn with leaves, a melancholy wind sighs through the barren trees that stand about her. She encounters darkly clad figures who turn their backs on her and is offered a glittering jewel (by implication a baby) by a girl dressed in black. She then goes over to a man by an overturned car whom she believes is Tomas, but when he turns to look at her he has the grim face of Death. Recoiling from this figure, Birgitta sees Peter take a plastic doll from a pan of water. In a moment the doll becomes a fish, which Peter destroys with wrenching twists of his hands before placing it back in the water, and Birgitta awakens.

After Birgitta returns to Peter and Linnéa, and Tomas's protective presence is removed when his wife, Sofi, appears and she and Tomas leave together, her desperation increases. Peter brings home one of his former clients and leaves him alone with Birgitta, even though he knows of the man's sadism; when Birgitta refuses him, he burns her with his cigarette butt, and she seeks sanctuary in the basement of the building. In the basement earlier she had met a small boy dressed in an Indian outfit who had sought to escape from his

Birgitta-Carolina alone in a basement hiding place as she prepares to slash her wrists. Bergman called *Prison* "a morality play for the cinema."

mother. The hunting knife he left behind now becomes the instrument of Birgitta's suicide: she cuts her wrists and dies slowly in the darkness. In death she lies in a shaft of light coming from a barred window, which Jörn Donner has called a "light of mysticism, a light of grace and mercy."[10]

In the course of the film, church bells are heard, and one notices that a number of characters have names with religious connotations—Tomas and Paul and Peter. But Peter here is merely a figure of destructiveness, at whose hands the girl is brought to misery and death. *Prison* ends as it began, with the film director and his colleagues in the studio. They discuss the professor's idea but conclude that it cannot be made into a film since it can have no resolution. If God does not exist, to whom can the question of meaningless suffering in life even be asked? As the group leaves the studio, an overhead light is left burning, providing a single shaft of illumination that seems to comment on the ray of "mystical" light falling over the dead Birgitta. Cigarette smoke hanging in the air has been marvelously photographed to give the impression of a white cloudlike luminousness, all around which lie emptiness and darkness.

Prison is the gem of Bergman's filmmaking in the 1940s, but it is also seriously flawed. At times it is difficult to follow, a problem compounded by the only available print of it for an English-language audience, in which the white subtitles are sometimes set against a white background and thus disappear. The film suffers, too, from Bergman's manipulation of Birgitta into martyrdom, and from its shaky thesis that Birgitta's experience proves that Satan rules the world. What gives excitement to *Prison* is Bergman's dramatic use of imagery that foretells his later work. Its emotional voltage comes in part, one would think, from Bergman's marital experience. Tomas stands in for him, a husband on the verge of breakdown and despair, an emotional state akin to the anguish of Bergman's childhood, reflected in Birgitta, of outraged innocence, paralysis, and fear of the outer world.

Three Strange Loves

(1949)

BIRGER MALMSTEN and Eva Henning, the unhappily married couple in *Prison,* reappear in related roles in *Three Strange Loves,* which was made in the same year as *Prison* but is strikingly different in form and style. Its source was a collection of three stories called *Törst* (*Thirst*) by Birgit Tengroth that had recently been published in Sweden. The screen adaptation was by Herbert Grevenius, who had collaborated with Bergman on the screenplay of *It Rains on Our Love* and would continue the collaboration in the next few years. At the inception of the project, Bergman was busy preparing to stage Jean Anouilh's *A Wild Bird* and Tennessee Williams's *A Streetcar Named Desire* at the Gothenburg City Theater, but the two conferred on a regular basis at a Gothenburg café after Grevenius concluded his writing for the day and Bergman finished his rehearsals.[11] Produced by Svensk Filmindustri, which with few exceptions would finance all of Bergman's films in the time immediately ahead, *Three Strange Loves* scored a modest success at the box office, doing better than any of Bergman's films up to that time.

Like *Prison,* the film reveals Bergman beginning to emerge from his apprenticeship. It creates a modern world, focusing on marital relationships, and with a new emphasis on women and their points of view. It also has a new ease and fluidity of movement in which seriousness is lightened by moments of humor. The picture incorporates three separate but interrelated stories, but the main one concerns a couple returning to Sweden aboard a train, in which the cramped quarters of their compartment reinforce the sense of their confinement within a marriage that is like a private hell. Bertil (Birger Malmsten), an art historian and collector of ancient coins, and his wife, Rut (Eva Henning), a former ballet dancer, are returning from a

above: Bertil (Birger Malmsten) and Rut, the unhappily married couple in *Three Strange Loves*. They have stopped at a hotel in Basel before continuing their train journey to Sweden. Even at the opening of the film it is evident that differences divide them.

trip to Sicily. First seen in a hotel room in Basel as they awake in the morning, they give the impression of being distant from one another. While Bertil lies in bed, Rut smokes a cigarette and broods. On the train, as the conflict between them grows more intense, their backgrounds are revealed in flashbacks. One shows Rut as a student in ballet school, where she is wholly absorbed by her dancing (Naima Wifstrand, as the ballet teacher who wears a black beret and has a cigarette dangling from her lip, is, as always, wonderful). Another goes back to an affair Rut had with an army captain that was broken off when his wife learned of it. After Rut tells him that she is pregnant, he denies that he is the father and pressures her into having an abortion, which leaves her unable to bear children. Now too old in early middle age to continue with her dancing, and unable to have a family, Rut seethes with frustration.

In crosscuts to other lines of plot, Bertil's former wife, Viola, played by Birgit Tengroth, who also wrote the book on which the film was based, is on the edge of a nervous breakdown. In an overwrought state she sees a psychiatrist, who tries to seduce her; later she meets a former friend from the ballet school who turns out to be a lesbian, and another seduction attempt occurs. A woman with a desperate longing to escape from herself and her situation, Viola projects a mood that parallels the state of mind of Rut on the train. Meticulous and pedantic, Bertil defensively studies an antique coin, and Rut, also locked into herself, drinks too much and has outbursts of hysteria in which she tells Bertil how much she hates him.

In a dramatic scene, without knowing that Bertil stands behind her in the corridor, Rut stares out the window of an unlocked exit door into the darkness that rushes past the fast-moving train. Realizing that she is on the verge of jumping, he steals up behind her, grasping her shoulder with one hand, and when she turns she falls into his arms while the train's whistle sounds a long, shrill scream. The film's ending juxtaposes scenes from its different plots. Viola drowns herself in Sweden on Midsummer's Night against an ironic background of music, dancing, and human contact, and Bertil has a nightmare in which he murders Rut, only to awaken in a sweat to find her alive. It comes to him now that he does not want to lose her, although nothing between them will change. To be alone, he tells her, "would be even worse than the hell we are living in. After all, we have each other." Bergman's use of multiple story lines relies at times on some rather strained points of intersection, most obviously when Rut and Bertil look out the train window to see Rut's captain and his wife in the window of a train passing theirs. But on the whole, the film is engaging and skillfully handled. One would like to see more of Rut and Bertil, whose marital ambivalence projects one into the near future of Bergman's films in which the situation of marriage is a distinctive, recurring theme. *Three Strange Loves*, written in the aftermath of Bergman's own marriage gone bad to Ellen Lundström, prepares the brew.

The Rose Period

To Joy

(1950)

Bergman filming *Summer with Monika* in the Stockholm archipelago. "For everyone," cinematographer Gunnar Fischer recalled, "it was our happiest film."

THE 1950s, which were to prove one of Bergman's richest periods in filmmaking, are often called his "Rose Period," a time when, as in the case of Picasso, to whom the term was originally applied, he found his distinctive style. But as the fifties began, Bergman's career was in trouble, and it was a time of lowered morale. Tired by the hectic pace of his stage and film work and dejected by the hostile reception of *Prison*, Bergman took a trip to the French Riviera with Birger Malmsten and during a two-month holiday wrote the screenplay of *To Joy*.[1] Its story of a troubled marriage derives from his Mediterranean afterthoughts about his marriage to Ellen Lundström. In the new film he places the blame for the failure of the relationship on the young musician protagonist, who has been so absorbed by his sense of his budding greatness as an artist that he puts his career above his marriage. His eventual recognition that he has overestimated his talent and his resigned acceptance of his limitations reflects Bergman's own state of mind when the script was written. "I thought to myself," Bergman remarks, "'even if one is only a mediocrity, still one must function.' So then I made up some sort of consolation for myself. That it's the infantry who are important in culture, not the more dashing cavalry."[2]

The movie begins with a rehearsal of the Hälsingborg Symphony Orchestra and a telephone call informing Stig (Stig Olin), a violinist, that his wife and one of their children have died in an explosion of a kerosene stove at their cottage in the Stockholm archipelago. A long flashback shows Stig as he is starting out with the orchestra, his vaulting ambition, humiliating failure as a soloist, the breakup of his marriage, and his eventual reconciliation with his wife. The picture ends in the present when, faced with his new losses, Stig recognizes the joy in life and art that lies beyond pain and despair. Bergman's direction of *To Joy*, which received miserable reviews, seems half-hearted. But the problem lies partly in his script, which is clichéd at important points. The sudden death of Martha (Maj-Britt Nilsson) and one of their children in the stove explosion is unconscionably melodramatic; and the concert-hall scene, where Stig's little boy looks on bravely as the orchestra plays the stirring "Ode to Joy" movement of Beethoven's Ninth Symphony, is too obviously designed to provide an emotional, uplifting ending. But there are some good things in the film. Victor Sjöström as the orchestra conductor Sönderby, who plays a mentor role to Stig, projects a rich humanity and has one of the great faces in Bergman's films. Maj-Britt Nilsson is also an asset and was praised by Bergman for "her way of letting everything be born on the spur of the moment. Her ability to express complexities . . . [her] absolute naturalness."[3]

While the City Sleeps
(1950)

BY 1950 the Swedish film studios were preparing to close down to protest the steep government tax on movie-theater tickets that was keeping audiences away from cinemas. Heavily burdened by his financial obligations to two ex-wives and five children, and alarmed by the prospect of being without work, Bergman resorted to a number of inconsequential film projects that could be made before the shutdown occurred.[4] *While the City Sleeps*, which was made at that time, is one of the worst films with which Bergman was associated. His connection with it, however, was merely marginal, since he did no more than provide a synopsis of Per Anders Fogelström's novel *Ligister* (*Delinquents*), which was then adapted for the screen by Fogelström and Lars-Eric Kjellgren, who directed. The movie concerns a group of Stockholm juvenile delinquents led by a particularly incorrigible type named Jompa (Sven-Eric Gamble), who burglarizes a house, gets his girlfriend pregnant, and after being forced to marry her steals money from his father-in-law's boss, stages a break-in of a pawnshop in the course of which he kills its owner, is pursued by the police, and is finally apprehended. The movie, which surprisingly is still in circulation (having been shown on Swedish television while I was in Stockholm in 1992), drags on without much point and without by the end being able to decide whether Jompa is the product of society's neglect of its lower-class youth or is innately depraved.[5]

This Doesn't Happen Here
(1950)

This Doesn't Happen Here (British title: *High Tension*), also shot in 1950, was made to capitalize on the vogue of the international spy thriller. Herbert Grevenius adapted it for the screen from Waldemar Brøgger's novel *I løpet av tölv timer* (*Within Twelve Hours*), and it was directed by Bergman. The film concerns Baltic refugees during the cold war attempting to defect to the West and is set in a country that is unnamed but obviously Sweden. Atkä Natas (Ulf Palme) arrives in the country on a diplomatic passport with incriminating papers in his briefcase. Before long he meets his wife, Vera (Signe Hasso), and many complications ensue. Natas is abducted and then becomes an agent for his abductors; police inspector Björn Almkvist (Alf Kjellin) becomes involved, and there are car chases across Stockholm. Cornered at the end, Natas jumps to his death from the terrace of the outdoor elevator of a tall building overlooking the harbor. Bergman's direction is a skillful parody of Hitchcock's, but the film is without substance, as Bergman well knew. It helped him to negotiate his survival, but embarrasses him today.

Summer Interlude

(1951)

A shot of Marie (Maj-Britt Nilsson) concentrating on her legs as she dances for Henrik (Birger Malmsten) in *Summer Interlude*. The scene occurs at her cottage in the Stockholm archipelago, where the summer romance ends abruptly with Henrik's death.

IN THIS SAME turn-of-the-fifties period of work for hire, Bergman made a film, *Summer Interlude*, that surpasses all others he had done up to that time. Shot in Stockholm and its archipelago in spring 1950 (but delayed in its release until 1951), it follows close upon *Three Strange Loves* and, like that picture, reveals the blossoming of new gifts and individuality. Bergman himself was conscious of *Summer Interlude* as the first film in which the medium of cinema "obeyed" him. "This was my first film," he remarks, "in which I felt I was functioning independently, with a style of my own, making a film all my own, with a particular appearance of its own."[6] The origins of *Summer Interlude* go back to a story called "Mari," written by Bergman in the summer before he entered Stockholm University. When he went to work for Svensk Filmindustri, he proposed it as the basis for a film, but the management had no interest in it, and Bergman revised the story thereafter a number of times. In 1950 he collaborated with Herbert Grevenius on a screen version that, at Grevenius's urging, was developed from the original draft.[7]

The movie opens in the present at the Royal Opera in Stockholm during a dress rehearsal of *Swan Lake*. The principal character is Marie (Maj-Britt Nilsson), a ballerina, to whom a book is delivered backstage. It is the diary she kept long ago on an island in the Stockholm archipelago when she and a university student, Henrik (Birger Malmsten), had a love affair that turned to tragedy when he died in a swimming accident. The diary, which has been sent by her Uncle Erland (Georg Funkquist) to spite her, awakens her memory of the past, and before long she takes a boat to the island where the love affair had taken place. The film employs several flashbacks—of her earlier boat trip to the island, her revisiting the cottage where she stayed when she and Henrik were in love, and her return from the island to the city. The picture ends in the present with the opening night of *Swan Lake*. Having confronted and relived the painful past,

Marie is now able to accept the still-remaining chance for life represented by David (Alf Kjellin), a journalist who waits for her in the wings. A remarkable feature of *Summer Interlude* is that although the underpinnings of the narrative (ideal love, tragic death, and self-recovery) are clichés, Bergman lifts the story into delicate and moving art.

One might wonder, in view of the emotional fidelity of Bergman's treatment, if the story did not have some basis in his own experience; and he has, in fact, acknowledged that Marie was inspired by a girl he knew in his youth who contracted polio. "I was writing," he remarks, "about something which had hurt." He adds that there are reflections of himself in a number of the characters: "There's an awful lot of myself in Marie, . . . the ballet-master, and the somewhat world-weary and scabby journalist."[8] His strongest involvement, however, is with Marie, and the film marks the point at which Bergman begins to identify with women, placing them at the center of consciousness in his pictures. Maj-Britt Nilsson is a sympathetic Marie, able to suggest a range of inner experience by subtle means, and in many ways *Summer Interlude* is her film.

Nowhere in Bergman before has there been such an enveloping poetic atmosphere, together with a sense of space and light, captured with luminous clarity in the camerawork of Gunnar Fischer. The Stockholm archipelago becomes the setting of a summer idyll that is at the same time filled with a sense of the imminence of death. The film works with many contrasts. Nature is associated with freedom and bounty, but also linked with the change of seasons, not only

opposite: Annalisa Ericson as Kaj, a ballerina, with Marie. The picture opens with a rehearsal of *Swan Lake* in all its splendor, but here we have a dose of backstage reality.

below: One of Bergman's scenes using a favorite prop, a mirror, which draws the viewer into the characters' subjective lives. Reflected in the left panel is Stig Olin as the ballet master in the costume of Coppelius, the master of marionettes. It is as if he controls the interior life of Marie, reflected in the panel at the right.

summer, when the love affair occurs, but also autumn, with which the film begins, when Marie is beyond her first youth. And the world of nature is contrasted with art, embodied in the Opera House setting where the ballet represents life frozen into a timeless perfection.

The movie develops through subtle patterns and motifs that act on one's consciousness, and it is haunted by death figures. During her love affair with Henrik, Marie comes upon a small, pathetic old woman garbed in black (Mimi Pollak) who is a prefiguration of death. She appears again later when Marie and Henrik go to Henrik's house, and he introduces her to this woman, his aunt. Dying of cancer, she is seated playing chess with a minister, who finds it interesting to observe the progress of her dying. The chess game they play looks ahead to the knight's playing chess with Death in *The Seventh Seal*. Bergman also makes a particularly striking use of mirrors in the film. In a memorable tableau, for example, Marie and the ballet master (Stig Olin), his face made up as he prepares for the role of Coppelius, are reflected in the adjoining panels of a double-paneled dressing-room mirror. The moment fixes an impression of her as a reflection of the ballet master, who keeps her encased within the museum world of his art.

Realistic as *Summer Interlude* is, it continually suggests a sense of fable. Embittered Uncle Erland, who takes Marie as his mistress after Henrik's death, thus removing her from the hazards of life, is not merely a misguided man. He is also an enchanter allied with death. When Marie walks away with him after Henrik's death, his figure casts a huge, sinister shadow on the corridor wall. It is also worth noting that the two ballets entering into the film are based on fairy tales.[9] In *Swan Lake*, Odette is held in thrall by the sinister Von Rothbart; and Marie has been in thrall to Uncle Erland, whose attempt to spite her has the reverse effect of bringing her to life. The *Coppelia* theme is introduced through the presence of the ballet master in the costume of Coppelius, the master of marionettes. His most cherished marionette is Coppelia who, because she "belongs" to art and is inanimate, is spared the pain of consciousness. At the end, when Marie is to meet David and to live for more than her career alone, "Coppelius" kisses her suddenly as he leaves the room and sets her free. Part of the film's richness and resonance flows from its shaping as a fairy tale, a dimension of Bergman's art that will affect even such apparently realistic films as *Wild Strawberries*.

Divorced
(1951)

TUCKED IN between two splendid films is another, very minor one, *Divorced*, which, although released in 1951, was shot a year earlier during the impending studio shutdown. *Divorced*, which was directed by Gustaf Molander from an original screenplay provided by Bergman and Herbert Grevenius, concerns a middle-aged woman, Gertrud Holmgren (Inga Tidblad), who has been married to an engineer for twenty years. One day her husband, Tore (Holger Löwenadler), tells her that he wants a divorce so he can marry a colleague who shares his interests. Gertrud, an unworldly and unassuming woman, then steps out into a new life and attempts to deal with the awkwardness of her situation. Renting a room in an apartment in the city, she meets her landlady's son, Bertil Nordelius (Alf Kjellin), a young doctor engaged to a woman of his own age. Nevertheless, Bertil becomes attracted to her, and they are on the verge of an affair when Gertrud has second thoughts because of the difference in their ages. She moves out of the room, and on a train trip finds herself in a compartment with a doctor of her own age whom she had consulted earlier and who now shows an interest in her. The film ends with the impression that she is moving out of a painful experience of divorce into a more confident future. Bergman and Grevenius created *Divorced* as a vehicle that would bring Marta Ekstrom, one of Sweden's great actresses, back to the screen after a serious illness. However, after the screenplay had been written and production at Svensk Filmindustri was about to begin, Ekstrom backed out and the role went to Inga Tidblad. Tidblad gives a sensitive performance, but Molander's direction lacks excitement, and the material is badly dated.

Secrets of Women
(1952)

THE EARLY fifties brought more changes in Bergman's life. In 1951 he married his third wife, Gun Hagberg, and in the following year was appointed director at the Malmö City Theater, initiating an illustrious period of new stage productions. In 1952 he also shot two new pictures, *Secrets of Women* and *Summer with Monika*, that would raise his status in the Swedish film industry. *Secrets of Women*, which was made soon after the studio shutdown ended, was developed by Bergman from an idea supplied by Gun Hagberg in which three wives each relate an incident from their marriages while they are together at a summer house expecting the return of their husbands, a set of brothers named Lobelius. The movie proved a distinct success both critically and commercially and established Bergman for the first time as a skillful practitioner of comedy.

Not that *Secrets of Women* (British title: *Waiting Women*) is entirely comic. An anthology film that weaves together three narratives within a single framework, it is amusing only sparingly in the first two episodes before becoming a polished comedy of manners in its final segment. The first story is related by Rakel (Anita Björk), the young and attractive but frigid wife of Eugen (Karl-Arne Holmsten), an older man who believes complacently that he is a satisfying lover as well as a good provider. As the drama begins, she is visited by Kaj (Jarl Kulle), a romantic attachment of her early youth, before the Lobelius husbands are due to return. Before long the two change into bathing suits, and after Kaj practices his arts of persuasion they go to bed together. Later Eugen arrives and as the three talk in the living room, Rakel makes a sudden announcement to her husband that she has never been fulfilled by him sexually.

The shaken Eugen plies himself with drink and speaks of a divorce, then lapses into a deep depression that sends him out with a rifle to the boathouse, where he plans to shoot himself. Rakel hurriedly summons his brother Paul (Håkan Westergren), who goes to the boathouse to reason with him. When Paul comes out of the building a short time later, he announces that the crisis has passed; the calming advice he has given Eugen, amusingly, is that "an unfaithful wife is better than no wife at all." The puncturing of Eugen's illusions about himself is accompanied by Rakel's own not unhappy recognition that the role she is qualified to play is as a mother to Eugen. In the meantime, another male ego has been damaged in that Rakel's sexual response to Kaj, who thinks of himself as a Don Juan, has also been tepid. He, too, is a posturing child.

The compromises that Bergman's characters make are also reflected in the second episode, which centers upon Marta Lobelius (Maj-Britt Nilsson) and her husband, Martin (Birger Malmsten). This portion of the film is much more adventurous technically than the first. It is set in Paris, where Marta leaves her American soldier fiancé for Martin, a painter resisting the efforts of the Lobeliuses to bring him into the family business. Marta and Martin have an affair, and Marta, without Martin's being aware of it, becomes pregnant. In a flashback Marta is in a hospital alone giving birth to her child, a painful experience that occasions a flashback within a flashback, in which moments of their affair in Paris and other aspects of her consciousness are rendered in an impressionistic delirium. When the baby is born, Marta realizes that she loves Martin, and they are later married. Martin is never substantially fleshed out, but it is apparent that without Marta and a place in the Lobelius family business, he would be a perennial adolescent. He is another "little boy."

Episode three, differently styled still, centers upon Karin Lobelius (Eva Dahlbeck) and her husband, Fredrik (Gunnar Björnstrand), a man of somewhat formal bearing who is head of the Lobelius company. A handsome couple now in middle age, they have grown apart in the course of time: Fredrik has been totally absorbed by business. One evening as they return from a social affair, Karin makes amusing jabs at her husband's dignity. She tells him that while he was talking with a man of title a dab of shaving cream could be seen clearly on his cheek ("Is that what he was looking at?" Fredrik asks). But these mischievous deflations of her husband are merely a prelude to what awaits him when they arrive home and take an elevator that becomes stuck between floors.

Scene from the first episode of *Secrets of Women*. Rakel (Anita Björk) at right is seen in multiple images created by another of Bergman's mirrors. Before the arrival home of her husband, Kaj (Jarl Kulle) shows a romantic interest in her.

Attempting to manage the situation, Fredrik presses an emergency button that plunges the car into darkness. On a second attempt to play the manly role, he releases a switch that sends the car careening down the elevator shaft—until coming to a halt suddenly and throwing them both to the floor. Fredrik's cries are heard, together with Karin's laughter. It is *she* who manages to restore the lights, which reveal Fredrik in his formal attire, his top hat now battered. Yet despite these farcical elements, the scene occasions sophisticated comedy and repartee in which the couple are observed obliquely in the mirrors of the car, as if to underscore the sense of their ambiguous relationship. Seated ludicrously on the floor of the car, they talk together as they have not done in years and even begin to feel amorously toward each other again. By the next morning, when help comes, they agree to start over.

Yet once they are in their apartment, the telephone rings, summoning Fredrik to a business appointment, and one understands that the moment of romance in the stalled elevator will be short-lived. Like the other Lobelius wives, Karin's romantic expectations in her man are dashed, and the most that she can look forward to is to continue to be Fredrik's mother. The episode in the elevator was the high point of the film; audiences loved it, and for the first time Bergman

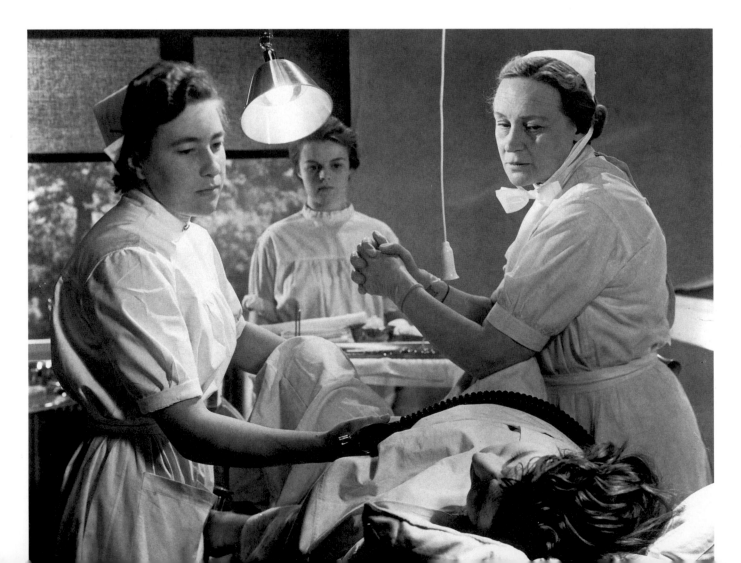

became recognized as a director with a gift for comedy. The film also marks the first appearance of Eva Dahlbeck and Gunnar Björnstrand in leading roles in Bergman's films. Both display remarkable talent for sophisticated comedy and play off each other superbly. Before long, to the delight of international audiences, they will appear together as a team in a series of other Bergman films.

An encompassing frame for *Secrets of Women* is achieved through the gathering at the summer house, where two additional couples enter into the story. Annette (Aino Taube) declines to relate an episode from her marriage to Paul Lobelius, with the implication that it must have been disillusioning indeed. At the end Marta's younger sister Maj elopes with a boyfriend on a motorboat out on the lake, and the last lines are spoken by Paul: "Let them leave. They will come back one day. Let them profit from their summer. They will know soon enough the wounds, the wisdom of life, and other silly matters." He sums up not only the acquired wisdom of the Lobeliuses at their summer house but also, as it were, of the human family. The spirit of the film is bittersweet, but it is generous.

Summer with Monika

(1953)

Summer with Monika, shot in the Stockholm archipelago shortly after *Secrets of Women* was completed, was written by Bergman with Per Anders Fogelström, with whom he had had a marginal association on *While the City Sleeps*. Bergman relates how they met one day on a Stockholm street and the idea for the film was conceived. "I asked him," Bergman recalls, "what he was doing. He said: 'I've got a thing in my head, but how it's going to turn out I don't know.' 'Really?' 'Yes, it's about a girl and a fellow, just kids, who pack in their jobs and families—and beat it out into the archipelago. And then come back to town and try to set up in some sort of a bourgeois existence. But everything goes to hell for them.' I remember jumping a yard high into the air and saying: 'We're going to make a film of this! Remember—we're going to make a film of this!' He thought so, too; but then other things came between. But each time we met, I asked him how things had turned out for that couple. And by and by, during the film stoppage I suppose it must have been, we got down to work on the script."[10]

When the script was presented to Svensk Filmindustri, Carl-Anders Dymling was enthusiastic but had difficulty getting it approved by his board; some of the board members, who considered the story too racy, are supposed to have resigned. It is not at all prurient but it is quite definitely sensual, thanks in part to Harriet Andersson, who plays Monika. Bergman discovered Andersson only a short time before when he saw her in a current film called *Defiance*, which convinced him that she would be the perfect Monika. Working with

above: Scene in the stalled elevator with Eva Dahlbeck as Karin Lobelius and Gunnar Björnstrand as her husband, Fredrik. The comic episode delighted audiences. "It was one of the happiest experiences of my life," Bergman told an interviewer, "to hang about in the foyer . . . and suddenly hear people inside howling with laughter. It was the first time in my life people had ever laughed at something I'd made."

opposite: Marta Lobelius (Maj-Britt Nilsson) in childbirth, a scene that occasions flashbacks in which she relives moments from her romance with her husband, Martin.

her and a relatively small crew (including cinematographer Gunnar Fischer) in the archipelago turned out to be an idyll for Bergman, for he soon became infatuated with his eighteen-year-old star.[11] It was during the making of the film that he began his relationship with her, which would last for the next several years, a time sometimes called Bergman's "Harriet Andersson period."

Summer Interlude anticipates the summer motif and Bergman's use of the Stockholm archipelago as the setting of a love affair between two young people, but *Summer with Monika* has no deep resemblance to it, nor is it like any other film that Bergman would later make. Monika (Harriet Andersson) and Harry (Lars Ekborg) live in working-class Stockholm; he is employed in a china-and-glass warehouse, and she has a small job in a wholesale fruit-and-vegetable business. Neither has a satisfactory homelife. Monika lives in a cramped tenement apartment with a family, including a father who drinks, that she would chiefly like to get away from; Harry, whose mother is dead, lives with his father, with whom he is not very close. The young people meet one day in a café and go out on a date to an escapist Hollywood movie. Then before long Monika, who is more spirited than Harry, leaves her job and after a quarrel with her father goes to see Harry. That night they sleep together in the small cabin of a motorboat belonging to Harry's father. The next morning Harry is late for work and is fired; then the two, with some provisions, head out for the archipelago in the motorboat.

Their life on an island in the archipelago at first seems ideal. They are like children (Lars Ekborg's finely cut, baby-faced features are just right) enjoying new freedoms. They dance to the music of a gramophone, make love, and swim naked. Trouble begins when a former, jealous boyfriend of Monika's arrives (by some great coincidence) and attempts to set fire to the motorboat; but Harry fights him, assisted by Monika wielding a frying pan, and he is routed. But other troubles come. They run out of food, and in a fine scene Monika steals some meat from the cellar of a summer house and is caught by the occupants but escapes before the arrival of the police. But Monika is by now pregnant, and the idyll is over. They return in the motorboat through a dour, choppy sea to married life in the city.

The baby arrives while Harry works in a factory and studies to become an engineer at night. Still an escapist, Monika is bored and unhappy taking care of the baby and before long is unfaithful. When Harry returns a day early from a trip, he finds her in bed with another man, and the marriage collapses. The final views of the two are revealing. Harry carries the baby in his arms as he stops before a store window; the reflection of them in the glass (another of Bergman's mirror devices) predicts his future. Monika, on the other hand, is shown in a café with a young man whose interest she has attracted. She turns suddenly to face the camera, and the long-held shot (an innovative technique at the time) records her expression of

opposite, top: Views of Harriet Andersson as Monika and Lars Ekborg as Harry, the young lovers in *Summer with Monika.* They have the look of children.

opposite, bottom: Love in the woods, with a gramophone nearby. The scene has a fresh intimacy, like the film itself.

overleaf, left: Monika in her natural state riled censors in the 1950s and fostered an impression of Swedish films as being in the vanguard of sexual freedom.

overleaf, right: A famous still of Harriet Andersson as Monika. Her defiant sensuality made a definite impression on the emerging New Wave in France.

defiance and indifference to what others may say. The sensuality that radiates from her is sizzling.

Before *Summer with Monika* was released, Swedish censors cut parts of it, including a scene in which, after the fight on the island, Harry gets drunk and he and Monika have sex. But even with these excisions, the film was considered provocative by the standards of the time—an impression hardly lessened by the studio's widely circulated publicity still of Andersson without brassiere in an erotic pose in which her partially unbuttoned sweater is draped down over her shoulders.[12] The movie did well commercially in Sweden and won the praise of cinephiles in France. Jean-Luc Godard called it "the most beautiful film of this most original of cinéastes,"[13] and François Truffaut would later pay tribute to it in *The 400 Blows*, in which his young hero goes to see a movie in Paris with the talked-about poster of Harriet Andersson displayed out in front.[14] *Summer with Monika* has a remarkable purity and freshness and is acted by Andersson and Ekborg with unfailing naturalness.

The Naked Night

(1953)

Summer with Monika was followed in the same year by *The Naked Night* (British title: *Sawdust and Tinsel*), which was unlike it in every respect. In 1952 Bergman showed his screenplay for the film to Dymling at Svensk Filmindustri, who turned it down; but not long afterward he talked to Rune Waldekranz, production head at another film company, Sandrews, who was interested. Waldekranz recognized that the movie would be a risky investment, but he speculated that a high-prestige picture by Bergman might attract attention in the European film market.[15] Bergman shot the picture in Arild in southern Sweden in the spring and summer of 1953, and it was quickly put into circulation in the autumn. Several cinematographers contributed to it.[16] Hilding Bladh and Göran Strindberg shot different segments of it; then, when Strindberg was called away to America, a young man named Sven Nykvist stepped in, anticipating his later collaboration with Bergman that would link them together in the public mind. Surprisingly, the work of the three cinematographers fused together seamlessly.

The Naked Night, which is set in 1900, employs a twenty-four-hour time frame and has something of the quality of a folktale. As the Circus Alberti approaches a small town at dawn, its owner, Albert Johansson (Åke Grönberg), awakes and climbs into the wagon beside its driver, Jens, who relates an incident that had occurred at this same place seven years earlier involving Frost the clown and his wife, Alma. The incident is visualized in a flashback in which Alma (Gudrun Brost) appears before a group of soldiers who are lounging on some rocks by the water cleaning their weapons. In response to

opposite, top: As clowns attempt to restrain her, Anne (Harriet Andersson) takes revenge on Frans (Hasse Ekman).

opposite, bottom: Anne with Albert (Åke Grönberg) after his beating. His desolation shows clearly in his bruised face.

overleaf, left: A memorable scene from *The Naked Night*: soldiers on the rocky beach laugh uproariously as Frost the clown (Anders Ek) witnesses the humiliation of his wife, Alma, who is naked before them in the water.

overleaf, top: Albert before his dressing-room mirror as he contemplates suicide. In the end he shoots the reflection of his face that stares at him from the mirror.

overleaf, bottom: In the center of the circus ring, Albert receives a brutal beating from the actor Frans. For Albert it has been a long day of humiliation.

overleaf, far right: Albert's mistress, Anne, in the theater, where she will be seduced by Frans. The wire mesh that casts shadows on her face emphasizes the sense of her exclusion.

their sexual taunts, Alma takes off her clothes and goes out into the water—much to the merriment of the men. A boy rushes away to the circus encampment to summon Frost (Anders Ek), who hurries to the scene in whiteface, dressed in his clown's costume that, grotesquely, has a clown's face embroidered over his genitals. Stripping off his costume, Frost goes out into the water to Alma, lifting her up into his arms so as to shield her nakedness, and struggles with her toward shore. On the shore sharp rocks lacerate the clown's feet; he stumbles, falls, and gets up again to continue with his burden in indescribable agony that is accompanied by the laughter and raillery of the soldiers. The episode is intensified and made to seem dreamlike by Bergman's use of harsh sunlight that becomes unnaturally white and blinding. A strange silence surrounds the clown (dramatic close-ups of the open mouths of shouting soldiers are shown but no sound is heard), who is mocked in his lonely, Christlike suffering.

The episode is a forecast of what is to follow. The action now centers on Albert and his young mistress, Anne (Harriet Andersson), who call at a local theater to ask for the loan of costumes, since their circus troupe is now close to destitution. The theater's manager, Mr. Sjuberg (Gunnar Björnstrand), allows them to have some castoffs while reminding them of their lowly status—the first of a long day's humiliations. Albert, who had formerly lived in the town, leaves Anne to call on the wife and two small boys he had abandoned. She now owns a successful shop, and Albert, envying their comfortable bourgeois life, asks her to take him back, since he is now thoroughly sick of his wandering, indigent circus life. But she does not want him. Anne, meanwhile, jealous of Albert's going to see his wife (and suspecting his motives), becomes involved with Frans (Hasse Ekman), a

Alma (Gudrun Brost) holds the anguished Frost as he lies exhausted on the beach. Their heavily made-up faces seem like grotesque masks.

handsome, if effete and wily, actor at the theater, who seduces her with what he claims is a valuable amulet, but which is actually worthless. When Albert and Anne meet on a street again after Anne leaves a pawnshop, where she has the amulet appraised, he senses that she has been unfaithful and is thrown into dejection.

At the circus performance, attended by members of the theater company, Frans taunts Anne publicly about his seduction of her. A gruesome fistfight ensues between Albert and Frans in the center of the circus ring. Overweight and clumsy, Albert proves no match for the cunning actor, who beats him brutally while the audience cheers and laughs uproariously at his degradation. In his trailer the stupefied and despondent Albert contemplates suicide with a pistol that lies before him by his dressing-room mirror. After a long, tense interval, he shoots his reflection in the mirror and then turns the weapon on Anne's ailing circus bear, a reminder of his own heavy, weary, and tethered self. The following dawn the circus moves on. Rather like the couple in *Three Strange Loves*, the truth of Albert and Anne's relationship is revealed as a form of hell, but as they face a bitter future they at least have each other.

Bergman makes sweeping use of the visual resources of cinema, but the film also has a relation to theater. Two scenes are set at a theater and the rest at a circus, a more rudimentary form of theater; and it deals with actors and performers who purvey illusion and are themselves victims of it. Moreover, it draws on Bergman's own early work as a playwright. A moment near the end of one of his plays, *Jack Among the Actors*, is insinuated into the film. Jack is steadily reduced in size and importance until the female character, Nelly, treats him as an infant, whom she feeds with a spoon, promising sleep and release from the pain of consciousness.[17] Rather similarly at the end of *The Naked Night*, Frost tells Albert (his alter ego) of a strange dream he has had in which Alma took him as a fetus into her womb where, rocked by her as in a cradle, he grew smaller and smaller. "Finally," he says, "I was no bigger than a seed, and then I was gone altogether." *The Naked Night* features strong performances by Grönberg, Ek, and Andersson and is Bergman's boldest and most brilliant film up to this time; but upon its release, it was savaged by critics. "Ingmar and I wept," Harriet Andersson told me, "when we read the reviews." The work on which Bergman had pinned his hopes as a serious filmmaker became a debacle.

A Lesson in Love
(1954)

IF ONE DID not know, one might well suspect that Bergman's next film, the sparkling comedy *A Lesson in Love,* which enjoyed considerable commercial success, was made to cover his losses on *The Naked Night*. But, in fact, it was shot in the summer of 1953 before the disastrous notices for *The Naked Night* appeared. The movie came about when Bergman and Harriet Andersson spent a holiday at a resort hotel in Arild, where he had shot scenes for *The Naked Night*. "I had just divorced my third wife [Gun Hagberg]," Bergman comments, "though I still liked her very much, and, therefore, began writing about her. In fourteen days I finished the script, and fourteen days later we began shooting the picture. The whole thing was just for fun—and money. I was very poor at the time, you know. I already had lots of children and a lot of women, and money had to be paid out. A good deal of my filmmaking in earlier days came from lack of money."[18] Bergman had Sandrews in mind for the picture but because everyone in the production department was away on vacation at the time, he showed it instead to Carl-Anders Dymling at Svensk Filmindustri, who liked it and rushed it into production.

above: David Erneman (Gunnar Björnstrand) with his daughter, Nix (Harriet Andersson), as she works at her pottery in *A Lesson in Love*. A generation of experience divides them.

As a comedy dealing with marriage and the need for compromise, *A Lesson in Love* is reminiscent of *Secrets of Women*, particularly in its final segment in which Eva Dahlbeck and Gunnar Björnstrand play a middle-aged couple still trying to get to know each other. The resemblance is heightened by the casting of Dahlbeck and Björnstrand in the principal roles of Marianne and David Erneman. David, a gynecologist, is seen at the beginning in his office, where his mistress, Suzanne, is giving him trouble; after sixteen years of married life he had felt the need to refresh his life with Suzanne, but she has already begun to bore him, and the sportive episode is over. Canceling his appointments, he hastily leaves to catch a train to Copenhagen. Once aboard the train, he enters a compartment where an attractive, well-dressed woman and another man are seated opposite each other. When the woman leaves the compartment for a few minutes, the man makes a bet with David that the woman will respond to his advances. David wagers that he himself will soon kiss her. Before long the other man is rebuffed by the lady, but she kisses David. Only late in the episode is it revealed that she is his wife, Marianne.

All is not well, however, since she is on her way to Copenhagen to marry the sculptor Carl-Adam (Åke Grönberg), whom years before she had almost married before marrying David. During the train journey a number of flashbacks occur that fill out the background of David and Marianne's lives. One returns to Marianne's near wedding to Carl-Adam, at which David is his best man. Just prior to the wedding ceremony, David discovers Marianne about to hang herself and is told by her that it is he she loves; they then go to the wedding ball to break the news to Carl-Adam, who becomes furious, and a wild, farcical melee ensues. In the end the wedding ceremony goes forward with David as the groom.

Two other flashbacks go back to a year before the present events. In the first, David visits their fifteen-year-old daughter, Nix (Harriet Andersson), a tomboy unhappily attempting to cope with the awkwardness of her sexual coming-of-age. David and Nix are at

58

above: Marianne (Eva Dahlbeck) and David Erneman in a comic scene in which Marianne reveals to David that it is he she really loves, not Carl-Adam.

below: A celebration before the wedding of Marianne and Carl-Adam (Åke Grönberg) that will turn into a wild melee.

different edges of sexual love, she rebelling against the disturbance it poses, and he, in middle age, bored by it as a nuisance. The second flashback shows David, Marianne, and their two children—Nix and Pelle—visiting his parents at their country home on a summer morning. It is the seventy-third birthday of David's father, who is fêted by his wife and offspring to a breakfast-in-bed ceremony; later they all drive out in the country for a family picnic. The scene introduces the motif of the stability of married life and the consolations it offers after the fires of romantic love have been banked.

The film approaches its conclusion when the train arrives in Copenhagen, and David appears at the gathering for Marianne and Carl-Adam at a pub prior to their expected marriage—an episode that is a replay of the wedding scene sixteen years before. At a critical moment, Marianne recognizes that she wants David, not Carl-Adam; the festivities are interrupted by their announcement and a wild fracas ensues in which Marianne takes part spiritedly. All ends well as Marianne and David enjoy a "honeymoon" in a hotel suite that David has booked *in advance*. In a closing shot, a sparkling, blonde-haired, diapered Cupid, equipped with bow and arrow, places a "Do Not Disturb" sign on their door. The comic conceit of the film springs from David and Marianne's misunderstanding of themselves. Twice Marianne almost marries Carl-Adam, whom she does not want, and David has an affair with Suzanne, whom he does not want either. Of the two, David seems more ambivalent about sex and is less sure of who he is. He needs Marianne to take him in hand. "A mature grown man is a rarity," Marianne remarks on the train, "so one has to find the child who suits her best." Her remark is underscored by the scene with the grandparents, in which the grandmother (Renée Björling) insists that her husband (Olof Winnerstrand) go back into the house before they begin their motoring trip and change into his long underwear, lest he catch cold. He grumbles and protests, but finally obeys his "mother." Bergman's warmly evoked sense of family and a settled place in life provide a sanctuary for father and son, who seem rather helpless.

Bergman refers to *A Lesson in Love* as "a *divertissement*," which would seem to dismiss it, but it is an expertly constructed comedy that succeeds well on its own terms. The film breathes and has an expansive openness that is not usual in Bergman. Dahlbeck and Björnstrand are, as usual, superb—incapable of the slightest false step. Åke Grönberg, who played the woebegone Albert in *The Naked Night*, is also delightful in the wholly different role of Carl-Adam, a burly man of irrepressible spirits. That the lighthearted *Lesson in Love* should follow so closely upon the bleak and somber *Naked Night* is curious and is a forecast of Bergman's constantly modulating vision that unfolds through the rest of the decade. Rather than one, there are many Bergmans, each demanding to be heard.

The International Breakthrough

Dreams

(1955)

IN BERGMAN'S next picture, *Dreams* (British title: *Journey into Autumn*), Dahlbeck and Björnstrand are featured again, but not as husband and wife. The film begins in a fashion-photography studio with a shot of a camera and then of an enlarged photograph of a pair of lips that comes into focus in a developing solution. The various individuals who work at the studio, including Susanne (Eva Dahlbeck), its early middle-aged fashion manager, and Doris (Harriet Andersson), a young model, are introduced; and the plot is set in motion by a trip that Susanne and Doris take to Gothenburg, where part of the fashion collection is photographed. In addition to the professional reason for the trip, however, there is another: Susanne is still desperately in love with a Gothenburg businessman, Henrik Lobelius (Ulf Palme), with whom she has had an affair that ended seven months earlier.

In Gothenburg Susanne persuades the reluctant Henrik to come to see her at her hotel room; when he joins her there, they talk at first, then go to bed together. But then his wife appears and coolly outlines to the pair why Henrik will remain with her and their children. His business is on the verge of bankruptcy but her own money is protected, and he needs her for this reason as well as for the reason that he is weary and weak-willed. "I have only said," his wife remarks, "what you yourselves know but refuse to think about." The Lobeliuses leave together, but a moment later Henrik returns, and Susanne, suddenly elated, exclaims, "You've come back." "I forgot my briefcase," her lover says sheepishly, and departs, grotesquely puncturing what remains of Susanne's illusions.

Like certain earlier Bergman films, *Dreams* interweaves separate tales within a single fabric. While Susanne's story unfolds, Bergman crosscuts to Doris as she stands gazing wistfully into the window of a fashionable shop. Suddenly, in the reflection of the glass, she sees a distinguished-looking older man—a diplomat named Sönderby (Gunnar Björnstrand)—standing behind her. Like a fairy-tale godfather, he

Bengt Ekerot in the costume of Death with Bergman, in a time-out in the filming of *The Seventh Seal.*

takes her to an expensive shop, where he buys her a dress, a pair of shoes, and a pearl necklace; they then go to his fairy-tale house, a mansion. Craving excitement, Doris asks Sönderby to take her to an amusement park, and as if by a miracle he arranges with a friend who owns one, and owes him a favor, to open it for them for the afternoon. Riding through the dark tunnel of the "Terror Express," Doris screams with delight as a papier-mâché skeleton, spider, and wolf leap out at them, but Sönderby is visibly shaken; on the way out he stumbles and falls, and his weariness and the difference in their ages make him seem rather pathetic.

Sönderby is dealt another blow when they return to the house and Doris intimates, grotesquely, that she might be willing to become his mistress if he would pay to have her teeth capped, produce a film in which she would star, and buy her a sports car and a summer house. At the same time we see what it is that has attracted him to her. As she stands by a portrait of his wife when she was young, it is clear that Doris looks almost exactly like her. Sönderby himself points out the resemblance, adding that his wife has been confined to an insane asylum ever since she became convinced that their daughter Marianne was born with the head of a wolf. Marianne (Kerstin Hedeby) then soon appears at the house. Cool and acquisitive, she treats Doris contemptuously as a thief attempting to make off with some of the Sönderby possessions that rightfully belong to her. By the time Marianne leaves, the fairy tale has shattered. Doris goes without taking Sönderby's gifts, and he is last seen in an upstairs window of his house, a prisoner of his own loneliness. The film ends in the Stockholm studio where it began, with Susanne and Doris deprived of their illusions.

A common pattern can be noticed in the film's separate but related stories. In both, for example, self-possessed women who understand the world humiliate the women from the fashion studio

above: At the fashion studio, Susanne (Eva Dahlbeck), at center, and Doris (Harriet Andersson), at right, as she peers into a mirror. At left is Magnus (Benkt-Åke Benktsson), the fashion director—a massive, mysterious figure who drums on the table with his fingers as the fashions are shown.

and dash their dreams. The photograph of a pair of lips in the developing solution at the beginning implies intimate contact, but all of Bergman's characters remain apart, enclosed within themselves. Sönderby's is the worst case because his isolation is so absolute and because he is the most haunted in his attempt to break out of his enclosure; his wolfish daughter and the vain Doris, as well as the egoism that is implied to exist within himself, are the reality that he does not want to see. The glamorous dream projections of the fashion studio offer a merely delusive escape from isolation and loneliness. *Dreams* is flawed in some respects; Sönderby is never fully developed as a character, nor is his adoption of Doris particularly believable. The film is interesting in its meditative and bleak interior mood; this very feature of the film, however, had little appeal for movie-house audiences. Rune Waldekranz at Sandrews, who had previously backed *The Naked Night*, produced the film and lost again at the box office.

Smiles of a Summer Night

(1955)

BY 1955 Bergman had assembled the preeminent repertory company in Sweden at the Malmö City Theater. The group was very close, and for his next film Bergman wanted to give the members of the company summertime film employment. The film itself, at the strictest insistence of Carl-Anders Dymling at Svensk Filmindustri, would be a comedy. But when Bergman wrote the screenplay in Switzerland, he was going through one of his darkest periods. "I was very depressed," he told an interviewer. "This was a terrible time in my life, . . . So, I went away to Switzerland and had two alternatives: write *Smiles of a Summer Night*, or kill myself."[1]

Set in 1901, the movie begins at the home of Fredrik Egerman (Gunnar Björnstrand), a middle-aged lawyer, and his second wife, Anne (Ulla Jacobsson), who is about nineteen and is still a virgin, although the Egermans have been married two years. The household also includes Egerman's handsome son by his late first wife, Henrik (Björn Bjelvenstam), a theology student. In the afternoon Fredrik, as an experienced man of the world, counsels his son, who is in a muddle because his lofty spirituality is in conflict with his no-longer-repressible sexual urges. That evening Fredrik and Anne go to the theater, where a famous actress, Desirée Armfeldt (Eva Dahlbeck), is performing. She is, as even the unworldly Anne soon recognizes, Fredrik's former mistress. Disturbed, Anne insists on leaving the theater early with Fredrik, but he returns to see Desirée backstage and accepts her invitation to call on her at her home. As he is arriving, however, he falls into a puddle of water, and Desirée, with barely suppressed mirth, has him change out of his wet clothes into a night-

left: Smiles of a Summer Night: the men in Desirée's life confront one another for the first time. Desirée Armfeldt (Eva Dahlbeck), center; Fredrik Egerman (Gunnar Björnstrand), left; and Count Malcolm (Jarl Kulle), right. Altogether an awkward moment for Fredrik.

right: Henrik (Björn Bjelvenstam) and Anne (Ulla Jacobsson), in foreground, share a passionate kiss, while in the distance, at right, Fredrik witnesses his wife's elopement with his son.

shirt and cap belonging to her current lover, Count Carl-Magnus Malcolm (Jarl Kulle). To complicate matters, Count Malcolm, a vainglorious, quick-tempered army officer with a reputation for dueling, arrives unexpectedly. In a threatening manner, he puts Fredrik out of the house, and Fredrik is forced to make his way through the city in his ridiculous attire.

The following morning, Desirée calls on her aged, eccentric, and wealthy mother (delightfully played by Naima Wifstrand) and persuades her to give a party at her country estate at Ryarp, to which the Egermans as well as Malcolm and his wife, Charlotte, will be invited. Desirée, who wants Fredrik, conspires with Charlotte (Margit Carlquist), who is still in love with her husband despite his infidelities, to win back their men. At dinner a bet is made (designed to make Malcolm jealous and thus renew his interest in his wife) that Charlotte cannot seduce Fredrik in fifteen minutes. Henrik, struggling to suppress his attraction to his father's young wife, is so disturbed by the group's talk of seduction that he dashes from the room; and when Anne goes after him to try to calm him, Fredrik is suddenly aware that, without their having admitted it, the two young people are in love. Anne retires to bed, and Henrik goes to his room and prepares

below: Petra (Harriet Andersson) and Frid (Åke Fridell) in an amorous game of hide-and-seek on the wooded grounds of the estate.

left: Petra and Frid in the hay field at the end. With outstretched arms to the dawn sky, Frid seems a celebrant of nature and sexual love.

opposite, top left: Henrik, left, and Anne, right. Between them, in the doorway, is the servant Petra, who attempts to snare Henrik—before finding her rightful partner in the coachman Frid.

opposite, top right: Naima Wifstrand as the rich, eccentric Mrs. Armfeldt, with her daughter Desirée. "One can never protect anyone," Mrs. Armfeldt tells her daughter, "from the least little suffering; that's what makes one so infinitely tired."

to hang himself. The room had once been occupied by the king and is equipped with a device that activates a revolving wall and causes his mistress's bed to come gliding into his chamber. As Henrik is attempting to hang himself, he accidentally activates the device, and the bed in which Anne lies sleeping suddenly coasts into the room. They now confess their love and with the help of Petra (Harriet Andersson), a maid, and Frid (Åke Fridell), a coachman, steal out of the house to elope. Standing in the distance in a poignantly rendered moment, Fredrik observes them as they leave the grounds in a coach.

But still another humiliation lies in store for Fredrik. He goes off to a tryst in the pavilion with Charlotte, but when Desirée observes that Charlotte may be serious rather than merely making her husband jealous, she alerts Malcolm, who appears at the pavilion with his dueling pistol. Malcolm and Fredrik go inside the building to settle accounts while the women wait anxiously outside. Malcolm challenges Fredrik to a game of Russian roulette, to which Fredrik, with some anguish, agrees; when Fredrik nervously holds the pistol to his temple and pulls the trigger, it goes off. Just before the report of the

opposite, bottom: The drawing room in Mrs. Armfeldt's country estate in *Smiles of a Summer Night*. Desirée, holding a guitar, is seated by the monocled Count Malcolm.

gun is heard, the camera cuts to the outside of the building, where the women stare with horror. Then the door opens and Fredrik appears, his face covered with soot, with which the pistol was actually loaded. A new pairing of couples now occurs—Anne and Henrik, the innocent young lovers; Desirée and Fredrik, who in marrying will give

legitimacy to Desirée's small son whom Fredrik, unknown to him until now, had fathered; Charlotte and Malcolm, now reconciled; and Petra, the servant girl, and Frid, the life-embracing coachman. The couples all find their rightful partners, and the film ends with a view of Petra and Frid sporting in the hay. In a mythic stance, Frid stands with his arms outstretched to the dawn sky like a celebrant of nature and sexual love.

According to Bergman, *Smiles of a Summer Night* was "based on a play by Marivaux, in the classical 18th-century manner."[2] He first conceived of the work, in fact, as a play rather than as a film, and a sense of theater is very strong in it. A French influence is clear in Bergman's construction of *Smiles* as a witty, sometimes aphoristic *pièce bien fait*; but in addition the film reflects Bergman's recent work in the theater at Malmö. Immediately before *Smiles*, Bergman had staged a production of Franz Lehár's operetta *The Merry Widow* that drew crowds in 1954–55 and was the most popular success in the history of the Malmö theater. At first Bergman thought of a contemporary setting, but then decided that it should take place at the turn of the century, exactly the time of *The Merry Widow*.[3] *Smiles*, which Bergman has called "a mixture of operetta and comedy,"[4] has the effervescence of *The Merry Widow* together with a reminiscent artificiality in its setting and in the turnings of its romantic plot. The relevance of theater to Bergman's films is nowhere more conspicuous than in *Smiles*. The movie unfolds in a series of dramatic scenes, often in drawing rooms or bedrooms. One of the main characters is an actress; a scene is set in a theater; and the party at Ryarp gives the sense of a theatrical entertainment transpiring there. The characters themselves all have their roles and masks and belong to one of life's jests.

But *Smiles* is not wholly a jest. The three smiles of a summer night of which Frid tells Petra at the close are those, respectively, for young lovers; for clowns and fools who cry out for or believe that they have found love; and for the sad, the frightened, and the lonely. Only the young lovers in *Smiles* actually possess love, their innocence shielding them briefly from the disillusionment experience brings. The deceptively happy ending is reminiscent of the ambivalent ending of *Secrets of Women* in which the young couple who are eloping are allowed to "have their summer"; but it has a sharper edge, since in this case what life holds is not only an exposure of the characters' illusions but also of the imminence of death. The moment when Fredrik pulls the trigger of the pistol in his "game" of Russian roulette with Malcolm brings the recognition that death is what underlies the charade of desire and self-importance. If Bergman's characters are fools in love, Fredrik, in marrying a nineteen-year-old girl in an attempt to recover his youth, is the greatest fool. In his relationship to a young girl, he resembles Sönderby in *Dreams*, and like Sönderby he sees the destruction of his illusions. At every stage of the film Fredrik suffers humiliation that strips him of his manhood and

Luncheon at Ryarp is a matter of some formality, but the conversation is piquantly sexual.

self-respect. Even his being united with Desirée at the end is more maternal consolation than love. *Smiles* is one of Bergman's most perfectly realized films. It is a triumph not only in its ensemble acting (including the accomplished performances of Dahlbeck and Björnstrand) but also in its precision of tone that accommodates the warmth of comedy with a chilly disenchantment.

When *Smiles* was shown to executives at Svensk Filmindustri, they had deep misgivings about it, fearing that it might even prove a fiasco. It was released in Sweden to mixed notices, and little was expected when the movie was routinely entered in competition at the 1956 Cannes Film Festival. Bergman was stunned and incredulous when word reached him that it had been awarded the festival's Special Jury Prize for "its 'poetic humour.'"[5] The attention it received gave Bergman his international breakthrough, and foreign sales of the movie proved a bonanza for the production company. Nor was the film soon forgotten. In 1973 Stephen Sondheim used it as the basis of his cool, sophisticated operetta *A Little Night Music*, and in 1982 it helped to inspire Woody Allen's picture *A Midsummer Night's Sex Comedy*.

left: Bo (Björn Bjelvenstam) at a teenage party with Kerstin (Bibi Andersson). Bo's coming of age proves confusing.

below: In Last Couple Out, Bo's relationship with his mother (Eva Dahlbeck) has evident Oedipal overtones.

Last Couple Out

(1956)

AS A THROWBACK to his concern with adolescent turmoil in his films of the 1940s, *Last Couple Out* seems out of place in Bergman's film chronology. Based on an early story by Bergman and written by him in 1950 when the studio shutdown was imminent, it was acquired by Svensk Filmindustri in 1952; and in the mid-1950s Alf Sjöberg accepted the assignment to direct it. The central character is an eighteen-year-old student named Bo Dahlin (Björn Bjelvenstam), the only child of quarreling upper-middle-class parents. Matters worsen when Bo discovers that his mother has been having an affair with a psychiatrist named Fårell (Jarl Kulle), and when he becomes involved with two teenage girls, Anita (Harriet Andersson) and Kerstin (Bibi Andersson). At the apartment of Anita, whose parents are away partying in Gothenburg, a teenage gathering Bo attends turns into a drunken debacle; and at Kerstin's apartment, her mother arrives to accuse Bo, wrongly, of having seduced her daughter. Angered by what he regards as the betrayal of parents, Bo at the end is advised by an understanding teacher to allow for the imperfection of the adult world into which he himself is about to enter.

The fault of *Last Couple Out* is not Sjöberg's but the material Bergman has given him, which consists of a string of incidents that lack dimension and cohesion. The picture has peripheral interest in the attractive performances of Harriet Andersson, whose affair with Bergman ended with *Dreams*, and Bibi Andersson, whose relationship with him had already begun. The film also has a highly personal subtext. The father (Olof Widgren) and mother (Eva Dahlbeck) have a decided resemblance to Bergman's own parents. The father is formal, distant, and weaker than his wife, whose affair with another man (like Karin Bergman's with Torsten Bohlen) creates a crisis in their marriage. But what is of greater interest is Bo's peculiar relationship to his mother, which is closer to that of a would-be lover than that of a son, a situation emphasized by the fact that Bo looks slightly older than a teenager and by the physical nature of certain scenes between them. In one, for example, the mother rests her head on his shoulder while he slips his arm around her waist. The family relationships are also reflected revealingly in mirrors. In one such shot, the mother is at the center of the frame, with her husband distinctly off to one side; while in another the mother and son are shown together in the center of the frame with his arms around her. Yet Bergman does not know quite what to do with this material, which does not relate clearly to the rest of the film. In this very slight film, which falls between two major ones, Bergman seems to be engaging in an Oedipal daydream.

The Seventh Seal

(1957)

AS BERGMAN tells it, he went in a determined mood to see Carl-Anders Dymling with his script of *The Seventh Seal*. "Carl-Anders," he remarks, "was sitting there selling *Smiles of a Summer Night* to every country you could think of and was in a state of euphoria, thinking how from now on he'd be able to sit on genuine Persian carpets and look at pictures by Picasso. . . . So I said: 'Now, Carl-Anders, it's now or never.' And plumped *The Seventh Seal* down in front of him, and said 'Come on now, make up your mind!'"[6] Dymling agreed to do the film, but only if it could be made on a low budget and with a shooting schedule that would not exceed

right: Bengt Ekerot as Death in *The Seventh Seal*, a film of striking theatricality. Bergman relates how he and Ekerot decided to make Death as a clown: "*Not* the beautiful clown, but the white clown, because for us children, when we were at the circus, the white clown always frightened us."

left: A theatrical interlude in *The Seventh Seal.* Jof (Nils Poppe), at left, plays a cuckolded husband. Skat (Erik Strandmark), at right, a Pan-like seducer, has designs on Mia (Bibi Andersson).

thirty-five days. Bergman shot the film exactly within these pinched time limits in midsummer 1956.

The interrelatedness of theater and cinema in Bergman's work can be seen not only in *Smiles of a Summer Night* but also in *The Seventh Seal*, which was originally a one-act play, "Painting on Wood." Inspired by a painting in an old Swedish church that he remembered from his youth, the play was written by Bergman for an acting class at the Malmö City Theater. "There were some youngsters there," Bergman comments, "eight or nine of them, and I was looking for a play to put on, for that's the best way of teaching. I couldn't find anything, so I took it into my head to write something myself. It was called *A Painting on Wood*. It is a pure training play, and consists of a number of monologues. All except for one part. One pupil was being trained for the musical comedy section. He had a good singing voice and looked very handsome, but as soon as he opened his mouth [to speak] it was a catastrophe. So I gave him a silent part. The Saracens had cut out his tongue. He was the Knight."[7]

After using "Painting on Wood" as an acting exercise, Bergman presented it at Malmö in March 1955, using a professional cast. Then in September the play was performed with a different cast at the Royal Dramatic Theater in Stockholm, where it was directed by Bengt Ekerot, who would play Death in *The Seventh Seal*.[8] Soon after the critically acclaimed production in Stockholm, Bergman decided to turn the play into a film. *The Seventh Seal* retains a number of the features of the stage work—its historical background, the burning of the witch, and the Dance of Death; and the dialogue of Jöns, the squire, is kept fully intact. But other elements were added, including Jof and Mia, and their child Michael, and the chess game that the knight plays with Death.[9] In this draft, too, the knight becomes a central, "speaking" character. *The Seventh Seal* also introduces two of Bergman's most faithful and versatile performers in leading roles— Bibi Andersson, who was not long out of drama school when she joined the Malmö company in 1956; and Max von Sydow, who had had only a few parts in films when he came to Malmö in 1955. With his austere, aristocratic features and commanding presence, Von

above: Death, impersonating a priest, hears the confession of Antonius Block, played by Bergman's new discovery, the twenty-seven-year-old Max von Sydow.

Sydow takes over the film, which catapulted him into international fame.

The story of *The Seventh Seal* is not at all complicated. After a ten-year absence in the Holy Land during the Crusades, a knight, Antonius Block (Max von Sydow), and his squire (Gunnar Björnstrand) return to their fourteenth-century Sweden, which is under the pall of the Black Plague. On the seashore where they stop to rest, the awesome figure of Death (Bengt Ekerot in a stunning performance) appears to claim the knight who, stalling for time, challenges him to a game of chess. The game is played with a number of interruptions, in the course of which one is introduced to other characters—a touring group of actors (very Bergmanesque); the juggler Jof (Nils Poppe) and his wife, Mia (Bibi Andersson), who possess an unspoiled innocence and moral beauty; the blacksmith Plog (Åke Fridell), whose wife, Lisa (Inga Gill), runs off with one of the actors, Skat (Erik Strandmark); and Raval (Bertil Anderberg), a depraved former student for the priesthood. In the end, the knight is defeated in the chess game and he, his wife, the squire, and others at the knight's castle are led away in a Dance of Death to the land of darkness. But not before the knight has distracted Death's attention and effected the escape of Jof, Mia, and their child—thus achieving the single "meaningful" act he has sought in his life.

Set against a background of disillusionment with the Crusades that have yielded nothing but slaughter, and the pestilence-ravaged countryside of the knight's homeland, the film addresses itself to final questions. The medieval village to which the answer-seeking, high-minded knight and his sure-footed, practical-minded squire return is a microcosm of humanity. The episode of Skat's wife-stealing provides comic relief, but cruelty and irrationality are never absent for long. Raval attempts to rape a young girl and later forces Jof to

right: Close-up of the theatrical entertainment focusing upon Jof, left, and Mia.

dance on a tavern table to the jeering accompaniment of a throng of drunken men. A young girl is burned at the stake as a witch, and a horrifying procession of flagellants bearing a huge cross arrives at the village and their fanatical leader harangues the onlookers for the sins that he claims have brought on the plague. The knight finds relief from such scenes in the companionship of Jof and Mia; the wild strawberries they share with him (reminiscent of the wild strawberries the young lovers Marie and Henrik enjoyed together in *Summer Interlude*) evoke the idea of redeeming grace afforded in a heightened moment of pure existence.

With its disillusionment and anguished questioning of final things, the film captures in an uncanny way the mood of a particular cultural moment: the angst-ridden aftermath of World War II and the birth of the nuclear age. Bergman's allusions to the Existentialists ("the meaningful act") were also timely, and critical articles were soon being written about Bergman in relation to them. But, in fact, he was not well versed in Existentialism, nor is the film the work of an intellectual. Despite its eschatological issues, *The Seventh Seal* deals most centrally with the knight's sense of isolation from others and the emptiness he feels as a consequence—a version of Bergman's own attempt at this point in his career to break out of his isolation through a saving relationship to others. It is this theme that links *The Seventh Seal* very closely, although they may appear dissimilar, with *Wild Strawberries*.

The rhetorical aspect of *The Seventh Seal* seems dated, yet the film still exerts a strong hold on the imagination, and it benefits everywhere by the camerawork of Gunnar Fischer, making his ninth film with Bergman. The scene in the tavern (with its lurid close-ups of debauched faces that make one think of Sergei Eisenstein), the procession of the flagellants, the views of the knight in the confession booth with Death and playing chess with him by the seashore, and the Dance of Death along the horizon are all bold and memorable. The film touches primary emotions like a black fable or fantastic fairy tale. When at the close Jof envisions the knight and the others being led away in a procession to the dark country "while the rain

left: Bergman directing the scene with the flagellants.

right: The procession of the flagellants halts at the settlement, where the fierce monk harangues the onlookers on their sins, which he tells them have caused the plague.

opposite: The knight, stalling for time, plays a game of chess with Death against an imposing background of sea and sky.

overleaf: Magnificent tableau of the Dance of Death. The knight and the others are led away by Death to the dark lands. According to Bergman the scene was shot hastily: "We'd packed up for the evening and were just about to go home. It was raining. Suddenly I saw a cloud; and Fischer swung his camera up. Several of the actors had already gone home. So at a moment's notice some of the grips had to stand in, and get some costumes on and dance along up there. The whole scene was improvised in about ten minutes flat."

washes their faces and cleanses the tears from their cheeks," he speaks for Bergman as a lyric poet.

In Sweden the critical reception of the movie was mixed, but internationally it elevated Bergman to the stature of one of the most striking filmmakers on the contemporary scene. *The Seventh Seal* received the French Motion Picture Academy's Grand Prix International du Film d'Avant Garde, as well as major awards in Italy and Spain; and in the United States it called attention to Bergman in a way that no previous film of his had done. Up until *The Seventh Seal*, there was a popular conception of Bergman in America as a director of erotic Swedish films; pirated prints of some of his earlier films such as *Summer with Monika,* with sex scenes spliced in, were shown at raffish movie theaters on Times Square. But *The Seventh Seal*, distributed by Cyrus Harvey's Janus Films at the beginning of a long association with Bergman and Svensk Filmindustri, radically altered Bergman's image. Together with Fellini, Antonioni, and Truffaut, he entered into the fledgling American art-house circuit, where he would acquire a devoted following.[10]

Wild Strawberries

(1957)

THE INSPIRATION for *Wild Strawberries*, which appeared later in the same year as *The Seventh Seal*, came to Bergman from an incident that occurred while he was driving early one morning to Dalarna. When he reached Uppsala, he decided on a sudden impulse to revisit his grandmother's apartment. "I went into the little cobblestone yard," he remarks. "Then I went up into the house and took hold of the door knob to the kitchen door, . . . and a feeling ran quickly through me: suppose I open it? . . . Suppose I could suddenly walk into my childhood? . . . That was the real starting point of *Wild Strawberries*."[11] In the spring of 1957, Bergman began writing the script, which would concern a doctor, "a tired old egocentric, who'd cut off everything around him—as I'd done."[12] His immediate choice for the role was Victor Sjöström, Bergman's silent-film idol and early counselor at Svensk Filmindustri, whom he had directed in *To Joy* eight years earlier. "Victor," Bergman remarks, "was feeling wretched and didn't want to [do it]; . . . he must have been seventy-eight. He was misanthropic and tired and felt old. . . . I had to use all my powers of persuasion to get him to play the part."[13]

Wild Strawberries, like *Summer Interlude*, is one of Bergman's "journey" films, in which a character goes back into the past to confront a deep problem within himself and, as a result, achieves a reintegration of personality. The movie, which takes place on June 1, 1957, has a twenty-four-hour time frame. It begins early in the morning at the home of Isak Borg (Victor Sjöström), a doctor and retired professor of medicine who is to receive a Jubilee Doctor degree from the University of Lund on the occasion of the fiftieth anniversary of his graduation. Still not quite awake, he has a disturbing, surrealistic dream in which he is alone in strong sunlight on an unnaturally quiet

left: A family outing at the Borgs' summer house is "witnessed" by Isak Borg as, in his imagination, he revisits the past.

right: The drive Isak Borg (Victor Sjöström) takes with his daughter-in-law Marianne (Ingrid Thulin) to Lund. Although sharing the same seat, they are set apart from one another and withdrawn into their own thoughts. En route, Marianne tells Isak that he is a cold, egoistic man who has destroyed his son's capacity for love.

opposite: One of a number of haunting scenes in which Isak is alone in the woods, silhouetted against dark tree limbs and an expansive sky. The figure of the old man by the cradle brings birth and death into dramatic relation.

and deserted city street. As he looks up at a clock, he notices that it has no hands; suddenly he observes the dark figure of a man standing with his back to him, and when he approaches and taps him on the shoulder, the man turns to face him. His crabbed and puckered face startles Isak, and a moment later the man collapses like a punctured balloon into a pool of dark fluid at his feet. Church bells ring, and a hearse drawn by a pair of horses appears in the street, strikes a lamppost, and disgorges a coffin that bursts open to reveal a protruding hand. As Isak comes closer and peers into the coffin, the hand reaches out and draws him close to the corpse within, whose face is suddenly revealed as Isak's own. Horrified, Isak awakens. It is the first in a series of dreams and dreamlike reveries that lay bare his isolation from others, his unlived life.

In the morning Isak leaves on his auto journey to Lund, accompanied by his daughter-in-law Marianne (Ingrid Thulin in her first appearance in Bergman's films), but en route they stop to look at the Borg family's old summer house. As they walk in the woods adjoining the large house, the sight of a patch of wild strawberries sets off a chain of associations. In reverie, old Isak returns to this spot in his youth, where he observes Sara (Bibi Andersson), the attractive young cousin Isak expects to marry, as she picks wild strawberries for her Uncle Aron's name day and is kissed by Sigfrid (Per Sjöstrand), Isak's more relaxed and pleasure-loving brother whom Sara will marry in his place. Isak's reveries ends with the appearance, in the present, of a vivacious girl also named Sara (and also played by Bibi Andersson), accompanied by two boyfriends who argue fruitlessly about the existence of God. These young people join Isak and Marianne on their trip to Lund.

Isak's personal history is filled out further when he stops to visit his ninety-six-year-old mother (Naima Wifstrand), whose emotional detachment from others is her legacy to her son. Later, in a strange dream sequence, Isak is examined in a lecture hall to determine his fitness as a doctor. When he cannot remember that a doctor's first duty is "to ask forgiveness," he is judged "incompetent" and is punished by being taken to a spot in the woods, where he is made to witness a scene from years gone by of his wife's infidelity with another man, which is attributed to his coldness toward her. Later still, in a flashback, one meets his son Evald (Gunnar Björnstrand), whose bitter self-enclosure has been affected by his father's lack of feeling for him. When Marianne tells him that she is pregnant, Evald insists that she have an abortion, having come to regard life almost solely in terms of pain. The picture closes with the ceremony at the university and Isak's retirement for the evening at Evald's house where, following all that has been revealed to him, he is moved by a new sensitivity to life and to others.

Wild Strawberries scored an enormous success both in Sweden and abroad and won numerous awards. It received the Golden Bear award at the 1958 Berlin International Film Festival, as well as signif-

above: Bergman, seated alone, while making *Wild Strawberries.* Ingrid Thulin described him at this time as "part devil, part man, with a touch of what you might call heaven."

below: On the set of *Wild Strawberries,* Bergman in conversation with Victor Sjöström. At left is Bibi Andersson, with whom Sjöström developed "an enchanting kinship."

above: Isak Borg prepares for his trip to Lund, while Agda, his housekeeper (Jullan Kindahl), packs his bag. His grumpy but affectionate relationship with Agda is one of the delightful features of the film.

icant awards in Italy, Norway, Denmark, and the United States. Despite its acclaim when it first appeared, however, *Wild Strawberries* seems flawed in at least one important respect. One never sees Isak in close relation to the characters he is supposed to have injured by his self-absorption. We have only Evald's word for it, for example, that his father has made him as he is. One sees an incident of Isak's wife's infidelity but the marriage has never been filled in. His wife tells her lover that Isak is "as cold as ice," but as far as one can see there is nothing whatever of a forbidding chill about the old professor. He is a lovable old soul (as can be seen in his slightly grumpy but affectionate relationship with his housekeeper Agda), who does not seem to warrant the harsh charges against him of other characters. The great problem for the film is that the beneficence Victor Sjöström projects is at odds with Bergman's conception of Isak as a man who is cold and withdrawn.

Yet in terms of emotive effect and richness of texture, Sjöström's performance is the most absorbing feature of the film. The humanity of his face is constantly fascinating, as Bergman himself notes in a diary he kept during the shooting of the movie. "I never stop pryingly, shamelessly studying this powerful face," he writes. "Sometimes it is like a dumb cry of pain, sometimes it is distorted by mistrustful cruelty and senile querulousness, sometimes it dissolves into self-pity and astoundingly sentimental effusions."[14] The movie ends with a "vision" of Isak as he looks across a stretch of water to a bank in the distance where his parents, as younger people, are together fishing; as his parents wave to him in recognition, his face

Isak comes upon the patch of wild
strawberries from his youth that
provokes a recall of the past.

suddenly brightens with an expression of openness and tenderness. It
is the most magnificent visual moment in a film that throughout has
been superbly lighted and photographed by Gunnar Fischer. All the
scenes in the woods where Isak is shown against a background of the
dark, gnarled branches of trees and a slate-gray sky are magical in
their atmosphere of longing for what has been lost. Isak appears in
his visions as an old man, an outsider, standing unseen in doorways
or looking in through windows at a young world. Poignantly, in one
of the woodland scenes Sara holds up a mirror to Isak's face so that
he may see himself, "a worried old man who will die soon." The
scene is set by the patch of wild strawberries that suggest the conse-
crated moment of deeply felt life that Isak has denied himself.

   Wild Strawberries also has a personal subtext, for it is not only
Isak who stands trial for not asking "to be forgiven" but also Ingmar
Bergman in his relationship to his father, from whom he had been
distant for two decades. When Bergman speaks of Isak as "an egocentric, who'd cut off everything around him—as I'd done," he is
acknowledging his early family wounds and their consequence: the

intellectual wall he had built around himself for self-protection. At the same time, not a little of Erik Bergman can be seen in the portrait of Isak. Frank Gado points out that when Bergman was writing *Wild Strawberries*, Erik Bergman had just retired as Royal Chaplain and pastor of Hedvig Eleonora. Like the elder Bergman, Gado writes, "Isak, at the end of an illustrious career, is a man whose public honor contrasts with his family's antipathy toward him. Significantly, Evald (at thirty-eight, exactly Bergman's age on June 1, 1957) cannot overcome his 'deep alienation' toward his father—and thus the film is cheated of the happy ending toward which it has been heading. And yet, despite the residual bitterness Bergman felt impelled to register in this final scene between father and son, the longing for his father's love remains the most powerful force behind the film."[15] In the previous year Bergman and his father had drawn somewhat closer together. The scene at the end in which the parents wave at Isak across the stretch of water is at least a nod in the direction of reconciliation, and on its primary level *Wild Strawberries* is a morality of "sin" and forgiveness. Considered purely in its imagery, the film is a marvel.

View of Isak's wife (Gertrud Fridh) in the woods as she studies her face in a mirror, gazing as it were into her soul. In another scene occurring in Isak's imagination, Sara, the girl he hoped to marry, holds a mirror to his face, remarking: "You are a worried old man who will die soon."

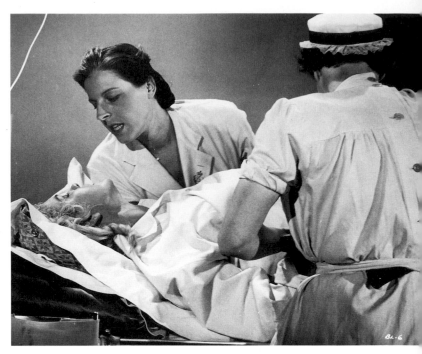

Brink of Life

(1957)

IMMEDIATELY after *Wild Strawberries*, Bergman made the short film *Brink of Life* (British title: *So Close to Life*) for Nordisk Tonefilm. Several years earlier Bergman had agreed to do a film version of Strindberg's *The Crown-Bride* for the company, but the project was abandoned when he became involved with other films. He felt that he owed them something, however, and in its place made *Brink of Life*, about several pregnant women in a Stockholm maternity ward.[16] The screenplay was written by Bergman with Ulla Isaksson and was based on a story in her collection, *Death's Aunt*.

The picture focuses first on Cecilia Ellius (Ingrid Thulin), a secretary with the state board of education, whose husband, Anders (Erland Josephson), visits her in the maternity ward—a scene providing a quick psychological probe of their marriage, which seems a very edgy affair. There is a subtle but distinct lack of communication between them. A rather dour, intellectual type, Anders shows scant enthusiasm about his impending fatherhood. The worst happens: the baby is stillborn, and Cecilia suffers self-blaming remorse. The second woman, Stina Andersson (Eva Dahlbeck), is, unlike Cecilia, an untroubled person who exudes health and looks forward expectantly to the birth of her child, and her working-class husband, Harry (Max von Sydow), is entirely supportive. Yet her childbirth experience, when it comes, is extremely harrowing, and the baby is born dead. The third figure is an unmarried nineteen-year-old girl, Hjördis Pet-

left: Hjördis Pettersson (Bibi Andersson), a pregnant, nineteen-year-old factory girl without a husband, enters into an understanding relationship with Cecilia Ellius (Ingrid Thulin).

right: Stina Andersson (Eva Dahlbeck) about to give birth. Her baby, however, will be born dead. *Brink of Life* attracted attention when it appeared because of its stark, documentary-like realism, but it also anticipates Bergman's "chamber films" that are harrowing and intimate.

tersson (Bibi Andersson), whose boyfriend has refused to marry her and who feels unready to assume the responsibilities of motherhood. Yet at the end, having matured through her association with the other women, she calls her mother and decides to return home to have her baby.

In keeping with its documentary approach, no moral is drawn in the film, which leaves the viewer with the puzzle of why the childbirth experience should bring suffering to some and renewal to others. *Brink of Life* is an austere film involving only a small number of characters within the limited setting of the hospital room. It has no deep resonance, chiefly because its characters are so strongly typed, but it is superbly acted, and its realistic techniques (a camera that is almost immobile and kept close to the characters) were considered innovative at the time the film was made. Swedish critics praised it, and at the 1958 Cannes Film Festival it received awards for Best Director and Best Actress (collectively to Thulin, Dahlbeck, and Andersson).

Brink of Life: Cecilia in an early scene in the maternity ward. Nothing goes well for her.

The Magician

(1958)

I N THE LATE 1950s, Bergman's recognition as a filmmaker was matched by the acclaim his stage productions at Malmö were receiving. In 1957, the season of *The Seventh Seal* and *Wild Strawberries*, Bergman staged Molière's *The Misanthrope*, starring Max von Sydow as Alceste, which became one of the highlights of his theatrical career—the "brilliant climax," one critic wrote, "of all Swedish theater in the fifties."[17] Shortly after its opening, Bergman wrote and began shooting *The Magician* (British title: *The Face*), which had its Swedish premiere in December 1958 and would go on to win the 1959 Special Jury Prize at the Venice Film Festival.

Set in Sweden in the 1840s, the movie begins with a view of a carriage as it travels through a dim, misty forest. Inside are various members of the Magnetic Health Theater—Albert Emanuel Vogler (Max von Sydow), a mesmerist and illusionist; Aman (Ingrid Thulin), Vogler's "boy" assistant who is actually his wife, Manda, in disguise; their stout, wily manager, Tubal (Åke Fridell); and Vogler's grandmother (Naima Wifstrand), an old crone who purveys potions and herbal medicaments. Vogler and his wife travel in disguise because of a scrape with the law in another locality that caused them to leave in the middle of the night, yet they have hopes of performing their magic before the king when they reach Stockholm. As they near the city, they stop to attend a drunken and dying actor named Spegel (Bengt Ekerot); seated in the coach beside them, he appears to expire, and they are faced with the prospect of arriving in the city with a corpse as their companion.

When they reach the city, the troupe is detained by police chief Starbeck (Toivo Pawlo) and invited by Councilman Egerman (Erland Josephson) to spend the night at his mansion, where Dr. Vergérus (Gunnar Björnstrand), the court medical officer, plans to examine Vogler and expose him as a charlatan. Vogler claims to be mute, but when Vergérus examines his vocal cords he can find no physiological explanation for the supposed condition and declares Vogler a fraud. His greatest wish, more chillingly, is to perform an autopsy on the mesmerist—to weigh his brain, open his heart, explore his nerves, lift out his eyes. Egerman and his friends enjoy a formal dinner, while Vogler and his troupe are sent to the kitchen to eat with the servants.

Their presence in the house, however, is a catalyst that brings characters into unexpected relationships. Tubal sells a love potion to Sofia Garp (Sif Ruud), the cook, and to two maids, Sara (Bibi Andersson) and Sanna (Birgitta Pettersson), with entertaining and comic results. Sofia, a widow, becomes attracted to Tubal and will leave him exhausted by her sexual insatiability. Simon (Lars Ekborg), the young coachman of the troupe, boasts of his virility and knowledge of the world to Sara, but reveals himself as a diffident, inexperienced boy when she seduces him in the laundry room. Unlooked-for interactions of characters belonging to the Egerman house and the Vogler troupe also extend to those upstairs. Mrs. Egerman (Gertrud Fridh) meets with Vogler and asks him to come to her bedroom at two o'clock in the morning; and after "Aman" is revealed as being Vogler's wife, Vergérus appears at her room with an interest in making love to her.

The next day Vogler is invited to demonstrate his magic before Egerman and his guests. Provoked by their treatment of him and by their failure to be convinced by his levitation of a table, he puts Starbeck's wife into a trance in which she gigglingly reveals that the police chief is a man lacking in any refinement and is not really the father of their children. In another demonstration of his powers, he binds Antonsson, Egerman's huge coachman, with an invisible chain from which he is unable to break loose. Enraged, Antonsson throttles Vogler, apparently killing him. Bergman's own conjuring tricks create a constant fluctuation between appearance and reality. Presumed dead, Spegel comes to life and, like a household ghost, steals brandy from the kitchen, then dies in fact and is placed by Vogler among his theatrical properties. When Dr. Vergérus goes to the attic to perform his much-desired autopsy of Vogler, it turns out that Vogler has merely feigned death and (in some never clearly explained way) substituted Spegel's body for his own.

At first Vergérus seems to triumph, having found nothing exceptional or abnormal in the corpse, and with some satisfaction proceeds to write his report. Yet as he does, a series of eerie events occur (a stopped clock begins to strike, an eyeball appears in Vergérus's inkwell, the face of the presumably dead Vogler appears in a mirror). Pursued by what seems Vogler's ghost, Vergérus screams and rushes down the attic stairs in terror. Yet still more reversals occur. In the stairwell, Vogler admits to the hoax he has perpetrated, and Vergérus, having regained his composure, displays his contempt for the pathetic and penniless illusionist. Then, with another swing of the pendulum, news arrives suddenly that Vogler's troupe has been summoned to perform their magic at the royal palace. Before their carriage rolls off triumphantly, a number of surprising role changes occur among the household and Health Theater characters. Tubal decides to stay with Sofia Garp, and Granny retires from her life as a necromancer to open a respectable chemist's shop in town. Sara, the maid, on the other hand, joins her newfound lover Simon for a life of adventure with the Voglers. The pairing off of these characters and the new roles they adopt suggest the ending of a comedy, which *The Magician* is in part.

But not entirely. Bergman first imagined the film as an erotic comedy (and persuaded Carl-Anders Dymling to approve it on this basis), but as he proceeded with the script its texture grew denser and more concerned with the debate between supernaturalism and science. He also began to explore the role played by the theatrical characters. The actor Spegel (whose name in Swedish means mirror) has taken to drink, seemingly because his profession no longer sustains him. He would if he could be the servant of a higher spiritual truth but is entrapped within his physical being, which he calls meaningless and absurd. Vogler, who is Spegel's character double, suffers from this dilemma too. When he first appears, his bearded countenance and dark, penetrating, soulful eyes seems to evoke him as a kind of Christ figure; but later, when he is alone with Manda in the Egerman house and removes his false beard and the rest of his disguise, he looks almost featureless. The spiritual role he assumes makes him a self-hating charlatan.

The focal confrontation of the film occurs between Vogler and Vergérus, who are allied, respectively, with spirit and intellect. Yet these two are more similar than they might at first seem. Vergérus's desire to expose Vogler rests on more than intellectual disinterestedness; it springs from a deep-seated fear that rationality itself may be inadequate to explain the mystery of life. Vogler's anguish is that the spiritual idea must prove inadequate when confronted by reason and science. The tensions of doubt are equally passionate in both men. The film has been set in an earlier age of confusion when science was as yet insecurely established and religion had begun to degenerate into theatrical supernaturalism. But one of the characters, Spegel, is modern in his implications, even existential. The agonist of a God who is silent, he announces as he dies that "we move step by step into obscurity; the moving tide is the only truth."

The Magician is one of Bergman's most theatrical films, consisting of disguise and exposure; sudden reversals of fortune; a central character who levitates tables; a doctor whose autopsies are like a performance; a brandy-swilling ghost; an apparent corpse that comes

A dramatic moment in *The Magician*, in which Dr. Vergérus (Gunnar Björnstrand) conducts a harsh examination of the supposedly mute Albert Vogler (Max von Sydow) and declares him a fraud. In the background is Vogler's wife, Manda (Ingrid Thulin), disguised as the boy Aman.

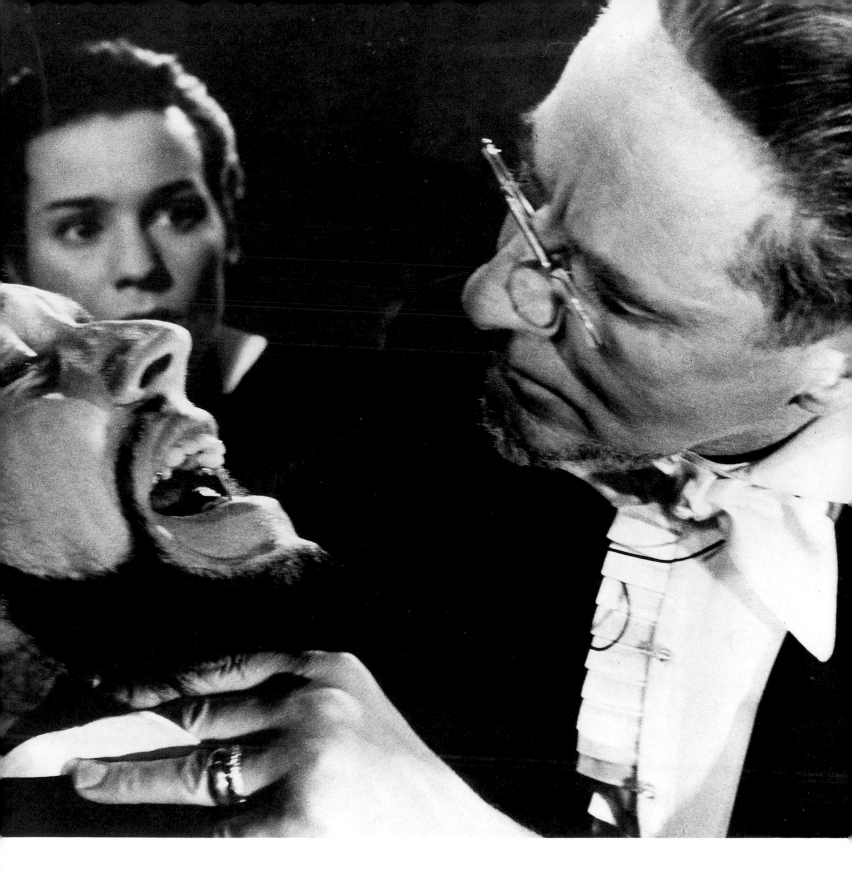

to life; a horror show in the attic; and much more. But its comedy darkens with the introduction of Bergman's existential theme, the removal of all certainties and the anguish felt by Vogler as he confronts his isolation. In this respect, *The Magician* is a pivotal film that leads Bergman from his bittersweet comedies of love and marriage of the 1950s to his explorations of forsaken characters in his movies of the 1960s.

The First Trilogy

The Virgin Spring

(1960)

B Y THE END of the 1950s, Bergman's personal and professional life had undergone a number of changes.[1] In 1959 he and Bibi Andersson ended their relationship, although not their friendship or professional collaboration, which has continued fruitfully into the present, and Bergman married his fourth wife, the concert pianist Käbi Laretei. In that year, too, he left Malmö to become a director with the Royal Dramatic Theater in Stockholm and shot his new film *The Virgin Spring*, based on the folk ballad "Töres dotter i Vänge," about the rape and murder of a young virgin and the revenge of her father on the perpetrators in fourteenth-century Sweden.

Bergman had read a version of the ballad as early as his student days. Later he suggested to the principal choreographer at the Royal Opera that it be made into a ballet, and later still he considered the possibility of developing it into a play. Finally, while shooting *Wild Strawberries*, it struck him that the material was, in fact, cinematic. "I went home," Bergman remarks, "re-read the ballad, and saw it materialize in scenes."[2] The screenplay was written in consultation with Bergman by Ulla Isaksson, who had written *Brink of Life* and is responsible for the film's historical accuracy. Gunnar Fischer was called away on assignment when Bergman was about to begin work on the picture, and in his place he used Sven Nykvist, who had been one of the three cinematographers for *The Naked Night*. Fischer would shoot Bergman's next film, *The Devil's Eye*, but thereafter Nykvist would be Bergman's cinematographer of choice and the look of his films would be altered—from the tense light-and-dark studies of Fischer to the subtler, more naturalistic compositions of Nykvist.

The plot of *The Virgin Spring*, set in a rural medieval world in which the pagan worship of Odin has begun to give way to Christianity, is simplicity itself. In the Christian household of Töre (Max von Sydow) and Märeta (Birgitta Valberg), their young, blonde-haired daughter Karin (Birgitta Pettersson) is to journey by horseback to a church in the region to offer votive candles for the Virgin Mary. Accompanying her is Ingeri (Gunnel Lindblom), her foster sister, who has a lowly position in the household, is jealous of Karin,

opposite: Winter Light: Bergman directing a scene in church. The settings in the film are unusually austere. "Bergman is the only practising director," critic Vernon Young declared, "who can make an eloquent film from a rag, a bone and a hank of hair."

91

left: The Virgin Spring: As she travels by horseback to a church in the region, Karin (Birgitta Pettersson) stops to speak to a neighbor. Like her father, he regards her as a little princess. During shooting, Bergman felt that *The Virgin Spring* was one of his finest films. Later, however, he spoke of it deprecatingly as imitation Kurosawa. "All that time," he commented, "my admiration for the Japanese cinema was at its height. I was almost a samurai myself."

above: Töre (Max von Sydow) rubs his hands together to warm them after entering his house. The day began in sunshine but the weather has now turned cold, and Töre and Märeta (Birgitta Valberg) are deeply concerned that Karin has not returned from her journey. Before long Töre will learn that the herdsmen-guests have raped and murdered his child and will take resolute revenge.

and wishes her ill. En route they encounter three itinerant herdsmen, one of them a boy, with whom Karin innocently offers to share her lunch. While Ingeri looks on at a distance, one of the herdsmen rapes and then kills the girl. Later the three herdsmen wander upon the dwelling of Karin's parents, who give them supper; but when, unaware that the couple are the girl's parents, they attempt to sell Karin's clothing to Märeta, she alerts her husband, who dispatches them. Töre sets out to find Karin's body and upon discovering it kneels, asks forgiveness for his violence, and promises to build a church on the site of his daughter's death. A spring suddenly wells from the soil as if to sanction the drama of Christian rebirth through sin and atonement.

Visually compelling and tightly constructed, *The Virgin Spring* is rooted in the historical past but speaks to universal human nature. The household at the beginning already contains incipient conflicts that the picture skillfully develops. Karin is a beautiful and innocent girl but she is also vain. Because she lacks a developed consciousness, she brings about her own undoing—first by dancing with the young man who is Ingeri's lover, thus setting Ingeri against her, and then by flirting innocently with the herdsmen, which leads to her rape and murder. She has no awareness of the darker passions underlying sexuality.

Her contrasting foster sister Ingeri, who is dark and sensual, is closer to the earth and to rudimentary instinct. Quick to resentment and jealousy, she seeks to bring the cosseted Karin down to her own level of basic sexuality. She casts a pagan spell on Karin and plants a live toad in the bread she prepares for her lunch; when Karin cuts the bread in the presence of the herdsmen, the toad, associated with sexuality in medieval folklore, leaps out and Karin becomes the object of their lust. If Karin is unconscious of the passional nature of sexuality,

Ingeri is blinded by her emotions to the consequences of the sexuality she evokes but also regrets. She is in conflict with herself, and the viewer is drawn partly into sympathy with her. Töre is an upright man, but when confronted by the murderers of his child becomes coldly homicidal; quickly forgetting his Christian principles, he kills not only the perpetrators of his daughter's violation but also the thirteen-year-old boy, whose guilt has been marginal. The boy's face, one notices, suggests a perhaps ruder version of Karin's innocence. But if a certain complexity exists within the principal characters, one also notes an ambivalence in the natural world through which the two girls ride, Karin mounted on a white horse, Ingeri on a dark one.

Just before making *The Virgin Spring*, Bergman studied the films of Akira Kurosawa, particularly *Rashomon*,[3] and the picture reflects the styling of Kurosawa in a number of respects. One thinks of *Rashomon*, for example, in the rape scene, which is reminiscent of the one in which the aristocratic wife of a samurai warrior is raped by a primitive, uncouth, lower-class bandit. Bergman also seems conscious of the Japanese director in the manner in which he places solitary figures against a vast outdoor background and in symmetrical relation to particular objects or furnishings of building interiors. Kurosawa's frequent passages of silence, too, have their counterparts in Bergman's film. Perhaps most of all, the forest setting (and the way it is lit) is strikingly like Kurosawa in being somber, ominous, and even frightening.

right: Karin with the boy (Ove Porath) and one of the herdsmen (Tor Isedal) in a lighthearted moment.

The *Virgin Spring* is one of Bergman's most striking, if also one of his most untypical, works. Only the Christian denouement mars it. Architecturally, the ending has a certain sense, since it shows the conquest of pagan worship by Christian moral law: the need for humility, restraint, and atonement. In other respects, it seems pietistic (a heavenly choir is heard at the end) and imposed upon the film. Although Töre kneels before his Christian God, He seems absent from the work. What excites Bergman and the viewer more is the ambivalence of pagan nature with its sexuality, mystery, and latent violence. A brilliant tour de force, *The Virgin Spring* made a strong impression and won numerous awards, including the International Critics Prize at the 1960 Cannes Film Festival and the 1960 Academy Award for Best Foreign Film.

The itinerant herdsmen, seated at a bench with their backs to the camera, have been invited to have dinner with Töre and his wife, Märeta, at his left.

The naïve pastor (Nils Poppe) in *The Devil's Eye* introduces his daughter, Britt-Marie (Bibi Andersson), to a stranger in their area. In reality, he is Don Juan (Jarl Kulle), on a mission from hell to corrupt the girl.

The Devil's Eye

(1960)

BERGMAN wrote *The Devil's Eye* at the same time that he and Ulla Isaksson wrote *The Virgin Spring*; the two films, in fact, were part of an arrangement worked out with Carl-Anders Dymling at Svensk Filmindustri. When Bergman proposed *The Virgin Spring*, Dymling was reluctant to support the film, which he did not think would have much appeal. But he agreed, provided that Bergman would make a comedy immediately afterward.[4] The comedy Bergman offered, *The Devil's Eye*, was based on a Danish radio play by Oluf Bang that Svensk Filmindustri had acquired sometime before. Its protagonist, Don Juan, the legendary seducer of women who is consigned to hell, was already familiar to Bergman, who had staged a popular production of Molière's *Don Juan* at Malmö in 1956. Unfortunately, *The Devil's Eye* followed so quickly after *The Virgin Spring* that Bergman had not yet had time to collect himself. He speaks of being tired during the making of the picture and of feeling unanchored by all the changes brought about in his life by his recent marriage and removal from Malmö to the Royal Dramatic Theater in Stockholm. All of these things, he remarks, "must have infected my work."[5] Part of the film at least fails to come to life.

The movie's plot, which involves Don Juan's leaving hell to visit Scandinavia to test a virgin's virtue, has comic potentialities. The epigraph for the film shown before the action begins, "A young woman's chastity is a stye in the Devil's eye," is attributed to a saying of the Irish, but it is Bergman's own invention, and it is one of a number of witty comments ("What would hell be without marriage?") that are sprinkled through the film. The picture opens in the Devil's fiery chambers, to which Don Juan is summoned on a mission to return to earth and compromise the virtue of a Swedish girl who is

left: Don Juan with his servant Pablo (Sture Lagerwall). While Don Juan pursues Britt-Marie, Pablo lays siege to the pastor's wife.

right: Don Juan with Britt-Marie, who will later tell her bridegroom the outrageous lie that she has never kissed another man.

about to be married and whose chastity has caused a painful stye to form on the Devil's eye. Don Juan (Jarl Kulle) and his squire Pablo (Sture Lagerwall) materialize in the Swedish countryside and before long are introduced into the household of a naïve parson (Nils Poppe), his wife, Renata (Gertrud Fridh), and their daughter, Britt-Marie (Bibi Andersson), the maiden Don Juan has been sent to corrupt. Don Juan makes up to Britt-Marie while Pablo lays siege to the parson's wife, but the intruders' plans miscarry. Don Juan refrains from seducing Britt-Marie when he recognizes that he is in love with her; Pablo goes to bed with Renata but the incident merely draws her closer to her husband, who forgives her infidelity. The two emissaries return to the infernal regions to face the consternation of the Devil (Stig Järrel). Yet Britt-Marie's virtue is compromised after all when, on her wedding night, she tells her bridegroom the outrageous lie that she has never kissed another man. The stye miraculously disappears from the Devil's eye, and hell triumphs once again over heaven.

The Devil's Eye has the styling of a stage work. It is introduced by a gentleman with a pointer (Gunnar Björnstrand) before the action begins in the Devil's chambers, and thereafter the film is divided into a series of acts, with brief appearances of the gentleman between acts. The Devil's chambers, with torches flaring behind rear windows, have the artificiality of a stage set, and the bewigged, supercilious eighteenth-century counselors to the Devil might have stepped out of a play by Molière. Bergman's humor in the hell sequence is strained, and the Devil, who wears a business suit, makes an unlikely ruler of the netherworld. Only in the vicarage scenes does the film engage the audience's interest. Bibi Andersson is charming as Britt-Marie, and Gertrud Fridh gives an understanding portrayal of the parson's lonely wife, who has expected little from her marriage but by the end expects a little more. Nils Poppe is ingratiating as the naïve-as-a-child parson who locks the demon, sent to keep an eye on Don Juan and Pablo, in a cabinet, and eventually becomes more conscious of his wife's needs and the world of reality that has all the while surrounded him.

Karin (Harriet Andersson) tells her brother, Minus (Lars Passgård), that she hears voices behind the wallpaper of an upstairs room and that God will come to her soon.

Through a Glass Darkly

(1961)

hrough a Glass Darkly takes its title from the Bible (Paul's First Epistle to the Corinthians 13:12): "For now we see through a glass, darkly; but then face to face: now I know in part; but then shall I know even as also I am known." In it Bergman returns to the religious questioning of certain earlier films, but in this case the characters, or at least two of them, the father and son, also come to know themselves and find a new relationship. The film announces a turning point in Bergman's career as the first of his spare "chamber works," which are influenced by certain of Strindberg's plays, but which Bergman also compares to chamber music, "music in which, with an extremely limited number of voices and figures, one explores the essence of a number of motifs."[6] Its single setting is a remote Baltic island; its action takes place within a bare twenty-four-hour time period—from dawn of one day to dawn of the next; and it involves only four characters: David (Gunnar Björnstrand), a novelist; his seventeen-year-old son, Minus (Lars Passgård); his daughter, Karin (Harriet Andersson), who suffers from episodes of schizophrenia and by the end of the film will pass into permanent madness; and Karin's husband, Martin (Max von Sydow), a doctor.

Among the "firsts" associated with *Through a Glass Darkly* is its setting on the island of Fårö, off the coast of Sweden, where a number of subsequent films will be set and where Bergman will take up residence later in the decade. The Orkney Islands were at first considered, but no suitable site could be found, and then someone suggested Fårö. "So on a nasty, wet day," Bergman remarks, "we went over there on the ferry. It was pouring. But I don't know why, it was a kind of instant love. I just felt this was my landscape."[7] The film also marks the point at which Bergman begins his consistent collaboration with cameraman Sven Nykvist. At first Bergman and

Nykvist considered shooting the film in color, but they were dissatisfied with the footage they tried, and the movie was made in black and white. The decision seems fortunate; its muted tones, often in shades of gray, capture the austerity of the drama perfectly.

The most far-reaching influence on *Through a Glass Darkly* was Bergman's background as a man of the theater. "Because I've always worked in the theatre," Bergman told an interviewer, "and always had a longing to write stage plays, some of my films have obviously been surreptitious plays."[8] *Through a Glass Darkly* is a case in point, as Bergman explains: "I felt I had to drop all artistic tricks and simply concentrate on the human drama. And that was how this play came into being—for a play it is. It's a surreptitious stage-play, you can't get away from that, with orderly scenes, set side by side. The cinematic aspects of *Through a Glass Darkly* are rather secondary."[9] The film was also influenced by Anton Chekhov's *The Sea Gull*, which Bergman was preparing at Dramaten while he was writing *Through a Glass Darkly* at Dalarna in the spring of 1960. The little play that Minus has written and puts on at the summer house is inspired by the play-within-the-play that young Konstantin stages at the family estate in *The Sea Gull*; in each case the plays expose the artistic limitations of an older, established writer—Trigorin in Chekhov and David, Minus's father, in Bergman. David resembles

left: Minus in the rotted hull of the ship with his sister, Karin, after their act of incest.

right: Through a Glass Darkly begins at dawn as the film's four characters return from a swim. It will be a long and harrowing day.

opposite, top: Bergman and Sven Nykvist during the shooting of *Through a Glass Darkly*. Often his own harshest critic, Bergman later spoke slightingly of the film: "It's an étude, a study, an exercise, it's a beginning, but it's a pudding. It's so far away, I can't be sure, but my feeling is that it is a pudding."

opposite, bottom: Bergman while making *Through a Glass Darkly*. While shooting films, his laughter could often be heard on the set.

Trigorin particularly in his obsession with his writing and compulsion to use everything from his experience for his next piece of fiction, even though he knows that his work is superficial. Like Trigorin, David is an egocentric, conscious of an emptiness within himself and of his inability to enter life.

Bergman's characters reflect back and forth on one another. Karin's husband, Martin, is another version of David; they are of about the same age and are both failed father figures to Karin. Their resemblance is dramatized when they are together in the rowboat and accuse each other of being emotionally shallow; David admits to Martin that he has been observing Karin's dissolution for his fiction, but he also senses that Martin secretly wishes Karin were dead. At the same time, David has something in common with his seventeen-year-old son. Minus has been writing plays but has no knowledge of life; his plays, which are very bad, are no deeper than David's novels. Entrapped within himself by his youth and the sexuality he has attempted to repress, he searches for a way into life. These three self-enclosed males all gravitate toward Karin, the most sensitive character. Because of her schizophrenia, however, she is also the most helpless. In a harrowing scene near the end she withdraws from the real world into a delusional one in which God appears to her as a monstrous spider that attacks and sexually assaults her. Although delusional, her vision is relevant to the real world, since it implies an empty and unloving landscape, one in which there is only egoism and selfishness.

In addition to Karin's crisis, two others are depicted in the film, those of David and Minus. David, too, has had a "vision," which both consoles and troubles him. Sometime before the events of the film occur he had attempted to commit suicide by driving his car over a cliff. But at the point of life and death, the car stalled, with the front wheels hanging over the edge of the abyss. After crawling to safety, and still gasping for breath, he was suddenly filled with a love for his family. Intangible and hard to grasp as it is, the presence of love as something real in existence is all that he has to sustain him. "I let my emptiness, my dirty helplessness," he tells Minus at the end, "rest in that thought." But when he goes on to assure the boy that "we can't know whether love proves God's existence or whether love is itself God. After all, it doesn't make very much difference," he seems to delude himself with muddled metaphysics. David's "God is love" pronouncement that opens a form of communication with Minus is totally unconvincing and was promptly regretted by Bergman.

But Minus, too, has a "vision" of release from dread and self-enclosure, one that is more powerfully evoked than David's. A risky conception, it occurs in the scene in which Minus and Karin commit incest (offscreen) in the leaking hull of a wrecked schooner lying off the stony beach. The womblike hull of the forsaken and rotting ship brings together motifs of death and rebirth, and the scene enacted there becomes Minus's rite of passage into life. Minus tells his father that "as I was sitting in the wreck down there, holding Karin, reality burst in pieces for me. . . . Reality burst and I fell out." Bergman elaborates on Minus's state in his stage directions in the printed text of the film: "Minus is sitting somewhere in eternity with his sick sister in his arms. He is empty, exhausted, frozen. Reality, as he has known it until now, has been shattered, ceased to exist. Neither in his dreams nor his fantasies has he known anything to correspond to this weightlessness and grief. His mind has forced its way through the membrane of merciful ignorance. From this moment on his senses will change and harden, his receptivity will become sharpened, as he goes from the make-believe world of innocence to the torment of insight."[10] Karin loses her life to madness, and Minus is reborn as he comes to know sorrow and love. His life has interfused with that of another human being; he has moved out of his former isolation and touched life deeply.

Through a Glass Darkly is certainly flawed, yet its effect at times is hypnotic and it has a deep resonance that lingers in one's imagination. It is splendidly acted, particularly by Harriet Andersson, who gives one of the great performances of her career. The movie was enthusiastically received in Sweden, and in 1961 won both the British Film Academy Award and an Academy Award in the United States for Best Foreign Film.

Minus's search for his disturbed sister leads him to a decaying vessel by a stone pier.

The Pleasure Garden

(1961)

IN EARLY 1961, between the shooting of *Through a Glass Darkly* and *Winter Light*, Svensk Filmindustri was thrown into a state of crisis when Carl-Anders Dymling fell critically ill with cancer. Because no one was yet available to replace him, Bergman together with four other senior people at the studio formed an interim team to manage the company. One of the first problems to confront them was that the studio's staff of a hundred and thirty-five people had nothing to do, since no scripts were ready for filming. Bergman and Erland Josephson, using the joint pseudonym of Buntel Eriksson, quickly put together a screenplay entitled *The Pleasure Garden*, which was directed by Alf Kjellin.[11] *The Pleasure Garden*, which is set in a small Swedish town at the turn of the century, revolves around the affairs of two male schoolteachers with ladies in the town that, after some plot complications, are resolved rather nicely. Gunnar Björnstrand as David Franzén, Sickan Carlsson as Fanny, his love interest, and Bibi Andersson as Fanny's daughter Anna all give polished performances. But critics dismissed the movie as slight when it opened in Sweden, and it has never been shown abroad.

Winter Light

(1961)

IN APRIL 1961, Bergman staged a notable production of Igor Stravinsky's opera *The Rake's Progress* at the Royal Opera in Stockholm. But most of his energies were devoted to his new film *Winter Light* (British title: *The Communicants*). Like *Through a Glass Darkly*, *Winter Light* is a chamber work in which a very small group of characters appear in a setting of extreme austerity. It is the second installment of a film trilogy that begins with *Through a Glass Darkly* and concludes with *The Silence*; but the trilogy was not consciously in Bergman's mind when *Winter Light* was made. It is, however, clearly intended as a "correction" of *Through a Glass Darkly*, whose "God is love" ending Bergman had repudiated. In the new film the pastor's "twaddle of 'God is love and love is God'" is mere self-deception.

Winter Light was inspired partly by a conversation that Bergman held with a clergyman in Dalarna, who told him of a fisherman who had come to him for spiritual help; they talked together but his counsel was unavailing, and the fisherman hanged himself. To this situation, which Bergman uses in the film, he added another dimension: that the pastor is himself undergoing a crisis of faith. To prepare for the film, Bergman traveled to the Uppland churches with his father, observing their dwindling attendance and the lax attitude of the clergy in performing their duties.[12] At one church, a clergyman arrived and announced that, because he was feeling poorly, the service would consist only of a sermon and two psalms, without communion at the altar. Bergman's father, old and frail, was indignant and took the service at the altar himself. "In some ways," Bergman remarks, "I feel the end of the play [note the word] was influenced by my father's intervention—that at all costs one must do what it is one's duty to do, particularly in spiritual contexts. Even if it can seem meaningless."[13] The church at Mittsunda was constructed on a studio lot, but not before Bergman and Sven Nykvist had patiently studied the quality of light in the model church during the changing hours of the day. In their use of it, light gives cold comfort and is one of the essential elements in a drama that is enveloped in a sense of chilliness.

The small cast of the film includes Gunnar Björnstrand as pastor Tomas Ericsson; Ingrid Thulin as his mistress, Märta Lundberg; Max von Sydow as Jonas Persson, the fisherman who talks to Tomas before committing suicide; and Gunnel Lindblom as Jonas's concerned wife, Karin. Like *Through a Glass Darkly*, *Winter Light* has the tight construction of a play and contains only a few settings. The lengthy opening section is set at the church at Mittsunda, where Tomas officiates at an early morning service attended by a pathetically small group of congregants and later gives faltering counsel to the desolate Jonas in the vestry. As the action progresses, Tomas drives to the spot by the rapids where Jonas's body is recovered from the water and then to a schoolhouse where Märta teaches and lives upstairs in an apartment with her mother. Tomas and Märta then drive to the Frostnäs church, where the final scene occurs and Tomas conducts a vespers service. By then he has been revealed nakedly as a man of faltering faith who cannot help himself, much less others. His life has been a lie, a shielding of himself from life, and during the course of the film he is forced, with considerable anguish, to confront the truth of his situation.

But if *Winter Light* is constructed like a stage work in its series of well-defined scenes, it also has the nature of a Passion Play. It takes place on a Sunday between noon and 3 P.M., the time of Christ's Passion; and like Christ, Tomas calls out, "God, my God, why hast thou forsaken me?" Märta offers herself to him for support but he recoils from her, for there is nothing about her that he can idealize, as he has mistakenly idealized his late wife. Märta is too *real* in her desperate need to find meaning in her narrow existence by being of use to another human being. Her unsightly eczema, probably a psychosomatic condition, makes her one of life's victims. Another is the rheumatically crippled Algot Frövik, the sexton at Frostnäs, who compares his suffering to that of Christ's but is admirable in his ability to bear his lot. Bergman's characters are all locked into their isolation without the intervention of a caring God. Tomas is revealed particularly in his relation to Jonas, who has a lonely vision of life as terrible. When they confront one another, Jonas is the more honest

Pastor Tomas Ericsson (Gunnar Björnstrand), left, attempts to counsel the despondent fisherman Jonas Persson (Max von Sydow) in *Winter Light*. In a way, the two are character doubles, since Tomas's faith has also faltered. Later in the film he will confess: "Every time I confronted God with the reality I saw, he became ugly, revolting, a spider-God—a monster."

with himself of the two and is unmoved by Tomas's counsel that God equals love.

After so much spiritual desolation has been revealed, the last words of the film, spoken by Tomas at the altar at Frostnäs, seem particularly mocking. "Holy, holy, holy," he announces, "Lord God Almighty. All the earth is full of his glory." But the picture is not wholly despairing. Communication between people may yet be possible, not on the plane of "God is love" but on a more starkly human one. Tomas has not quite closed the door on a renewed relationship with Märta. When Bergman showed the film to his wife Käbi Laretei, she said: "Yes, Ingmar, it's a masterpiece; but it's a dreary masterpiece."[14] Its dreariness—the winter light without relief in which the suffering of the characters is captured—acts on the viewer's nerves and prevents any escape from the hard reality of Mittsunda and Frostnäs. The film is acted to perfection by a splendid cast who in a number of cases are playing against type. Gunnar Björnstrand, often seen in worldly parts, has here become a cleric; Max von Sydow, commanding in appearance, has somehow the look and bearing of a small, defeated, and inarticulate man; and the beautiful Ingrid Thulin is a stiff spinster with spectacles and severely combed-back hair. *Winter Light* is one of Bergman's most nearly perfect works.

The Silence

(1962)

SHOT IN THE late summer of 1962, *The Silence* followed quickly upon *Winter Light*. In *A Film Trilogy*, the published text of the three chamber works, Bergman notes: "The theme of these three films is a 'reduction'—in the metaphysical sense of that word. *Through a Glass Darkly*—certainty achieved. *The Communicants* [*Winter Light*]—certainty unmasked. *The Silence*—God's silence—the negative impression."[15] *The Silence* is set in what appears to be an East European city, where a foreign language made up by Bergman is unintelligible to the principal characters—two sisters in their thirties: Ester (Ingrid Thulin), a translator dying of consumption; Anna (Gunnel Lindblom), an attractive but morally aimless woman; and Anna's ten-year-old son, Johan (Jörgen Lindström). The name of the city, Timoka, an Estonian word meaning "pertaining to the executioner," was supplied by the title, noticed by Bergman, of a book that the Estonian-born Käbi Laretei happened to be reading. Its connotations are appropriate to the city, which evokes the idea of death (the death of God) and human disintegration.

The movie caused something of a sensation when it was released because of its sexual explicitness, which includes scenes of masturbation, lesbian eroticism, and sexual intercourse. Prior to its release it was reviewed by the Swedish censorship board, which approved it without cuts, a decision that altered the censorship laws in Sweden. It also stirred controversy abroad, and in Germany it was discussed in the Bundestag before the German censorship board finally approved it. Commercially the movie was an enormous success. In Sweden over six hundred thousand people went to see it during the first seven weeks of its showing; and in Europe, Britain, and America it attracted audiences in the millions.[16]

Johan (Jörgen Lindström), fourth from right, has wandered into the suite of the performing dwarfs. The dwarf on the bed wearing a monkey mask has been jumping up and down excitedly before Johan, whom the dwarfs have got up in a dress.

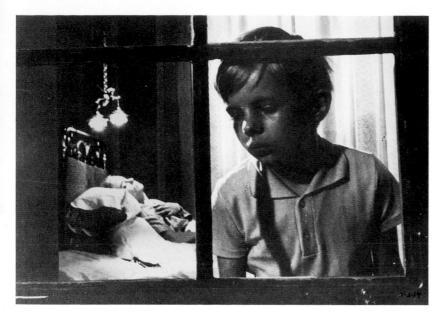 

left: Window tableau using dramatically contrasting panels. Ten-year-old Johan at right, his dying aunt Ester (Ingrid Thulin) at left. Bergman called *The Silence* "a sort of personal purgation: a rendering of hell on earth—my hell. . . . Some of the scenes I liked so much that I was astonished."

right: The Silence: a revealing spatial perspective of the principals, emphasizing their separateness from one another. Ester, at left; her sister, Anna (Gunnel Lindblom), seated at center in the adjoining room; Johan between them. "Ingrid Thulin once told me," critic James Monaco writes, "that at an initial stage Bergman had considered asking her to play both sisters."

The Silence has been conceived by Bergman as a cinematic dream. It has no flashbacks containing dream sequences; rather, the entire film is dreamlike. The strangeness of the city is complemented by the nineteenth-century hotel, built on a grand scale with high-ceilinged corridors, where Ester, Anna, and Johan stay. The only other guests shown, with expressionistic effect, are a troupe of dwarfs who perform in a cabaret revue. Ester and Anna, as different in their natures as intellect and instinct, interact in part on an abstract level; and their relationship, especially at the beginning, is probed subtly rather than dramatized through rapid action. More immediate action at first occurs at the edges of the film through Johan and his exploration of his newfound hotel world, which exercises a certain fascination for him but is also filled with threat. His consciousness at the opening ties him closely to his physically attractive, warm, and sensual mother. In the hotel suite he soaps her back as she takes a bath and then takes a nap with her; as she lies naked under a sheet, he curls up beside her in a fetal position. He looks to his mother for protection from the outer world, relying otherwise on the cap pistol he carries as he wanders the mazelike corridors. In one way or another his wanderings bring him into contact with sexuality. One of his encounters is with the elderly floorwaiter with big horse teeth who seeks to befriend him but whose overtures have sexual connotations. The floorwaiter pursues Johan through the corridors and gets hold of him for a moment before the boy wriggles away; later he entices Johan with a candy bar to his alcove room, where he waits to answer room-service calls. There he gives him photographs of his mother lying dead in an open bier with mourners around her, which link intimations of sexuality with death—specifically with the death of a mother figure.

In another sequence, Johan stands in a corridor looking up at a large painting of a hairy-legged satyr seducing a compliant nymph. The moment is followed by his entering the room of the dwarfs, who frolic about and put a dress on him while one of the dwarfs leaps up

105

and down excitedly on the bed wearing a grotesque monkey mask. Johan's most painful exposure to sexuality occurs when, standing alone and unseen in the corridor, he observes his mother and a café waiter (Birger Malmsten) she has picked up go into a room to have promiscuous sex (like the satyr and nymph in the painting). After he tells Ester what he has seen, he improvises a puppet show for her in which Punch beats Judy brutally—an expression of his anger at his mother, who has violated the supposedly protected center of his world. Bergman continually crosscuts between scenes with the boy and those with Ester and Anna, between his dawning consciousness and the destructive relationship of the adults.

That the sisters inhabit a God-forsaken world is implied in their references to their late father, a four-hundred-pound man who had once held authority but is now a faded memory. Ester, the attractive, slightly masculine sister, has attempted to take his place. As her translating work implies, she has cultural and intellectual interests but, as she recognizes, they have now come to seem meaningless. Moreover, a gulf exists between her and her sensual, instinctive sister, who resents her and wishes her dead. Her attempts to make contact with her sister, to express love, have at times lesbian overtones; but the only sexual experience Ester has in the film is with herself, an act of isolation and futility. The film has been lighted and photographed by Sven Nykvist with consummate skill that makes revelations of small moments, but it also draws intensity from the conflict between the sisters and the deterioration of Ester, who coughs up blood and has a horrifying fear of death. The old floorwaiter who attends her with fumbling solicitude is one of Bergman's recurring figures who usher characters into the land of the dead.

If Ester attempts to preserve what is left of a fading order, Anna attempts to throw off the prohibitions of the past through sexual indulgence. When she leaves the hotel, she attracts the interest of a café waiter, and then goes to a neighboring cinema to distract herself.

106

opposite, left: Johan stares up at a large canvas of a satyr seducing a compliant nymph. His wanderings through the corridors of the hotel have a dreamlike dimension.

opposite, right: When Ester comes into the room where Anna is in bed with the café waiter (Birger Malmsten), Anna rages at her: "I hate you because you make everything so important! I'm fed up with your principles. When Father died, you said you didn't want to go on living. Why are you still living then?"

below: Anna in a slatternly pose, while the café waiter faces away from her. The scene is a concise nightmare of empty lust.

She is in time to see the end of a stage revue featuring the dwarfs, who leap over one another like trained dogs under the direction of a handler and then glide grotesquely across the stage like a centipede, their bodies pressed so tightly together as to suggest a daisy chain of buggery. Their performance is a parody of sexual dehumanization. After the movie comes on, Anna observes a man and woman coupling in the darkness and, stimulated by what she sees, leaves the movie house and makes an assignation with the waiter, with whom she has sex in the dark corner of a church. Later they go to a room in the hotel for further sex, but the scene that ensues ends in squalor and misery. As the waiter (whose face is as expressionless as a mask) penetrates her from behind, she weepingly grips the rods of the bedframe, which resemble the bars of a prison. One of her legs strikes a nearby lamp, which crashes to the floor with an exploding flash of stark white light that is like a nightmare revelation of the emptiness of her experience.

But if the film visits hell, it does not seem purely hopeless. Johan undergoes an interesting change in the picture. At first he does not allow his aunt Ester to touch him; only his mother has that privilege. Later, however, when it is revealed that his mother cannot protect him from life or offer him guidance, he draws somewhat closer to Ester. He goes to her when she is dying, and she gives him a "secret message" in the form of a letter in which she has translated several Timokan words for "spirit," "anxiety," and "joy." In the final scene, when Johan and his mother are aboard a train leaving Timoka, after Ester has been left in the hotel to die, Johan reads and puzzles over their meaning. A dawning consciousness begins to occur to him as the result of his hotel experience. It is at least hinted that the gulf between people may be bridged to some degree, that "spirit" and "joy" might be present in life as well as "anxiety."

Unlike *Through and Glass Darkly* and *Winter Light*, which still adhere to conventional narrative form, *The Silence* introduces a new dimension in Bergman's conception of cinema. Realistic perception is replaced by a total immersion in a subjective world in which characters embody psychic states. Just as Federico Fellini shifts to a more abstract style at this time, Bergman in *The Silence* announces a new and more subjective film aesthetic. The movie looks immediately ahead to *Persona*, which also uses two young women who are alter egos and embody metaphysical ideas, and in which the same boy appears who is played by the same actor, wearing the same glasses and reading the same book, as in *The Silence*. In *The Silence*, Nykvist's camera dwells on the faces of the sisters, and in one scene shows them standing close together with the face of one toward the camera and the other in side profile—exactly as in a well-known still of Elisabet and Alma in the soon-to-be-made *Persona*. Bergman has said that in *The Silence*, Ester and Alma are different parts of a single psyche. In *Persona*, the psyches of the two young women actually merge.

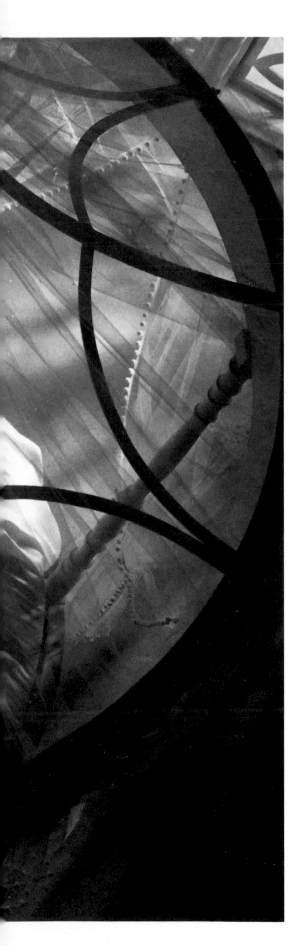

Persona *and the Second Trilogy*

Now About These Women

(1964)

INTERVENING between *The Silence* and *Persona* is a *divertissement*, *Now About These Women*, that Bergman wrote with Erland Josephson under the joint pseudonym of Buntel Eriksson. Bergman feared, incorrectly as it turned out, that *The Silence* would do poorly at the box office and that a comedy would now be helpful. Bergman and Josephson enjoyed working together on the script, but on its release the movie failed to amuse, and it is commonly considered Bergman's worst film. It revolves around a famous and greatly gifted cellist named Felix, who lives at a large ornamental estate called the Villa Tremolo with his wife and a bevy of mistresses. His privacy is invaded by the self-promoting music critic Cornelius (Jarl Kulle), who is writing a biography of the great man and believes that with enough spying on his personal life he will be able to account for his genius. The film is partly a satirical spanking of presumptuous critics and partly a comment on the elusive nature of genius and its transience. It is intermittently lively with slapstick that owes something to Mack Sennett and Jacques Tati, but it is also curiously melancholic.

With his current wife and circle of devoted mistresses, Felix might have stepped out of one of Fellini's dreams, but he points specifically to Bergman himself. Personal, too, is Bergman's irritation at critics who pry into his private life. Cornelius's affectations include a long black cigarette holder and flamboyantly plumed pen, and he is ridiculed and subjected to all sorts of humiliations, including a revelation of his impotence that is accompanied by a rousing rendition of the 1920s song "Yes, We Have No Bananas." But Cornelius is totally uninteresting, and the viewer quickly tires of such a straw horse.

opposite: An unusual shot in *Now About These Women,* looking down from above at a bed in which the ridiculous music critic Cornelius (Jarl Kulle) and Felix's mistress, Bumble Bee (Bibi Andersson), are lying asleep. Cornelius will be awakened suddenly by the appearance of a woman in black firing a pistol at him.

Some spirited and genuinely funny episodes occur in the film, such as Cornelius's accidentally igniting a mammoth stock of fireworks, but these are set pieces in a movie without any flowing movement and without a hero. Felix is never seen (except for a glimpse of his back), remaining an idea of the artist whose only responsibility is to his artistic integrity. He has instructed his wife that at such time as he betrays that integrity she is to shoot him, which she does when he stoops to playing a composition of Cornelius's. Felix dies, and almost immediately a new genius arrives to take his place.

That the essence of creativity lies beyond explanation makes a statement but not necessarily a film, for none of the characters has any dimension. Talent has been lavished on the film in the female characters who surround the maestro and include Eva Dahlbeck as Felix's wife, Adelaide; Harriet Andersson as Isolde; Bibi Andersson as the cellist's "official mistress," Bumble Bee; and Gertrud Fridh as Traviata—all of whom appear as versions of characters they have played in Bergman's films. But they have nothing of any substance to work with and have nothing to do. *Now About These Women* is Bergman's first movie in color, but here too there is a problem, since its sickly pastels offer no refreshment for the eye. Everything seemed to go wrong for Bergman at this moment. He had worked all winter preparing his stage production of Harry Martinson's *Three Knives from Wei*, which opened to savage reviews. Three days later *Now About These Women* premiered and was torn to pieces by critics. "I had two fiascos," Bergman remarks, "in one week."[1]

left: Cornelius, right, after his injury from accidentally igniting fireworks. Felix's manager, Jilker (Allan Edwall), left, proposes to Cornelius that if he wants to meet Felix he should dress up as a woman.

center: While snooping in the corridors of Felix's home, Cornelius discovers Bumble Bee, who invites him to her bedroom.

opposite, top: Scene following Felix's death. Personal details about him become confused. It is claimed that he was short, but Bumble Bee, standing on a chair to demonstrate, insists that he was tall.

opposite, bottom: The "woman" by the piano is Cornelius in drag. He has resorted to this disguise as a means of meeting the womanizing Felix. One critic called *Now About These Women* "a laborious effort at farce."

Persona

(1966)

AFTER making *The Silence*, Bergman was busy with new stage productions at Dramaten that included Edward Albee's *Who's Afraid of Virginia Woolf?* and Henrik Ibsen's *Hedda Gabler* and began arrangements to stage *The Magic Flute* in Hamburg. He was also at work on a new film script called *The Cannibals*, planned as a four-hour movie to be shown in two parts, with filming to begin in mid-1965.[2] Other events occurring at this time were to affect Bergman both personally and professionally, for it was then that he met the young Norwegian actress Liv Ullmann.[3] Although as yet unknown to the larger film world, Ullmann had made a strong impression in Norway. In 1960 she won acclaim in her stage debut in a production of *The Diary of Anne Frank* and went on to other successes in Norway on the stage and in film. In 1962 she appeared with Bibi Andersson in the Scandinavian film *Short Is the Summer*, an adaptation of Knut Hamsen's novel *Pan*, and the two actresses became friends. When Ullmann was in Stockholm, Andersson introduced her to Bergman with the thought that he might be interested in using her in his movies. Bergman was particularly struck by her resemblance to Andersson, an observation that would materially influence his conception of *Persona*.

Persona was born in a difficult period in Bergman's life.[4] In January 1965, he developed pneumonia and soon after contracted penicillin poisoning. Then a viral infection in his inner ear began to bring on attacks of acute dizziness that left him unable to work, and the production in Hamburg of *The Magic Flute* and his ambitious new film *The Cannibals* both had to be cancelled. Through much of March, April, and May he languished at the hospital at Sophiahem-

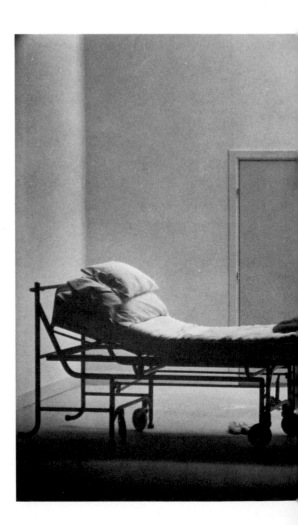

met staring at a black spot on the wall. If he turned his head, the entire room began to spin. It seemed to him that he would never be able to create again, yet during an interval of improvement the idea for a new film came to him that was suggested by the resemblance he noticed in Ullmann and Andersson: the two young women in the picture would in some way "lose their identities in each other."[5] The short, inexpensive film that would not tax his energies too severely was promptly supported by Kenne Fant, who by then had replaced Carl-Anders Dymling at Svensk Filmindustri. Because of his illness, Bergman began writing the script very slowly at the hospital, managing to work at it no more than an hour a day; then in May he had a relapse and could do no work at all. But in June, while convalescing at Ornö in the archipelago, he began to recover and commenced shooting the film in July on the island of Fårö.

During this same period, Bergman received the prestigious Erasmus Prize in Amsterdam, honoring exceptional achievement in cinema. He could not attend the presentation ceremony but sent a statement to be read entitled "The Snakeskin" (later included as a preface to the published text of *Persona*), which expresses his mood while making the new movie. In the statement, rather startling for an occasion honoring cultural solidarity, Bergman denies that art in any form is any longer relevant or capable of containing the reality of experience. "Art is free, shameless, irresponsible," he comments, "and, as I said, the movement is intense, almost feverish; it resembles, it seems to me, a snakeskin full of ants. The snake itself is long since dead, eaten out from within, deprived of its poison; but the skin moves, filled with busy life."[6] What drives him forward in his work, he remarks, is not a belief in the relevance of art but an insatiable and unappeasable curiosity. Bergman's statement has an obvious bearing on *Persona*. Elisabet Vogler, an actress who breaks down during a performance of *Electra* and withdraws into muteness, is a reflection in part on the incapacity of art to comprehend reality.

Elisabet Vogler takes her name from Albert Vogler in *The Magician*, a performer claiming to have something of spiritual significance to offer but who hides behind a mask, feigns muteness, and is tormented by a sense of emptiness within himself. But it is *The Silence*, with its dreamlike atmosphere, its two adversarial young women, and its theme of breakdown in an empty world that most directly prepares for *Persona*. *Persona* exceeds even *The Silence* in its audacity and technical virtuosity. It is Bergman's sparest and most economical film while at the same time having unusual complexity and density. It makes inordinate demands on the audience, yet compels its fascination if not always its comprehension. In a number of respects, the movie reflects Bergman's appropriation of the avant-garde filmmaking of the 1960s. Conventional narrative is dispensed with in favor of a procedure that cuts back and forth between the action of the film and moments that interrupt the action and direct the audience's attention to those who are involved in making the film. A horn

below: In *Persona*, Elisabet Vogler, in her hospital room, stands before a glowing television screen.

sounds alerting the crew that shooting is about to begin; conversations of the crew can be detected in the background; and the voice of Bergman is heard introducing a change of scene.

One of the controlling metaphors of the film is the motion-picture projector, which appears not only at the beginning and the end, but also when the storm of emotion between Elisabet and Alma becomes so intense that the film in the projector appears to burn up and the screen goes dark. The intrusion of the filmmakers within the film suggests that just as Elisabet and Alma have artificial identities, the film itself is an artificial construction rather than a reflection of truth. At one point Elisabet takes a picture of the film audience with her camera, with the implication that the horror of emptiness she and Alma confront within themselves is also the audience's.

The movie begins with the lighting of the arc lamps of the projector and the passage of a reel of film through the spools that creates a montage of disjointed images—among them a spider, a spike driven into a hand, and a brief segment of a silent-film comedy depicting a man in a nightshirt being chased by Death that Bergman had used in *Prison*. With the effect of concise momentary dreams, they recapitulate Bergman's earlier film work. They are followed by an interior view of a morgue and other images, including a young boy under a sheet on a slab; although apparently dead, he is awakened by the sound of a ringing telephone—which intimates Bergman's arousal by calls from the studio while he lay ill at the Sophiahemmet hospital, adjoined by a morgue. The boy runs his hand gropingly along a translucent screen, attempting to touch the face of a woman on the other side. Then a blurred whitish figure appears on the film that finally comes into focus as Alma (Bibi Andersson) in her nurse's uniform. As she enters the office of a female hospital psychiatrist and is assigned to attend Elisabet Vogler (Liv Ullmann), the film begins.

Persona is often oblique but it has a clear line of development. Alma, a naïve young woman, becomes the actress's companion, first at the hospital and then at the psychiatrist's summer house on an off-shore island. Alma reflects complacently on the usefulness of her work and the satisfaction she will have in her marriage to her fiancé, Karl-Henrik, but she is also obviously fascinated by the glamorous actress. It seems to her that she even resembles her and that she would like to *be* her. Before retiring on the first night, she speaks the magic words "Elisabet Vogler" that are like the incantation of a spell. One night at the cottage, tipsy after a few drinks, she reveals some of the most intimate facts of her life to the silent Elisabet, who comes to her late that night while she is sleeping—or, rather, appears to come to her in Alma's hallucination. But as they approach a psychic merger, they also become combatants. Alma opens a letter that Elisabet has written to the psychiatrist, which reveals that she has been "studying" Alma and finds her "amusing" in her naïveté. The trust that has characterized Alma up to now is shattered; her complacency is shocked, and although she will retaliate savagely, leaving a shard

above: Alma and Elisabet at the summer house, where their psychic interaction becomes intense.

below: Elisabet recoils from the sight, on television, of a Vietnamese monk setting himself on fire.

114

of broken glass on the terrace so that Elisabet will step on it in her bare feet, she is a step closer to Elisabet's vision of life as cruel, empty, and formless.

Much of the film deals with Alma's gradual entering, sometimes in the form of dreams, into Elisabet's consciousness. In one of these dreams, for example, Alma is made love to by Elisabet's husband and experiences her recoil from the marital role she plays. In another scene, which is actually a dream, she becomes Elisabet's accuser, laying bare Elisabet's rejection of motherhood and her small son. Remarkably, Alma's lines are spoken first with the camera on Elisabet's face, and then repeated by her almost word for word with the camera on her own as it dawns upon her that what she has been saying of the other woman is also true of herself. In the most baroque image in the film their faces suddenly converge to form a composite face, a face threatening disturbingly to tear apart in its tension and conflict.

Having been drawn to a psychic merger with Elisabet through much of the film, Alma now attempts to disengage herself from her; in doing so she attempts to deny the revelation that her complacent assumptions about the satisfaction she receives from her work and her forthcoming marriage have been lies. At the end of the film, as Alma prepares to leave the cottage to resume her life, she stops for a moment to examine herself in a hallway mirror, brushing back some hair with one hand, and in a vision behind her Elisabet makes the same gesture with the implication that she will continue to be part of her, that things will never be again for Alma as they were. At moments the encounter with emptiness and the vampire theme (of the artist feeding on life to renew itself and the audience feeding on art for sustaining illusion) has the shock effect of a fright film; yet the work is extraordinarily subtle and stands with *Citizen Kane* as a milestone in innovative filmmaking. It was awarded the National Film Society awards for Best Film, Best Direction, and Best Actress (Bibi Andersson) and is altogether a great moment in Bergman's career.

Stimulantia

(1967)

Persona was also a turning point in Bergman's personal life, for while shooting the film in 1965 he and Liv Ullmann entered into a relationship (described revealingly by Ullmann in the "Islanders" chapter of her memoir *Changing*) that would last for the rest of the decade.[7] Bergman was forty-six at the time and Ullmann twenty-five, and both were married. After making the film, Bergman decided to move to Fårö and to build a house for Ullmann and himself. Ullmann's daughter Linn, by Bergman, was born in 1966. Professionally, their relationship proved enormously fruitful; Ullmann

above: After Alma reads Elisabet's letter, a confrontation ensues. The two struggle, and Elisabet has Alma on the defensive. A moment later, Alma will threaten Elisabet with a pot of boiling water, and Elisabet breaks the silence by saying, "Please don't."

would win numerous honors and international recognition for her roles in Bergman's films during the twelve-year period from *Persona* to *Autumn Sonata*. In 1966 Bergman was immersed in the theater, staging productions of Peter Weiss's *The Investigation* and Molière's *The School for Wives*, but the year also saw the death of Karin Bergman, Ingmar's mother, who had played a key role in his emotional life and would continue to be much in his thoughts in the future.

In March 1966, from home-movie footage taken in 1963–65, Bergman put together a sixteen-minute sequence called "Daniel," which records scenes of his son Daniel Sebastian, by Käbi Laretei, from infancy to age two. The sequence, in both black and white and color, was part of a Svensk Filmindustri production, *Stimulantia*, bringing together brief works by eight different Swedish directors. One sees Daniel reacting while Käbi Laretei plays "Ah, vous dis-je, Madame" by Mozart; romping in the nude and collecting mushrooms; lying in a hammock with his grandmother; and drinking mineral water from a glass. He is a healthy little specimen with blue eyes that the camera continually reverts to, a penchant for sucking his thumb, and is the picture of unself-conscious innocence. Bergman introduces the film and at the end comments on the guilt-and-punishment God of Christianity. "Out of what fear of corruption," he remarks, "did this monster emerge which is called the forgiveness of sins, the resurrection of the dead and life everlasting? Instead to make contact with a human being, to take hold of him, to know him in all his thousands of varying moods. To live together in a common reality." The infant, after all, holds a moral.

Hour of the Wolf

(1966)

THE TITLE *Hour of the Wolf* is explained in a quotation that appears before the opening of the film: "The hour of the wolf is the hour between night and dawn. It is the hour when most people die, when sleep is deepest, when nightmares are most real. It is the hour when the sleepless are haunted by their greatest dread, when ghosts and demons are most powerful. The hour of the wolf is also the hour when most children are born." Curiously, Bergman claims to have been personally acquainted with demons. In an interview he explains, apparently quite seriously, that while writing the script in a bedroom-study, he was visited by demons, who sometimes stood at his bedside and talked to him.[8]

Hour of the Wolf begins with a prefatory statement by the filmmaker that the story was based on a diary kept by Johan Borg and given to him by his widow and on what she herself told him—the classic distancing effect of the ghostly tale. Then Alma (Liv Ullmann) comes out of her cottage on the windswept Frisian island of Baltrum

opposite, left: On a rocky beach where Johan (Max von Sydow) is fishing, a young boy appears and seems to entice him sexually. Before long a physical struggle ensues between them in which the boy cries aloud with the "cawing" sound of a bird. Bird imagery and associations are prominent throughout the work. "I am terribly afraid of birds," Bergman comments. "I become frightened, extremely frightened, when a bird gets into the room if I am sitting there."

opposite, right: In the crypt of Baron von Merkens's castle, Johan confronts the "dead" Veronica Vogler (Ingrid Thulin). When he pulls away the sheet to stroke her naked body, she rises up suddenly, laughing wildly.

On the set of *Hour of the Wolf*, Ingmar Bergman, left, and Max von Sydow, seated opposite, train their attention on Liv Ullmann, center.

and speaks to the camera, as if to an unseen listener, about her marriage to the now-deceased painter Johan Borg (Max von Sydow), with whom she had lived for seven years. A flashback takes us back to their arrival on the island, where Johan eventually became obsessed by demons lurking in the vicinity. One day while Johan is away from the cottage sketching, an ancient woman (Naima Wifstrand), wearing a large hat that shadows half her face, appears and tells Alma that Johan keeps a diary that she would do well to read. When Alma finds and begins reading it, its entries prompt a series of flashbacks within the flashback. In the first of these, Baron von Merkens (Erland Josephson), who lives in a castle at the northern end of the island, appears while Johan is outdoors sketching and invites him to dinner. After he leaves, Veronica Vogler (Ingrid Thulin), the former mistress of Johan and now the mistress of Von Merkens, appears to Johan in a brief vision of erotic enticement. Soon afterward Johan is approached by the curator Heerbrand (Ulf Johanson), and after Johan strides away from him angrily and the curator follows after him, Johan turns on him, strikes him across the face, and leaves him lying on the ground with a bleeding nose.

Arriving at the castle for dinner, Johan and Alma are introduced to Von Merkens's group, who could as well be members of the Addams family. The circle includes Von Merkens's mother (Gudrun Brost); the Baroness (Gertrud Fridh), whose beauty (to quote from the printed text) "is unusual and rather frightening";[9] the Baron's brother Ernst (Bertil Anderberg), who has a "tormented face";[10] and Lindhorst (Georg Rydeberg), the archivist, who has the face of "an aged youth."[11] The names of Heerbrand and Lindhorst are drawn by Bergman from the tales of E. T. A. Hoffmann,[12] and there is, indeed, a Hoffmannesque quality—half-real and half-fantastic—about Von Merkens and his guests. Lindhorst stages a sequence from *The Magic Flute* in the form of a puppet show, which becomes disturbing when one recognizes that Tamino, in quest of his ideal love for Pamina, is a real man in miniature, a homunculus, manipulated by Lindhorst like an evil deity. In place of Pamina, who promises the highest truth and enlightenment, Veronica Vogler will lead Johan to destruction.

In a later diary flashback, Johan goes to the castle alone in response to an invitation by Heerbrand. The scene at the castle becomes phantasmagoric and culminates in an episode in which Johan visits a vault in which Veronica Vogler lies naked under a sheet as if dead. When Johan removes the sheet and strokes her body, however, she rises up with mocking laughter, while a chorus of cackling

below: Near the end of *Hour of the Wolf*, Von Merkens and members of his circle take the form of a gathering of ghouls, who mock Johan's dark obsession with Veronica Vogler.

Erland Josephson as Baron von Merkens in *Hour of the Wolf*. At the opening he pays a call on Johan, inviting him to his castle.

laughter is heard from Von Merkens and his friends, who have been witnessing the scene. Following this flashback, Alma resumes her narration to the camera, relating that she last saw Johan in the depths of the forest being destroyed by demons (did this actually happen or has Alma, too, become delusional?). *Hour of the Wolf* is unlike any of Bergman's other films in its appropriation of the horror-movie genre. As Robin Wood has noted,[13] Lindhorst bears a striking resemblance to Bela Lugosi's Dracula, and the interior of the castle and incidents occurring there evoke a number of classic Hollywood horror films. Nor can one miss Bergman's allusion to Alfred Hitchcock's *The Birds* in this film in which predatory bird imagery is used throughout.

Bergman acknowledges that birds have always frightened him, and they appear in the film in many guises, beginning with an opening scene between Johan and Alma by a clothesline draped with sheets that flutter and snap in the breeze like the flapping wings of a large bird. In a dreamlike sequence that may be delusional, Johan is attacked and bitten by a young boy, and as they struggle together the boy cries out with birdlike cawing sounds. At the dinner at the castle, the movement of Sven Nykvist's camera simulates the darting of a bird from one shoulder-perched view of a guest's face to another, then executes a whirling movement halfway around the table like a bird in flight. Toward the end the bird imagery becomes more horrific. When Lindhorst leads Johan through a dim passageway to the vault where he is to confront Veronica Vogler, hundreds of birds fly madly around them, and Lindhorst extends his arms in a gesture like that of a vampire bat. In the climactic scene in the forest, Johan is pecked to death by monstrous birds that include a half-man, half-pheasant, the shape that Lindhorst has now taken. The expansion of this ornithic imagery is extremely theatrical and contains expressionistic effects that are fascinating; but its artificiality also works against a need to take Johan's inner horrors seriously.

Bergman calls *Hour of the Wolf* an "extremely personal" work, and a number of clues within the film point to Johan Borg as his stand-in. At the dinner, Johan speaks of "the unimportance of art in the world of men" and of his creativity as deriving from nothing more than compulsion—words that echo Bergman's bleak assessment of the artist's role in his Erasmus Prize statement "The Snakeskin." Moreover, Johan tells Alma of his being punished as a child by being locked in a closet with, he believed, a demon—which comes from Bergman's own often-repeated account of his boyhood. Alma, splendidly played by Liv Ullmann as a blonde earth mother of naïve purity, represents a vision of wholeness that Johan longs for but cannot attain because he has been psychically damaged. The set of obsessions of fear, guilt, and humiliation that agitate Johan are also those of Bergman; but they have been used to uncertain artistic purpose in the film. *Hour of the Wolf* is imaginative but as elusive in the end as the demons that stood by Bergman's bed and talked to him.

Shame

(1968)

IN APRIL 1967 Bergman's production of Luigi Pirandello's *Six Characters in Search of an Author* opened at the National Theater in Oslo, and while there Bergman worked on several new film scripts, all dealing with related themes of emotional stress and psychological deterioration. One of them became Bergman's next film, *Shame* (British title: *The Shame*). With the outbreak of war and the disbanding of the orchestra in which they have performed as violinists, Jan Rosenberg (Max von Sydow) and his wife, Eva (Liv Ullmann), have gone to live on a small island off the mainland and managed to survive by selling berries that they have grown in a greenhouse by their cottage. Now the island itself is invaded. When their house comes under bombardment, they travel across the island in their car past scenes of conflagration and death and are detained and interrogated by the invading soldiers. Neither Jan nor Eva has any political views or even any sense of what issues are involved in the warfare, but a televised interview that the soldiers stage with Eva, subsequently doctored, is made to give the impression that she supports the "liberators" of the island. When the invaders are routed before long by the occupation forces, the Rosenbergs are arrested and accused of collaborating with the enemy.

They are spared, however, by the intervention of Jacobi (Gunnar Björnstrand), the mayor of a town on the island who knows them and has thrown in his lot with the occupation forces. To manage their survival, Eva accepts Jacobi's gifts and enters into an affair with him.

But the pendulum swings again; a resistance unit takes over the town, Jacobi is arrested, and because he cannot produce the money to buy his freedom (the savings he has put in safekeeping with Eva have been stolen by Jan), he is executed. Jan himself, on the order of the soldiers, pulls the trigger. With the stolen money, Jan buys a place for himself and Eva on an open boat. Adrift in the ocean, the huddled occupants of the boat quickly run out of food and fresh water, while all around them, as in a nightmare, float heaps of dead bodies from a torpedoed ship. The movie ends with a sense of doom.

Although *Shame* has the appearance of documentary realism, it has the shape and texture of a dream. At the opening, church bells ring for no reason, and when Eva picks up the telephone that keeps ringing, no one answers at the other end. These incidents introduce the theme of a breakdown of communication and intelligibility. The war that is being waged, in which no ideological differences in the opposing forces can be discerned, reinforces the idea of radical confusion. The Rosenbergs are artists, but by the time the film opens their professional identities have receded into a dreamlike past. With the loss of their former supports, they sink into a state of fear and demoralization. Their marriage itself deteriorates, becoming a conflict within the conflict. Ullmann is splendid as Eva, who manages to retain what is left of civilized values in a collapsing world, while Von Sydow as Jan is a weaker figure, feckless at the beginning and morally callused at the end.

In the dream state the movie evokes, both Jan and Eva relate dreams and dreamlike sensations they have had. Jan tells Eva at the beginning of his dream of their being back with the orchestra, thankful that what has happened to them on the island was only a dream, only to have awakened weeping. At the midway point Eva explains that everything seems to her like a dream, yet not her own but "someone else's, that I'm forced to take part in. . . . What do you think will happen when the person who has dreamed us wakes up and is ashamed of his dream?" At the very end, in the open boat, Eva relates a surrealistic dream she has had in which she is on a beautiful street with her six-month-old daughter in her arms. Cold, dark green water runs by the street, along which is a high wall overgrown with roses. Then aircraft appear and set fire to the roses, which burn with a clear, beautiful flame. "I knew the whole time," she says, "that I ought to understand something important that someone had said, but I had forgotten what it was. I pressed the baby close to me and I could feel that she was heavy and wet and smelled good, as if she had just had her bath. And then you came on the other side of the street and I thought that you would be able to tell me about the important thing I had forgotten." The terrible, lyrical dream in which love, beauty, and human closeness dissolve in the face of nightmarish destruction sums up the film concisely and is its emotional center.

Shame won the 1965 National Society of Film Critics awards for Best Film, Best Direction, and Best Actress (Liv Ullmann), but critical

reaction was mixed, both in Sweden and abroad. When the film was released, the Vietnam War was escalating and Russian troops had marched into Czechoslovakia; against such a background Bergman's dream war struck many critics as naïve. In cancelling out any difference between the combatants, it seemed to them, he was refusing to take a stand or to engage the real world. It would be wrong to dismiss the film because it is not politically correct; human beings are, after all, caught up in senseless conflagrations. There is no doubt, however, that Bergman's war is extremely private; Jan and Eva share with Johan Borg a sense of terrifying powerlessness in the face of the outer world, and it is no coincidence that they are or have been artists.

The Ritual

(1969)

BETWEEN the writing of *Shame* in the spring and its filming in the autumn of 1967, Bergman wrote the script for *The Ritual* (British title: *The Rite*). "So, in a rather vague sort of way," Bergman remarks, "I began. And before I could say knife, there it was—a play! The direction script, it's true, reads like a film script. But there are no stage instructions. It's just dialogue, right through. . . . It was a wonderful feeling, suddenly writing a play—to be able to forget all about cinematic considerations, and just write dialogue."[14] *The Ritual* was put aside while *Shame* was being made, but in the late spring of 1968 Bergman gathered together a few actors and held rehearsals for four weeks, then shot the film at a Stockholm studio in a mere nine days. It was made for Swedish television by Cinematograph, a company organized by Bergman that would pro-

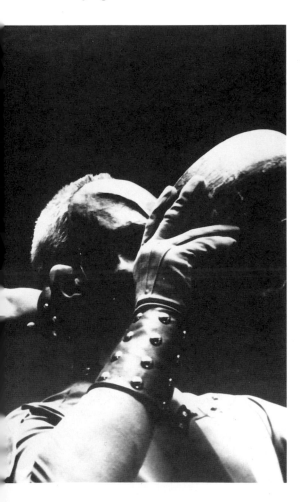

duce or co-produce many of his films in the future, and was later distributed as a theatrical release abroad. A relatively brief work, it is interesting as a variation on the disintegration theme of *Hour of the Wolf* and *Shame*.

The Ritual concerns several cabaret artists—Hans Winkelmann (Gunnar Björnstrand), the manager of the troupe; Thea (Ingrid Thulin), his wife; and Sebastian Fischer (Anders Ek), a high-strung "romantic" artist and Thea's lover—who are summoned to the office of Judge Abramsson (Erik Hell) to answer charges of having performed an act of obscenity in their revue. The film opens with Abramsson's looking at a photograph of the performers in costume through a magnifying glass that reveals a frighteningly enlarged image of his eye and introduces the motif of his shameless curiosity about them and his search into every aspect of their lives, both personal and professional. The interrogation becomes a ritual of his humiliation of the performers, but by the end the tables are turned and the judge is humiliated in a ritualistic performance staged by the actors. Visually the film is unrelievedly drab and claustrophobic, although intentionally so since all of its characters feel trapped—the performers by their profession, Abramsson by the sterility of his life.

In certain respects, *The Ritual* resembles *The Magician*, in which a troupe of suspect performers are "invited" to the home of Councilman Egerman, where their legitimacy is challenged by Dr. Vergérus. Both *The Magician* and *The Ritual* take the form of duels between the artist and society, with first one side and then the other having the upper hand. Albert Emmanuel Sebastian Fischer is linked specifically with Albert Emanuel Vogler in *The Magician* through his name; and Bergman has commented on the resemblance between them with the difference that while Vogler "still had vitality, spiritual strength,"[15] Fischer is burned out. So, for that matter, is Winkelmann, whose words reflect the sentiments of Bergman's Erasmus Prize statement. "Service to an artistic ideal," he declares, "was once an ennobling ambition, but I've grown tired of our so-called artistry. I no longer believe in what we're doing. I think we're meaningless, disgusting, absurd. We're not relevant any more." Although apparently bound to each other indefinitely, the performers have a frayed relationship and would like to disband their act; and Winkelmann particularly longs to adopt a quiet bourgeois life.

But just as the desperation of the performers is exposed, so too is Abramsson's. At first an inquisitor, Abramsson before long begins to break down; although he fears the artist's "freedom," he is drawn to and fascinated by it. In the scene in which he interrogates the unstable, nymphomaniac Thea, he breaks down shockingly, attacking her sexually. The mask he wears as a defender of social conventions falls away as he confesses his fear and loneliness. His longing for release from himself, for humiliation and purgation, is realized when the performers, in an act of revenge, stage a pagan rite revealing the death of God and the terror of reality. At a climactic moment, Abramsson suf-

123

fers a heart attack and dies. Thereafter the performers pay a small fine and leave to continue their work in another country. In ritualistic form, the film dramatizes the transactions between artists and the public, including the government bureaucracy, which attempts to regulate them yet has an ambivalent attitude toward them inasmuch as their art provides a catharsis of their own innermost psychic stresses. Bergman acknowledges that writing the film was a form of personal release after resigning as head (from 1963 to 1966) of the Royal Dramatic Theater. It expresses, he comments, "my resentment against the critics, audience, and government, with which I was in constant battle."[16]

The Passion of Anna
(1969)

The Passion of Anna (British title: *A Passion*), Bergman's second film to be made in color, is like *Hour of the Wolf* and *Shame* in that it is also set on a remote island and has the nature of a sustained dreamlike experience. If violence intrudes upon the characters' lives in the form of war in *Shame*, it appears nightmarishly in *The Passion of Anna* in the form of a brutal and irrational violation of innocent animals on the island. Andreas Winkelmann (Max von Sydow) lives a reclusive life at his cottage. In the past he had been married but, in a Pinteresque way, his earlier life is never filled in—except that he had behaved erratically, having forged checks, struck a policeman, and been fined for drunken driving. One day Anna Fromm (Liv Ullmann), a woman who uses a cane as the result of injuries suffered in an automobile crash, appears at his house to use his telephone, and an ominous involvement between them is set in motion.

Andreas meets Anna again when he is invited to dinner at the home of his neighbors Elis Vergérus (Erland Josephson) and his wife, Eva (Bibi Andersson), with whom she is staying. Elis is a successful architect who at the dinner describes the cultural center for Milan that he has been commissioned to design as "a tombstone over the total meaninglessness in which people of our sort live." His wife suffers from chronic insomnia and is troubled by the emptiness of her life. Both she and Elis have been hurt, in part by their child's having been born dead, leaving them without a future. Elis's cynicism is a wall that he erects against the cruelty of the outer world. But a wall also exists between Elis and Eva, who lack intimacy and have an uncertain relationship to one another. There is something vaguely menacing about Elis, a potential for aggression that lies beneath the surface of his composure. After Andreas sleeps with Eva, Elis plans some punishing act against him. Strangely, however, although typical of the film's foreshortened effects, the Vergéruses disappear from the picture at a midway point, never to be seen again.

above: The Passion of Anna: Andreas Winkelmann (Max von Sydow) with Johan Andersson (Erik Hell), who will be martyred by vigilantes as irrationality and violence sweep the island.

below: Andreas Winkelmann turns on Anna Fromm (Liv Ullmann) in a fit of rage.

overleaf: Anna is attacked by Andreas with an ax. Physical and emotional violence stands in the background and sometimes erupts in the foreground of the film.

But they introduce immediately the motifs of the film: a troubled couple and the impending threat of violence. Violence from without begins early when Andreas finds a puppy hanging by a noose from the limb of a tree. He cuts him down and nurses him back to health at his cottage, but other animals are mutilated by some unknown party on the island in escalating cycles of violence. Andreas and Anna, who before long comes to live with him, are opposite in type, but in neither case is one permitted to know how they came to be as they are. Andreas calls himself "a whipped cur," a man without self-esteem, "humiliated at heart, half-stifled and spat upon." Anna, on the other hand, is an unyielding moralist about whom, Bergman remarks, there is something "monstrous, something frightfully dangerous." She loved the first Andreas, her late husband, "to the point of madness," even though at some level she knows that her "perfect marriage" to him had been a lie. Almost as soon as they meet at the dinner, Andreas becomes drawn into her obsession and finds himself "becoming" the first Andreas. When he leaves the Vergéruses and returns home, he begins drinking heavily and wanders stupefied on the heath shouting his name, as if warding off an identification with the other Andreas that Anna seems to be imposing upon him.

Throughout the film, characters lapse into dream states, often withdrawing into unconsciousness. When Eva visits Andreas at his house, she is overcome by a need for sleep. Anna's sleep is disturbed by nightmares in which she calls out Andreas's name; and a disturbing dream she experiences is visualized in a monochrome sequence that seems related to her guilt over her child's death. Andreas collapses into a coma on the heath, and later, seated at his desk, falls into a trancelike state. The sense of Andreas's reenacting the experience of his namesake is the film's dominant "dream." His brief affair with Eva duplicates that of the first Andreas, and when Anna moves in with him he becomes involved ever more deeply in Anna's torment. One is always conscious that her marriage to the first Andreas had led to catastrophe. He had warned in a letter discovered by Andreas Winkelmann that if they continued to see each other, "physical and mental acts of violence" would ensue. When the first Andreas is about to leave her, Anna crashes the car in which they are driving, killing him and their child. Anna's life with Andreas Winkelmann is filled with tensions that point toward a similar outcome.

These tensions erupt in small incidents at first; when a fissure begins to show in their relationship, Anna drops a bowl of milk that crashes loudly on the kitchen floor like an explosion. The tensions steadily mount until Andreas, while chopping wood, hurls an axe at Anna and beats her savagely. In a climactic scene when they are together in Anna's car, Andreas tells her that he wants his "solitude back," and they don't really love each other. "Let us tell the truth for once," he says. "It was all lies." As she accelerates the car, Andreas grabs the wheel to avert a crash and gets out. The camera follows him after Anna drives off as he paces back and forth across a bleak stretch of ground while a clock is heard ticking. Then the screen goes snowy, and Andreas slumps to the ground as if falling into a coma. "This time," Bergman's voice announces, "his name was Andreas Winkelmann." The screen goes blank and the film ends.

When it appeared, a number of critics found *The Passion of Anna* cryptic beyond the point of comprehension, but it is not as impenetrable as it might seem. The ticking clocks heard in the film are a reminder of the temporal world in which the characters live that, because it admits of no transcendence, condemns them to struggle within fruitless patterns of repetition. Another Andreas will appear to repeat the experience of Andreas Winkelmann, just as he has relived the experience of the Andreas before him. No answering God exists in Bergman's vision to lift his couples into spiritual communion. The lie of the individual's possible oneness with another fills the world with lonely embitterment in which, in a manner similar to that of Nathanael West's *Miss Lonelyhearts*, there are only victims and victimizers, in which the victimized vent their rage upon the innocent. The outer world is thus ruled by a logic that is violent and destructive. A television screen shows a notorious moment in which a young Vietcong prisoner is shot in the head by his captor in a Vietnam street, and allusions occur to Martin Luther King's being assassinated at Easter, as if in angry denial of his vision of brotherhood.

Violence in the outer world is played off dramatically with the psychic violence of Anna, whose rage for a nonexistent moral order subjects Andreas to intolerable stress. Christian imagery appears at various points. Johan of Skir, the aging recluse who is innocent of all wrongdoing but is brutally beaten and humiliated by inhabitants of the island as the supposed defiler of the animals, and who then hangs himself, has affinities with Christ. In a fine, quiet scene, Andreas visits the bare, shabby room where Johan lies dead on a bed, with a picture of Christ on the wall behind it. As Andreas touches Johan's folded hands with his own, one is struck by their likeness as humiliated figures who have come to live alone at the bare margin of life. Yet there is no redemptive Christ in the picture, and there is no forgiveness. Anna's "passion" signifies merely suffering and isolation. Her attempts to affirm a perfect union between herself and the Andreases—a kind of religious thinking—lead to frustration and destructiveness.

Of the films making up Bergman's second trilogy of the 1960s, which involve disintegration and give focal attention to the psychic states of characters struggling with a loss of meaning in their lives, *The Passion of Anna* is the most powerful and the most highly charged with dramatic conflict. It also provides the fullest exploration of couples and their distance from one another and as such marks another turning point for Bergman. In his films of the 1970s, he will explore marital relationships elaborately, the baffled attempt of men and women to meet in what Johan Borg, in *Hour of the Wolf*, calls "a shared reality."

The Marriage Scenarios

B Y 1970 the Swedish film industry had fallen on hard times. Hurt by television, attendance at Swedish movie houses fell off sharply, and some houses in the regions beyond the larger cities closed. This happened, moreover, at the same time as the decline in popularity of Swedish films abroad and the soaring cost of producing films. No longer able to rely on the studios with which he had previously worked, Bergman turned to television as a vehicle for his films. The transition to television altered the appearance and the format of his pictures, since it restricted the use of medium and long shots and involved a severe emphasis on close-ups. It also meant that his films would be made in carefully shaped episodes for installment viewing. In many cases, Bergman would make two different versions of a film: a long, episodic one for TV and a shortened, edited one for theatrical release abroad. Another option available to Bergman was to make films that were financed abroad; but this, too, had its drawbacks. International financing involved using foreign actors in prominent roles, a disruption of Bergman's use of all-Swedish casts with whom he had established a close rapport. Although Bergman made several financially successful films in the 1970s, others failed to show a profit, and with each box-office failure foreign investment became more difficult to find.

Fårö Document

(1970)

A FTER HAVING made a series of films set on Fårö in the late 1960s, Bergman decided to make the island the subject of a documentary, which was produced by Cinematograph and presented on Swedish television on New Year's Day 1970. Sven Nykvist shot the film, in which Bergman himself acts as interviewer and commentator, with a small crew that traveled around the island in a house trailer. The interviews with a hand-held 16-mm camera are in black and white, while scenes of Fårö's landscapes, which evoke

opposite: Scene from *The Lie.* Frank Findlay and Gemma Jones are in the British production, and George Segal and Shirley Knight Hopkins in the American.

the passage of the seasons, appear in color. The sea is a strong presence in the documentary, which focuses on the raising of sheep and the traditional ways of life to which the island's seven hundred inhabitants still cling. But the film also has a message to convey to the mainlanders—improved facilities are needed to keep the young people from abandoning the island and more subsidies must be given to its hard-pressed farmers. It is surprising to find Bergman in the role of an activist challenging the national government. "My political act," he remarked, "is to try to stop this island and its people [from] being crushed."[1] Attention was paid, nearly half of Sweden's population having watched the program on television with keen interest.[2]

The Lie
(1970)

I N MAY 1969, Bergman completed a play for television that was presented in 1970 as its first feature by a consortium called Eurovision. Its Swedish title, *Reservatet*, means "The Sanctuary" or "The Preserve," but in subsequent English-language versions the play is called *The Lie*. The Eurovision production was directed by Jan Molander and starred Gunnel Lindblom, Erland Josephson, and Per Myrberg. As *The Lie*, it was presented in 1970 on BBC television in a production that was directed by Alan Bridges and starred Frank Findlay and Gemma Jones. An American version was also produced in 1972 as the initial program for the short-lived revival of CBS television's "Playhouse 90," which was directed by Alex Segal and starred George Segal and Shirley Knight Hopkins, with a supporting cast including Robert Culp, Louise Lasser, Victor Buono, John Ritter, and Dean Jagger.

The Lie, subtitled "A Tragic Comedy About Banality," evolves from *The Passion of Anna*; Anna Fromm in that film gives her name to Anna Fromm in *The Lie,* and her husband's name, Andrew, is a variation on the name of the two Andreases in Anna's life. As an architect, moreover, Andrew has the same profession as another of *Anna*'s characters, Elis Vergérus. Instead of living on a remote island, the couple in *The Lie* are members of the comfortably settled upper middle class of mainland Sweden. Yet ominous outer forces break in upon the Fromms in their "sanctuary," as it had upon Anna and Andreas on their island, when they discover that their marriage, considered to be ideal by others, has been a lie. The bottom suddenly drops out of Andrew's life when the ambitious architectural project he has been planning is rejected by the government bureaucracy for which he works, and when he learns that Anna is involved in an eight-year affair with another man. Anna's bedroom becomes their battleground; like Andreas in *The Passion of Anna,* Andrew wields an axe, breaking open the door of the room in which Anna has

130

locked herself and beating her savagely. Although the couple will apparently remain together, a gulf between them has opened that can never be bridged. The American production is set in no clearly specified place and tends to be slow and uninvolving. The Bridges version, however, is the one to see, and it benefits from being set distinctively in London; it is a skillfully controlled and finely acted mood piece that reveals a mysterious emptiness at the center of the couple's world.

The Touch

(1971)

Bergman on the set of *The Touch* with Elliott Gould.

IN MAY 1970, while rehearsing his stage production of *Hedda Gabler* at the National Theatre in London, Bergman met with Leonard Goldenson, president of the ABC Corporation, and Martin Baum, head of the company's new motion-picture production division. After outlining the story of his new film project, *The Touch*, he quickly gained their interest in producing it. The terms that the ABC executives struck with him were generous. They would pay $1 million for the completed film, plus the salary of an American actor whom he would choose for the male lead; and Bergman would have control over the final cut.[3] Bergman wrote the screenplay in July, and the film went into production immediately, with shooting completed in the autumn. Dustin Hoffman was approached for the male lead but had other commitments, and Bergman then selected Elliott Gould.

Two of the principal characters in *The Touch*, Karin Vergérus (Bibi Andersson) and her doctor husband, Andreas (Max von Sydow), have the names of characters in *The Passion of Anna*, but *The Touch* has closer links with *The Lie* in its situation of an extramarital affair and the disruption of the lives of an upper-middle-class couple in contemporary Sweden. The movie opens with Karin's appearance at a hospital room where her mother has just died. When she leaves the room after being at her mother's bedside, she encounters a man in the corridor who, noticing her trouble, attempts to speak to her; but she wants to be alone in her sorrow. Soon afterward, however, Andreas brings him to their house and introduces him to Karin. He is David Kovac (Elliott Gould), one of his patients and an archaeologist working at a dig in the region. In the course of the evening, David tells Karin suddenly that he is in love with her, and before long they enter into an affair.

David, who is Jewish, has led a wandering life. His earlier years were spent in Berlin, but during the Nazi era his father sent him, with his mother and sister, to Switzerland, where they lost touch with the father and other relatives, who died in concentration camps. After the death of David's mother, he went to Israel, where he received his training as an archaeologist, lived for a period in the United States, and now resides in London but travels continually in the course of his work. Unlike the Vergéruses, David is a deracinated outsider who lives a life of unrest and self-hatred. But his "touch" brings Karin to new consciousness. She is quickened by him in a way that she had not been by her decent, orderly husband and discovers a dimension of her nature that has until now lain dormant. At his small, untidy, and claustrophobic apartment where she visits him secretly, David responds to her ambivalently—with love and sexual hunger, and with anger and rejection. He cannot sort out his feelings, and at one point turns on her violently.

Despite their difficult relationship, the affair continues but Karin increasingly feels the guilt of her betrayal of her husband and their two children. After David abruptly leaves her, Karin goes to London and looks up his sister, who suffers from a disease (like that which ran in the Bergman family) involving progressive muscular atrophy; when the sister reveals that she and David are inseparable and that he will never leave her, Karin returns in a sobered mood to Sweden. Because her husband has by now learned of the affair, she is pressed to decide with which of the men she will remain. At this point David comes back and asks Karin to live with him, but she decides instead to return to her husband. Bergman speaks of Karin as a character who is "much more alive than anyone else. She knows she has enough warmth and human resources to make both men happy and create a new sort of life. She has a richness that he [David] has made her understand."[4] The final moments of the film show Karin standing alone by a pond in the park that reflects a perfect, inverted image of her and implies a double self. It is, in fact, exactly like the image of Alma as she is reflected in the water in *Persona*, and it implies that part of her life, her passional existence, will go underground in the resumption of her life with Andreas.

Bibi Andersson, who gives one of her finest performances, is a sympathetic character, but one responds uneasily to David, a vague and elusive figure. Although he is implied to have a passionate inner life, what one sees in him chiefly is an adolescent self-centeredness and bad temper. At the beginning he wears a black beard and has a certain mystery about him; but when he returns clean-shaven near the end and has, as it were, dropped his mask, he is revealed as irresponsible and immature. Why Karin would have been attracted to him in the first place, have allowed his abusive treatment of her, and still be in love with him at the end is hard to fathom. The casting of Elliott Gould as David compounds the problem, since he seems unsure of what he is supposed to be conveying. *The Touch* did poorly at the box office, and critics found it thin and oddly unlike Bergman's other films.

It does, however, have a personal subtext. In April 1970, Bergman's father died, and one can detect in the film another of Bergman's meditations on his parents' marriage. Karin's arrival at the

above: At the end of *The Touch*, Karin Vergérus (Bibi Andersson) tells David Kovac (Elliott Gould) that she is returning to her husband and family.

hospital too late to see her mother before she died parallels the experience of Bergman, who had reached the hospital only shortly after his mother's death. Karin has the same given name as Bergman's mother, and like her she has a passionate extramarital affair but remains in the end with her conventional husband and her children. Bergman's mother even appears obliquely in the film. When David shows Karin a photograph of his late mother, one notices, a little startled, that it is the face of Karin Bergman in a family photograph. Karin Bergman's was a double life, her passional nature concealed beneath the formal requirements of her marriage; it is her crisis and, as Bergman now sees it, her inner growth that are reflected in Karin Vergérus's story. In its subtext and in its interior mood, the film belongs very much to Bergman.

Cries and Whispers
(1973)

FINANCING FOR Bergman's next film, *Cries and Whispers*, was difficult to find, since a series of Bergman films preceding it had been commercial failures. In order to make the picture, Bergman had to commit his own funds to it and arrange with Sven Nykvist and his principal actresses to accept a share of the film's future earnings in lieu of their usual fees.[5] The movie is set at an eighteenth-century manor house at the turn of the century, where Agnes (Harriet Andersson)—an unmarried, thirty-seven-year-old woman—is dying of cancer, and where her sisters, Maria (Liv Ullmann) and Karin (Ingrid Thulin), have come to be with her. Agnes is attended by her maid Anna (Kari Sylwan), a large-boned, doggedly faithful woman who lavishes the love she felt for her dead child on her mistress. These four women belong to what might be considered a chamber work, although one that is not quite like any other Bergman had yet made.

Bergman outlined his intentions as well as a detailed synopsis of the story in a fifty-page letter (later printed as the film's text) to his cast and crew, in which he commented that the picture would give the sense of a "dream state." From the moment the movie opens with a view of the park grounds adjoining the estate, shrouded in an early morning mist, Bergman creates a sense of a heightened reality. The camera then moves to the interior of the house, where Agnes is confined by the experience of her dying; but here, too, one is aware of a dramatic heightening. Strangely, the rooms are predominantly in red (including walls and carpeting), with whitish light flowing into the rooms through white-curtained windows. Women in white period gowns pass through the rooms mysteriously; fade-outs and fade-ins are seen through a red filter; and voices whispering unintelligibly of the past are heard in the background.

below: Bergman on the set of *Cries and Whispers* with Ingrid Thulin and Liv Ullmann. The dining room, like the other rooms of the house, is dominated by the color red. "Ever since my childhood," Bergman told an interviewer, "I have pictured the soul as a moist membrane in shades of red."

133

opposite: A flashback sequence early in *Cries and Whispers,* in which Agnes remembers her mother (Liv Ullmann in a dual role) as she walked alone on the grounds of the family estate. "I loved Mother," Agnes says. "Because she was so gentle and alive."

above: The doctor (Erland Josephson) with Maria (Liv Ullmann) in a scene in *Cries and Whispers.* They played so well together in the film that Bergman paired them again in his next film, *Scenes from a Marriage.*

As in a moral fable, the characters have an archetypal dimension. Agnes, in the extremity of her situation, is suffering innocence, while her sisters register a loss of innocence in their worldly experience. Maria is like a spoiled child, taken up, as Bergman writes, "with her own beauty and her body's potentialities for pleasure."[6] Bergman focuses upon her early in the film when the family doctor (Erland Josephson) calls on Agnes, and Maria tempts him sexually. A flashback reveals an earlier occasion when the doctor had come to treat her children, and she prepares a dinner for him and arranges for him to stay overnight. Nykvist's camera frames them provocatively with their faces close together while the doctor is eating his meal and Maria speaks to him with an erotic smile at the edge of her lips. When she comes to his bedroom later that night, the doctor has her look at her image in a mirror while he points out the lines of "indifference, impatience, and ennui" now beginning to appear in her face. This striking sequence ends with Maria's commenting: "I haven't any need of being pardoned." Yet in the next fade-in, which seems to be actually happening but must be understood as a dream, Maria discovers that her husband has stabbed himself in the chest with a paper knife because of her infidelities. She stares at him in the doorway expressionlessly for a long moment, then a slight smile appears on her lips. At this moment she has a kind of romantic enlargement: her lack of feeling becomes horrible.

135

Karin is also revealed in her circumstances and in her essence. Married to an older, wealthy, and distasteful man, she plays the part of an exemplary wife. "Deep down," Bergman comments in the text, "under a surface of self-control, she hides an impotent hatred of her husband and a permanent rage against life."[7] A more complicated character than Maria, she longs to reach out to others but recoils from their contact, particularly that of her husband. When they dine together elegantly at the manor house and her husband announces that it is time for them to retire to their bedroom, she upsets and shatters her glass, and the wine spills out like blood over the luminously white tablecloth. Bringing a shard of the broken glass with her, she goes to the bedroom, is undressed by the maid Anna, and when she is alone proceeds to mutilate her vagina with the sharp fragment of glass. When her husband comes into the room attired for bed, she smears blood from her wounds across the top of her mouth with a horrible smile. One recognizes after the fact that the scene is a fantasy but this hardly lessens its grotesque impact.

The married sisters, who represent a failure of love and human contact, are contrasted with another pair of characters who are "sisters" in a sense—Agnes (whose name implies the "lamb of God" or Christ) and her devoted maid Anna. Agnes's dying is hard and pitiable, yet her sisters shrink from her, from giving their hearts to her. Anna, on the other hand, is compassionate and loving. In a startling scene Anna gets into bed with Agnes when she cries out for help, bares her large breasts, and lays Agnes's head on her lap. The tableau, reminiscent of the iconography of the *Pietà*, is perhaps too staged, yet it is not wholly out of place in a film having the nature of a fable. Bergman's Christian theme, without a conviction of God, is dramatized in a remarkable scene in which a parson (Anders Ek) invokes a prayer over the dead Agnes. It begins with a repetition of the conditional clause "if it is so," and before long becomes both per-

left: Harriet Andersson as Agnes, half her face in the shade cast by her broadbrimmed hat.

right: Maria sucking her thumb as she lies in bed, surrounded by her large collection of dolls. In some respects she is still a self-centered child.

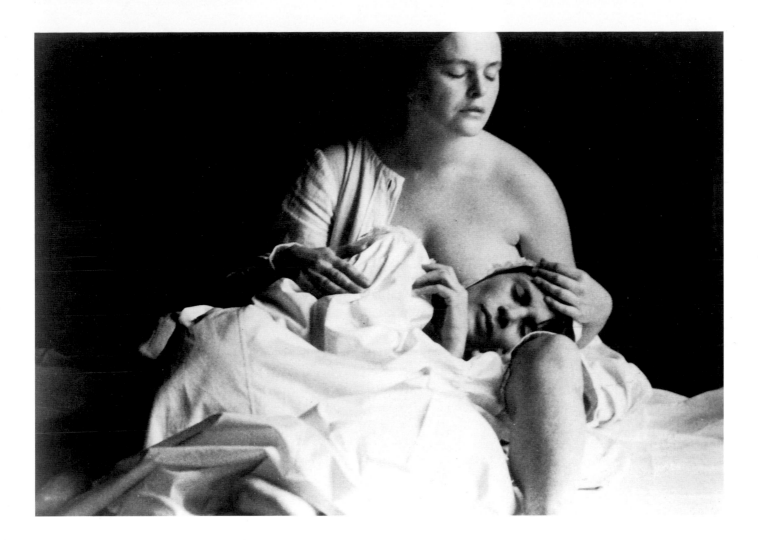

A striking scene in which the faithful servant Anna (Kari Sylwan), a kind of earth mother, comforts the dying Agnes. Bergman modeled the shot on the *Pietà*.

sonal and anguished. "If it is so" that Agnes will meet God, he asks her to "pray for us who are left here on the dark, dirty earth under an empty and cruel Heaven. Lay your burden of suffering at God's feet and ask Him to pardon us. Ask Him to free us at last from our anxiety, our weariness, and our deep doubt. Ask Him for a meaning to our lives."

The central figure in the film, Agnes has been carefully placed by Bergman in relation to the past and particularly to her mother. The mother appears briefly in a flashback in a family scene and is played by Liv Ullmann (taking a second part), who has been made up to resemble Bergman's mother as a young woman. Agnes was not the mother's favorite among her children, and at times her mother could be cold and indifferent to her. Yet Agnes writes in her diary: "I loved Mother. Because she was so gentle and beautiful and alive. Because she was so—I don't know how to put it—because she was so *present*. . . . now that I'm older I understand her much better. I should like so much to see her again and tell her what I have understood of her ennui, her impatience, her panic and her refusal to give up."

The mother is implied at the end in a passage from Agnes's diary that Anna reads and is visualized on the screen with stunning pictorial imagery. When the sisters come to see Anna in this visualization, the three stroll the lush park grounds wearing white formal dresses and carrying opened white parasols. They sit together in an old swing that Anna pushes back and forth, and it seems to Agnes that she has returned to her childhood. "I closed my eyes tightly," she comments, "trying to cling to the moment and thinking: Come what may, this is happiness. I can't wish for anything better. Now, for a few minutes, I can experience perfection. And I feel a great gratitude to my life, which gives me so much." The film begins in the park, moves to the interior of the house where the characters are revealed in their suffering or separateness from one another, and returns at the end to the openness of the park in a liberating vision of the human spirit set free. Like the lyric ending of *Wild Strawberries* in which Isak Borg is released from his confinement within his own egoism to enter into a form of communion with his parents, the concluding scene of *Cries and Whispers* offers a vision, even if elusive and momentary, of wholeness and communion within the family. Bergman has said that all three sisters represent aspects of his mother, but in a fuller sense the film's subtext is about his mother and himself. Although the movie is harrowing in its exposure of suffering and isolation, it reaches at its emotional core toward forgiveness and human closeness, which in secular terms becomes a kind of saving grace.

Cries and Whispers is one of Bergman's major films. It has the assurance of a master craftsman in full possession of his material, and the quality of its ensemble acting is as distinguished as the film's visual style. The movie proved an enormous success both commercially and critically when it opened in the United States. It was showered with prizes, including the 1972 National Society of Film Critics awards for Best Script and Best Photography; the 1972 New York Film Critics awards for Best Film, Best Script, Best Direction, and Best Actress (Liv Ullmann); the 1973 National Board of Review Award for Best Direction; and the 1973 Academy Award for Best Photography.

Scenes from a Marriage
1973

BY THE TIME *Cries and Whispers* was filmed, the relationship between Bergman and Ullmann had lapsed; by then he had fallen in love with a longtime acquaintance, Ingrid Karlebo, who at the time was married to Count Jan Carl von Rosen and was the mother of four children. Ingrid von Rosen married Bergman in November of 1971, when she was forty-one and he was fifty-three.[8] Bergman's fifth marriage has now lasted for over twenty years. The vicissitudes of marriage were on Bergman's mind in his next movie, *Scenes from a Marriage*, which was produced by his company, Cinematograph, and sold to Swedish television. In the spring of 1972, after his production of Ibsen's *The Wild Duck* opened at Dramaten, Bergman and his wife went to Fårö, where Bergman wrote the sce-

The three sisters, with the servant Anna, stroll the grounds of the estate, an episode that prompts Agnes's lyric recall of her childhood. *Cries and Whispers* evolved from a recurring dream in which Bergman "saw four white-clad women whispering in a red room."

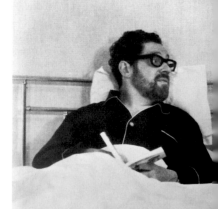

nario for the new picture. Liv Ullmann and Erland Josephson came to the island in the summer, were rehearsed by Bergman, and shooting began in midsummer. The film was planned in six fifty-minute episodes, which were aired on television from April 11 to May 16, 1973. The series scored an extraordinary success, giving Bergman a mass popularity such as he had never before known.

Bergman then edited the 252-minute TV version down to 155 minutes, or nearly three hours, for theatrical release in the United States in 1974. Part of the original version (which has been printed in book form) had to be sacrificed ruthlessly. The effect of the editing tends to deprive Johan and Marianne of their associations outside their marriage; Marianne's pregnancy and abortion, although relevant to the deterioration of the relationship, are eliminated; and the couple's two children, while acknowledged, virtually disappear. Yet all the essentials of the story remain intact. The appearance of *Scenes from a Marriage* as a feature film was dictated by its having been shot in 16 mm for television and blown up to 35 mm for international release. Scenes are shot almost entirely in close-up and without the cinematic resourcefulness characteristic of Bergman; there are no flashbacks or flashforwards or dream sequences. Nevertheless, the film is absorbing, and its reception in America was extremely favorable.

The picture is made up quite literally of scenes, which are like stages in the marital experience of Johan (Erland Josephson), a forty-two-year-old professor at the Psychotechnical Institute, and his wife, Marianne (Liv Ullmann), a thirty-five-year-old divorce lawyer. They are introduced in scene one as they celebrate their tenth wedding anniversary and are interviewed by a woman from a magazine who wants to learn about their "ideal" marriage. They are confident that it is a sound one and are somewhat complacent about it. In the evening another couple, Peter (Jan Malmsjö) and Katarina (Bibi Andersson), come for dinner, and the horror of their marriage is revealed in lacerating exchanges that cast Johan and Marianne temporarily into the shade. Fissures in their own relationship begin to show in scene two, and by scene three Johan announces that he is moving out to live with a young woman named Paula. In scene four, Johan returns to see Marianne, having had second thoughts about Paula; but, now beginning to gain confidence in herself after the upheaval of Johan's desertion, she will not have him back. In scene five pent-up emotions erupt; Johan beats Marianne, and after they begin to regain their composure they sign their divorce papers. In the sixth and final scene, occurring ten years after the opening, and entitled "In the Middle of the Night in a Dark House Somewhere in the World," Johan and Marianne have both remarried but have affairs on the side. They go to a cottage in the country belonging to a friend of Johan's to enjoy sex together without illusions or commitment, which had turned their marriage into a battle of wills. Yet their bedroom scene raises doubts that they have found their way out of their

below: Johan (Erland Josephson) and Marianne (Liv Ullmann), who consider themselves an ideally married couple at the opening of *Scenes from a Marriage*. They will have much to learn.

Marianne and Johan at the end of *Scenes from a Marriage*. Divorced and remarried to other partners, they meet for uncommitted sex. Johan's self-image has diminished in the course of time; he describes himself as "a child with genitals, a fabulous combination when it comes to women with maternal feelings."

confusion. In shedding his illusions, Johan has nothing to believe in, and Marianne has a dream in which she wants to reach out to Johan but has no hands. Whether married at the beginning or related to each other ambiguously at the end, they are essentially alone.

In his preface to the printed text, Bergman remarks that the film "took three months to write, but rather a long part of my life to experience."[9] The experience shows: the writing is sharp and unsparing, yet one feels Bergman's affection for his characters. Johan is sympathetic in many ways in the losses he sustains; his professional life is disappointing, and his intellectual-spiritual aspirations are unfulfilled in the course of the film. While he undergoes diminishment, Marianne grows in self-sufficiency and achieves more dimension than Johan. The performances of Ullmann and Josephson are flawless. Josephson plays Johan with such self-effacement that one is never conscious that he is acting, and Ullmann is a fascinating mixture of strength and vulnerability. They are so totally convincing together that one has the conviction that one knows them. They are the people next door.

The Magic Flute
(1975)

IN THE SPRING of 1965, Bergman agreed to stage *The Magic Flute* with the Hamburg Opera, but the project had to be canceled when he fell ill. An opportunity arose in the early 1970s, however, to make a cinematic version of the work for television that would also be released for movie-theater audiences. Laying plans to celebrate its fiftieth anniversary, Swedish Radio commissioned Bergman to prepare a production of *The Magic Flute* that would be broadcast on television on New Year's Day 1975. By Swedish standards, the $1 million cost of the production represented an extremely large investment, and it required elaborate preparations.[10]

opposite: Papageno (Håken Hagegård) discovers his true love in Papagena (Elizabeth Erikson).

140

above: Bergman was entranced by *The Magic Flute* and referred to it as "the world's best musical." Among the mythological beasts in the work is the monstrous dragon appearing at the opening.

opposite: Pamina (Irma Urrila) goes up in the balloon with the three boys to be reunited with Tamino (Josef Köstlinger).

overleaf, top: As vapor rises around them in the realm of night *(left)*, Tamino—with Pamina at his side— plays his magic flute. *(center):* Before Tamino and Papageno set out on their journey, three cherubic boys, guardian spirits, descend in the basket of a balloon to advise them. *(right):* The assembly of the brotherhood in *The Magic Flute*. Sarastro (Ulrik Cold) announces his intention to turn over his kingdom to Tamino and Pamina, subject to Tamino's passing a series of arduous tests. The members of the brotherhood pray for his success.

Bergman selected the Drottningholm Court Theater outside Stockholm as a close facsimile of the eighteenth-century Theater auf der Weiden in Vienna, where Mozart's opera had its premiere in 1791. But because the Drottningholm Theater could not accommodate Bergman's crew of technicians, the set was reconstructed in a Stockholm studio. Bergman began his search for singers (the opera would be sung in Swedish rather than German) as early as 1973. He insisted that they should have the physical appearance matching the parts they play, be able to act, and have voices that were "vibrant and alive." The cast he chose was international in scope but predominantly Scandinavian. The score was first recorded by the Swedish State Broadcasting Network Symphony Orchestra under the direction of Eric Ericsson and then played back in performance until a perfect match was achieved between the music and the lip synchronization of the cast.

Filmed operas are often static, but Bergman wanted *The Magic Flute* to appeal to audiences in an involving way. Thus rather than opening with the curtain going up, Bergman begins with panning shots of the grounds, ornamented with eighteenth-century statuary, of the Drottningholm Theater. The camera then moves to the interior of the theater, where an audience has assembled and the overture is played. The audience itself becomes a vital part of the intimacy of the

production. The camera moves over the faces of the audience to reveal members of Bergman's personal and professional family: one notices his wife, Ingrid, his former wife Käbi Laretei, his daughter Linn Ullmann, Erland Josephson, and Sven Nykvist. It is evident, too, that the audience is made up of people of different races, nationalities, and ages. A young girl (Helene Friberg) is shown in the audience at the beginning and at later points in the performance, and the expression on her face makes it clear that she has succumbed to the opera's fairy-tale enchantment. The opera thus belongs not only to a particular historic moment but also to more timeless, universal experience. Another feature of Bergman's concept is that the camera goes backstage to observe the machinery of scene changes and actors as they are captured unawares. Brushing up for his next role, Sarastro pores over the score of *Parsifal* and nearly misses his cue; and a boy, one of Sarastro's minions, is spied reading a comic book. These backstage views are also part of the magic of the theater.

The keynote of Bergman's *The Magic Flute* is exuberance; the work is nothing if not great fun. Tamino (Josef Köstlinger), a handsome young knight out of a fairy tale, is attacked by a dragon and saved by three handmaidens of the Queen of the Night (Birgit Nordin), who, after learning of the incident, sends him a medallion of her daughter Pamina (Irma Urrila), with whom he falls in love on

below: As Tamino plays his magic flute in the forest, he charms wild beasts in the vicinity, including a black bear who comes closer to listen.

below: The Queen of the Night (Birgit Nordin) beseeches Tamino to rescue her daughter Pamina from the sorcerer Sarastro.

sight. When the Queen of the Night then meets Tamino, she offers him her daughter in marriage if he can rescue her from the girl's father, Sarastro (Ulrik Cold), supposedly an evil enchanter. To aid him in his quest, she provides him with a magic flute and a companion, Papageno (Håkan Hagegård), a forester who offers comic relief. At the palace of Sarastro, however, in a sudden plot shift by Mozart and Schikaneder, his librettist, it turns out that the Queen of the Night, rather than Sarastro, is the evil spirit. Sarastro wishes to marry Tamino and Pamina, now much in love with each other, but first Tamino must undergo a series of trials proving his worthiness, as must Papageno, who by now has found an admirably suited mate in Papagena (Elizabeth Erikson). Armed with his magic flute, Tamino leads Pamina through the underworld and is united with her. The Queen of the Night is driven from the scene, and Sarastro turns over his spiritual kingdom to the young couple. The opera ends in celebration. In its theme of a quest for ultimate truth and harmony, the opera has a darker dimension: art and imagination are a fragile stay against despair. The extraordinary beauty of the music, played throughout at a fast tempo, is joyously seductive; and the work's lively inventiveness and comedy (Håkan Hagegård is a delightful Papageno) shimmer with immediacy. *The Magic Flute* is one of the splendid moments of Bergman's filmmaking.

Exile and Return

Face to Face
(1976)

WITH *Cries and Whispers, Scenes from a Marriage,* and *The Magic Flute,* Bergman carried off three triumphs in a row that revived his popularity in America, but his next picture, *Face to Face,* failed with both critics and audiences. *Face to Face* was produced by Bergman's Cinematograph, with financing from Dino De Laurentiis in Los Angeles. A longer treatment in four fifty-minute episodes was made for Swedish television and shown in April–May 1976, while a version reduced to 135 minutes was prepared as an international film release.

Face to Face was inspired, according to Bergman, by the painful case of a woman he knew, as well as by his own experience of having lived for some time "with an anxiety which has no tangible cause"[1] that he wished to investigate in the film. At the opening, Jenny Isaksson (Liv Ullmann), a psychiatrist in her late thirties attached to a hospital clinic in Stockholm, confers with a female patient, a young lesbian named Maria (Kari Sylwan), who has suffered a devastating nervous breakdown. As they talk together at the clinic, Maria accuses Jenny of being in need of treatment herself, of being unable to feel or express love. The patient's diagnosis of the caregiver proves to be only too accurate; before long Jenny's rigid self-control begins to crack. Jenny's husband, also a doctor, is in America attending a conference, and while their new house is being built, she moves into the apartment of her grandmother (Aino Taube) and grandfather (Gunnar Björnstrand), who had raised her following the death of her parents in an automobile accident. Jenny's returning to live with them reawakens her early childhood traumas. Other subordinate characters also enter into the story: Dr. Wankel (Ulf Johanson), who has the most serious doubts that psychoanalysis can effect cures in their patients; Wankel's wife (Sif Ruud), who has become infatuated with a homosexual actor named Michael Strömberg (Gösta Ekman); and Tomas Jacobi (Erland Josephson), a gynecologist and Jenny's confidant who, too, is homosexual.

At a midway point, Jenny is the victim of an attempted rape, which precipitates her breakdown and suicide attempt by swallowing

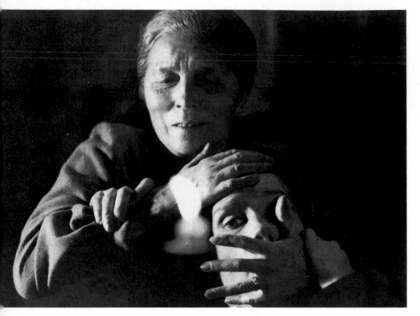

fifty Nembutal capsules. She is taken to the hospital, where she drifts in and out of a coma in the course of which she has disturbing, surrealistic dreams that reveal and become a partial purgation of her childhood anxieties. It becomes apparent, however, that Bergman is analyzing not only Jenny but also himself. A fear of death and other traumas involved in her parental relationships that lead to an inability to love and an obsession with controlling her life, and even a childhood incident of being punished by being locked in a closet, are wheeled out once again as part of the Jenny-Bergman childhood. At the end, Jenny's situation is not wholly changed, although she now knows herself better and has been brought to a new and more empathetic relation to her grandparents. The grandfather is becoming senile and, like Bergman's father in his seventies, suffers from paralysis in his legs. The grandmother, who was once tempted to leave him but remained when she realized how lonely he would be, provides the chief emotional support for her failing husband. Bergman's compassionate depiction of their closeness in old age, revealing a love that "embraces all, even death," implies his forgiveness, once again, of his parents.

Unfortunately, Jenny is less fully a character than a chart-and-graph illustration of how a denial of love leads to neurotic anxiety. Her experience is terrain that Bergman has covered before and better; even the dream sequences, with their death figures and flaming coffin, have a déjà vu quality. Nor has Bergman managed to make Jenny believable as a psychiatrist. Presumably a psychiatrist would have undergone extensive psychoanalysis before being ready to treat others, but Jenny lacks self-awareness, has no inkling of the dynamics of her inner life. Moreover, she has only the vaguest links to the characters who surround her. What do all the homosexual characters mean in terms of Jenny's story? It never becomes clear. Strangely, Jenny's husband comes from America to see her at the hospital, but after exchanging a few words with her he flies back across the Atlantic.

left: Grandma (Aino Taube) with Jenny (Liv Ullmann).

right: Jenny by the flaming casket. Revisiting her buried past proves a purgatory of suffering.

opposite: Ullmann runs the gamut of emotions as a psychiatrist who suffers a devastating nervous breakdown.

Bergman directing a scene in *Face to Face*.

Why did he come at all? Jenny's relationship with Tomas seems to be leading somewhere, but near the end he simply departs for Jamaica to pursue his interest in boys. What emotional intensity the film possesses is due to Liv Ullmann's performance as Jenny. She gives herself to the role totally, is equal to its most exacting requirements. Relating the rape incident to Tomas, she begins laughing in hysterical fits that come and go, then build to wild laughter that changes to sobbing. Bergman calls her acting in this sequence "one of the golden moments in my life as a film director."[2] Ullmann is this fuzzy film's indisputable glory.

The Serpent's Egg

(1977)

ON JANUARY 30, 1976, events occurred that would make international headlines and shake the life of Ingmar Bergman to its foundations.[3] At noon that day two plainclothes policemen appeared at Stockholm's Royal Dramatic Theater to see Bergman. They were told that he was rehearsing Strindberg's *The Dance of Death* and could not be disturbed until after the production's premiere, but they insisted on seeing him and before long confronted him backstage. The upshot of the encounter was that Bergman was hurried off in a car to police headquarters, where he was interrogated by Inspector Bo Stolpe in connection with his income-tax filing in 1971. Bergman was grilled by the inspector for three hours, and when he returned to his apartment under police escort, policemen searched his rooms and confiscated his passport and private papers. "Bergman," Frank Gado writes, "was in a state of shock. Three days later, suffering from the delusion that he was being pursued by a spectral self, he entered a mental ward. His confinement—first at the Karolinska hospital, then at Sophiahemmet—lasted almost two months."[4]

opposite: Manuela (Liv Ullmann) and Abel Rosenberg (David Carradine) in a cabaret raided by Nazi thugs. They look on helplessly as the leader of the band repeatedly bashes the Jewish owner's face against a table.

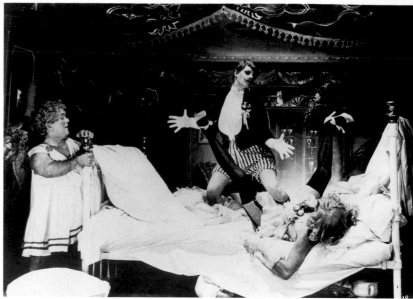

What provoked this extraordinary incident was that the Swedish tax authorities concluded that Bergman had underpaid on taxes for his company Persona Ltd. Persona had been set up in 1967 in Bern, Switzerland, by Bergman's attorney Sven Bauer in order to finance certain productions anticipated outside Sweden. Its revenues were to be used specifically to finance a two-part film, *Love Duet*, to be made with Fellini—a project that was canceled when Fellini was unable to provide a script for his part of the movie. Persona's funds were then reserved for a film Bergman was to make for Italian television about Christ's last days; but this project, too, foundered. The company was then dissolved and its funds were returned to Sweden, with a capital-gains tax paid to the government. Although the tax department approved the transaction, officials in its upper echelons decided that a much larger assessment was called for. Since the company had engaged in no real business, they argued, its funds should be taxed as personal income at eight times the capital-gains rate. And because the statute of limitations was about to run out, they acted precipitously. In March authorities acquitted Bergman of any wrongdoing, and the ugly affair should have ended there; but the tax department, unwilling to let the matter rest, reviewed Bergman's financial records and prepared a new set of charges. In early April they informed him that the Persona funds must be taxed as part of the profits earned by Cinematograph in 1975. The funds would thus be taxed twice, at an aggregate rate of 139 percent. They would, however, forgo this levy if he agreed to their original demands.

Bergman responded with an angry letter to the press decrying the state of affairs in which individuals are set upon by an irresponsible bureaucracy and announced his intention to leave the country. In the weeks that followed, scouting for a new place in which to live and work, Bergman and his wife toured foreign cities, including Paris, New York, Hollywood, Copenhagen, Oslo, and Munich. With its thriving cultural life, which included two symphony orchestras, two opera companies, and thirty theaters, Munich struck Bergman as particularly agreeable; in some ways it reminded him of Stockholm. After meeting with Kurt Meisel, head of Munich's Residenztheater, Bergman signed a contract as a director, and for the next eight years would make Munich his base of operations. During his self-imposed exile in Munich, the issues of Bergman's tax case continued to reverberate in Sweden. In autumn of 1976, the Social Democrats lost control of the government for the first time since 1932; their defeat, even if by a narrow margin, may well have been due to a growing feeling, highlighted perhaps by the Bergman case, that the government was imposing too rigid a control over people's lives. The Bergman case dragged on until autumn 1979, when the courts ruled that Bergman need pay only $35,000, a mere seven percent of the tax department's original claim. In addition, the state was required to pay all court costs, a figure amounting to $500,000.

Bergman wrote the script of *The Serpent's Egg* two months

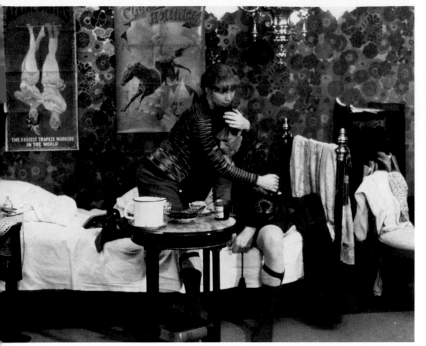

before the Swedish tax authorities descended on him at the beginning of 1976. It was to have been made in Sweden, but plans were now arranged to shoot the film in Munich,⁵ with financing of something close to $4 million coming from Dino De Laurentiis. It was shot with a German crew (except for Sven Nykvist) and a chiefly German cast. Because it was made with an international audience in mind, an English or American actor was needed for the leading role. Dustin Hoffman and Al Pacino were considered for the part before Bergman decided on Richard Harris; but then Harris became ill and Bergman chose David Carradine, who had impressed him in *Bound for Glory*. Re-creating Berlin in the 1920s proved a vast undertaking and involved in part the use of several thousand extras.

The Serpent's Egg, which is set in Berlin during the week of November 3 to 11, 1923, concerns several characters—Abel Rosenberg (David Carradine), his brother, and his brother's wife, Manuela (Liv Ullmann)—who are partners in an aerial act with a circus. When Abel's brother injures his wrist, the three lay over in Berlin, where they become involved in a cultural nightmare. As the film opens, Abel goes to see his brother at a boardinghouse, only to find that he has just put a bullet through his head. Abel is called in for interrogation by police inspector Bauer (Gert Fröbe) about his brother's death as well as the mysterious deaths of other individuals, with some of whom Abel has had contact, but because he is not as yet directly under suspicion, he is released. Abel then looks up Manuela, now surviving as a small-time cabaret singer and part-time prostitute, and he stays for a time at her lodgings. An American of Russian-Jewish origin, Abel suffers from a sense of guilt and takes refuge in drink as he wanders through the city. Some frightening scenes show him confronting his Jewishness—a sequence in a deserted street at night where he is menaced by Nazi thugs, an episode in a "decadent" cabaret where a band of Hitler's supporters smash the furnishings and the owner's face.

Yet these incidents are merely part of a larger, more enveloping malaise that leaves the characters debilitated, alone, and without a sense of identity. At the cabaret where the tarted-up and green-wigged Manuela performs, an obviously evil man named Hans Vergérus (Heinz Bennent) appears, and by the end of the film it is revealed that he is responsible for the trail of mysterious deaths. For it comes out that he has a secret headquarters hidden away in the bowels of St. Anna's Clinic, where he experiments on people with drugs that test their reaction to enormous psychological stress, often destroying their minds in the process and causing them to commit suicide. This blonde, blue-eyed, pure-bred Aryan keeps elaborate files that will prepare for the control of human beings in a scientific, totalitarian future. The present time, he tells Abel in the film's *denouement*, is "like a serpent's egg. Through the thin membranes you can clearly discern the already perfect reptile." When the police close in on him, Vergérus kills himself by swallowing a cyanide capsule; by no coincidence the thwarting of his experiments, for which the time is not yet quite ripe, coincides exactly with Hitler's early setback in his Munich beer-hall putsch. Bergman is clearly concerned with evoking the psychic breakdown of a community and its members, but his conception of Vergérus as a mad scientist belongs to melodrama and is more naïve than horrifying. Nor do Bergman's dimensionless characters ever really come to life as they wend their way through a murky and artificial plot. The film is an embarrassment and was a commercial disaster.

Autumn Sonata

(1978)

*A*utumn Sonata was produced by Personafilm, a company Bergman formed in Munich, with principal financing coming from Britain's Lord Lew Grade and his American colleague Martin Starger. It was shot in Oslo in the autumn of 1977, shortly before the opening of *The Serpent's Egg*. The movie is notable for Bergman's casting of Ingrid Bergman as the mother of Liv Ullmann. The story of how Sweden's two famous Bergmans agreed to work together, and of their at times difficult collaboration, is recounted in Bergman's autobiography *The Magic Lantern* and in Ingrid Bergman's memoirs, *Ingrid Bergman: My Story*, written with Alan Burgess and published posthumously in 1980.[6] Years before, Ingmar and Ingrid had met in Stockholm, and in the course of conversation Ingmar reflected that it might be fun to do a film together based on their namesake, Hjalmar Bergman. They then exchanged some letters about a film they might do, perhaps one that Ingmar himself would write. Several years later at the Cannes Film Festival, where Ingrid was president of the jury and Ingmar made a rare guest appearance in connection with *Cries and Whispers*, she reminded him of her interest in making a film with him. Then two years later, while Ingrid was staying on Fårö, Ingmar telephoned her to say that he would like her to star in a film he had written called *Autumn Sonata*, and she immediately agreed.

As soon as they started on the film, problems began. *Autumn*

above: While filming *Autumn Sonata* on a cold autumn day in Norway, Liv Ullmann and Ingmar Bergman, in buttoned-up overcoats, break into smiles.

Ingrid Bergman as Charlotte, a famous concert pianist and neglectful parent, is forced to confront herself when she pays her daughter a long-postponed visit.

Sonata was originally to have been a four-hour movie, which Ingrid considered too long (it was, in fact, drastically shortened). She made her own deletions in the script and prepared her role with an acting style ("So many false intonations," Bergman remarked in his autobiography, "had not been heard since the 1930s")[7] that conflicted with his direction of his actors as an ensemble. After the first read through and the terrific clash that developed between the two Bergmans, Liv Ullmann left the room and wept, convinced that the film would never be made. Yet after two weeks of rehearsals, an accommodation was reached between Ingmar and Ingrid, who also formed supportive friendships with Ullmann and other female members of the company. They were especially important because soon after beginning work on the film, Ingrid suffered a recurrence of malignant cancer. She was absent briefly for some relatively uncomplicated surgery in London; her working hours were shortened; and everything possible was done to assist her. In the end, the movie was completed successfully, and Ingrid was gratified by the results. What she did not know at the time was that while the picture was being shot, Bergman was filming a documentary, using a hidden camera, about the making of the movie. Two years later when Ingrid visited Ingmar on Fårö, he showed her the film, which she called "the best documentary on the making of a movie I've ever seen."[8] The work, as far as I know, has never been screened publicly.

Autumn Sonata has a cast of only four central characters: Charlotte (Ingrid Bergman), a famous concert pianist slightly over sixty who has been preoccupied with her career and has not seen her daughter in seven years; Eva (Liv Ullmann), Charlotte's daughter,

Ingmar Bergman directing Ingrid Bergman in a scene in *Autumn Sonata* in which the character Ingrid plays will cower before the terrible accusations of her daughter Eva. Liv Ullmann is at the left.

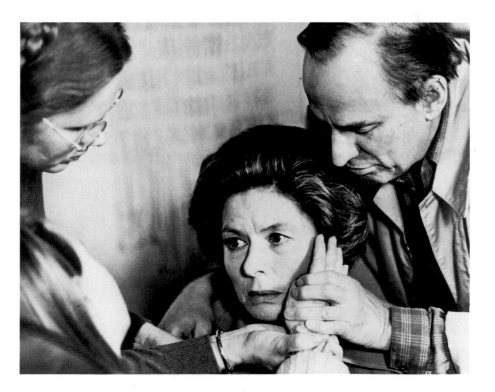

perhaps in her mid-thirties, whose love-hate relationship with her mother is explored in the film; Eva's pastor husband (Halvar Björk), a kindly, self-effacing man whose role in the film is rather incidental; and Helena (Lena Nyman), the crippled sister Eva has taken out of an institution to live with her and her husband in their remote Norwegian parsonage. The film is in essence a chamber work and strongly resembles a filmed play in its limited setting and stagelike character confrontations. Bergman employs a number of brief flashbacks, in some of which characters are shown but do not speak, but they are not in the text and have obviously been added in an attempt to give some cinematic dimension to Bergman's starkly scenic drama.

The film begins with Eva's letter to her mother, inviting her to visit after they have not seen each other in seven years. Charlotte soon arrives, and mother and daughter are reunited; but their

above: The two famous Bergmans, Ingrid and Ingmar, working together on a film at last. Ingrid remarked of Ingmar: "Of course his reputation is formidable. I heard he was a beast, very temperamental, always yelling and screaming, but he never raised his voice to me. He was a lamb. . . . He's very flexible and open."

opposite: Liv Ullmann as Eva and Ingrid Bergman as her mother Charlotte in *Autumn Sonata*. A stunning study of faces.

158

reunion soon develops into a duel between them, tense at first and then ferocious in its recriminations. A neglected child with a weak sense of self-worth, Eva has become a lonely neurotic who accuses her mother of having destroyed her life. Under Eva's assault, Charlotte breaks down and pleads for mercy, revealing that she, too, had been a neglected and unloved child whose only outlet for her emotions had been in her music. Unable to cope with the emotional demands of motherhood, she has built a protective, professional wall around herself, but with the recent death of her longtime lover

Leonardo she is confronted once again by the loneliness from which she had attempted to escape. The film, which deals with maiming as it descends from one generation to the next, reflects partly on Bergman's own guilt in having neglected his children; but even more importantly, through Eva, it suggests his early anguish as the love-starved child of a refusing mother.

Some complexity enters the film in that Eva's accusations are partly the distortions of her unstable mind. She has come to blame Charlotte, rather than herself, for many of the events in her life that she has regretted and has even gone so far as to hold her responsible for her sister Helena's illness, although it is of an organic nature. Paralyzed and helpless, gurgling and uttering sounds that painfully approximate human speech, Helena is a Gothic figure in Bergman's drama. She is, as Bergman never lets the viewer forget, the incarnation of a child's victimization; as an adult, she still resembles a child and has its terrible quality of helplessness. While Eva and Charlotte reveal the source of their trouble in childhood, Helena suffers on a visceral level. Projecting herself onto the floor from her criblike bed, she drags her body to the top of the staircase, where she calls out words that can barely be made out as "Mother, come." Her presence in the film, however, may be too staged, and certain other aspects of the work can be faulted. The movie is carried in part by great acting. Ullmann is remarkable as the plain-featured, resentful, and emotionally stunted daughter; and Ingrid Bergman, who was nominated for an Oscar for her role, is a commanding presence, egocentric yet vulnerable and with a fully dimensional humanity. As a consciously "great actress," she may not be quite in key with Ingmar Bergman's ensemble style, but no one has any right to complain. She gives glowing warmth to Bergman's stringent vision of characters locked away in the prison of self but who may yet, it is implied at the end, have opened the door a crack to love and forgiveness.

Fårö Document 79

(1979)

ALTHOUGH BERGMAN left Sweden in the spring of 1976 to make films abroad, he returned quietly to Fårö that summer, where he conceived the idea of making a second documentary about the island that would be an update to the one he filmed in 1969. For two years, beginning in the autumn of 1977, cameraman Arne Carlsson shot scenes of the island and its inhabitants, accumulating twenty-eight hours of footage that Bergman edited into a film of one hour and fifty-eight minutes. The film—which was shot in color and narrated by Bergman, who also interviews local people using a hand-held microphone—was produced by Cinematograph, shown on Swedish television on Christmas Day 1979, and released in the United States in the autumn of 1980. Its tone is more optimistic than that of the previous documentary: the fishing industry has started up again, more job opportunities are available, and more young people have chosen to remain.

Fårö is captured in its changing seasons. Bathers are seen swimming and on a sandy beach; white-capped waves break against a fishing boat that bobs on the water; an autumn wind blusters in the boughs of trees along the stony coast; snow falls over the landscape, blown by a howling wind. The daily work life is chronicled, from trawler fishing for flounder and salmon and the harvesting of crops to the shearing of lambs and slaughter of a hog. A group of men join in roofing a new farm building and afterward sing together at a thatching party dinner; a funeral is held in a small graveyard while snow falls and the sound of the sea is heard in the background. Bergman's camera continually crosscuts to the young people—on a school bus, at a dance, on the beach. A fisherman is shown alone preparing his fish dinner, a patient ritual, and then begins to eat it in his small kitchen. In a splendid shot, he is viewed through a window at night as he chews his food; the camera slowly recedes from the window until the little rectangle of light grows smaller and disappears in the darkness. Like the rest of the film, the moment focuses upon the beauty of the austere, upon lives lived far from the madding crowd.

From the Life of the Marionettes
(1981)

A fateful night for Katarina (Rita Russek), the prostitute in *From the Life of the Marionettes*.

IN THE MID-1970s, Bergman announced that before long he would retire from making feature films. Few people believed that he really would; his prodigious energy and the steady outpouring of his films over three decades argued against it. But in July 1979, he wrote the screenplay of *Fanny and Alexander*, which would be his valedictory film. In the meantime he had one more project to see to completion. The principal characters in the picture, Peter and Katarina, had appeared as the quarreling couple in the opening section of *Scenes from a Marriage*. Now wishing to enlarge upon them, he introduced them into an ambitious film concept, *Love Without Lovers*, which never reached the screen. But by 1979 he developed a new scenario, *From the Life of the Marionettes*, in which they are focal characters.[9] The movie was shot in Munich using German actors with the Residenztheater who had never previously appeared in films and was financed by Lew Grade and Martin Starger's ITC production company.

"I found it was fascinating," Bergman told an interviewer, "not only to work with actors who had not been before the camera before, but also to have a film without a plot. Just to make an investigation, like an operation: very, very clear, very simple, very sterile, but not to find the truth."[10] The movie begins and ends in color, but what comes between is filmed by Sven Nykvist in black and white. At the opening, Peter Egerman (Robert Atzorn), a successful businessman in his thirties, is locked overnight in a brothel with a young prostitute whom he begins to make love to but then brutally murders. At this point Bergman begins his investigation of what drove Peter to commit this mad act. A police official interrogates people who know him, and earlier scenes from his marriage are shown. The trouble with his marriage to Katarina (Christine Buchegger), a partner in a fashion-design company, has a central interest. A sense of reality has drained out of their marriage. They still love each other, yet they constantly quarrel. Although they "live close together and know everything about each other," as Katarina says, they cannot "see" each other. Katarina has not been fulfilled by Peter sexually and has had lovers, yet she is bound to him as to another self; the pain he feels is just as sharply felt by her. For some time Peter has had a dreamlike presentiment that he is going to kill Katarina. In killing the prostitute, whose name is also Katarina, he murders a surrogate of his wife—and in doing so effectively ends his own life.

"All roads are closed," Peter says in the brothel, and it is as if his act is preordained by some demonic power that has control over him and that he does not understand. Tim Mandelbaum (Walter Schmidinger)—middle-aged, Jewish, homosexual, and a partner in Katarina's fashion business—is particularly revealing in his relation to Peter. In a long, extraordinary monologue, he tells Katarina of his inmost nature. Possessing aesthetic refinement and longing for intimacy, he is yet impelled toward self-degradation in picking up "brutal, filthy trade . . . not exactly nearness and tenderness." He is, he declares, "governed by forces I cannot master . . . hidden forces. Forces I can't control." By giving Peter the name and address of the prostitute, he betrays Katarina, whom he claims to love, and sets the catastrophe in motion. Without fully understanding his motives, he had hoped to detach Peter from his painful marriage to Katarina and in some way come to possess him himself. What results is violence and destruction.

The tawdry, claustrophobic brothel, shot in lurid red tones, is a meeting ground of erotic desire and frustration; and it is notable that Peter's murder of the girl occurs by a bed on the brothel's performing stage. The homicide is a ritualization of the marionette theme. Earlier in the film, Katarina tells Peter that they are both children who do not want to grow up, and Tim describes himself as a "mere child" and a "childish old man." Their child's longing for love and closeness can find no realization in the adult world. Peter, in fact, returns to childhood at the end, hugging a teddy bear in his room in a mental hospital and playing chess with a computer that suggests both his distance from the real world and his dehumanization.

The film's characterization of Peter contains many allusions that point to Bergman himself. In his childhood, Peter was sickly and terrified by the dark and by birds, had a younger sister with whom he

Peter Egerman (Robert Atzorn), the conflicted protoganist of *From the Life of the Marionettes,* holds a razor at the throat of his wife, Katarina (Christine Buchegger).

staged puppet shows, and an older brother who would later occupy a prominent position in the country's diplomatic service. Peter enjoyed trips with his father but also regarded him far into adulthood as an oppressor, a tyrant, and as a result of his upbringing would later become a "punctuality neurotic." All these features of Peter's background have their equivalents in Bergman's own experience. The film also interweaves a number of Bergman's preoccupations, such as the theme of human beings as marionettes. In *Howards End,* E. M. Forster remarks, "only connect," but in *From the Life of the Marionettes,* Bergman's characters can connect with nothing, are unable "to become real."

Speaking of his murder of the prostitute, Peter remarks: "Am I in

Katarina Egerman with her husband, Peter, right. A strange logic of destruction looms over their marriage.

fact alive or was the dream, in the shape it took, my one brief moment of life, of conquered and experienced reality? The mirror is smashed, but what do the splinters reflect?" The psychiatrist Mogens Jensen (Martin Benrath), an unsympathetic figure (like Bergman's earlier psychiatrists), neatly sums up Peter as a latent homosexual whose suppressed emotions explode in violence. Yet what is true of Peter is also true of the other characters, who are thwarted in their attempt to become deeply connected with others. Peter, his mother, Katarina, and Tim all long to find a oneness with another individual only to be confronted by their isolation. *From the Life of the Marionettes*, which had respectful if puzzled reviews, may be too airless, but it is skillfully executed and contains uniformly controlled performances (Robert Atzorn is particularly good as the handsome yet faceless protagonist). As an observation of the rituals of half-alive characters, the film creates a pensive mood that lingers in the mind and in which all attempts at certainty dissolve into mystery.

Bergman's use of mirrors again to create multidimensionality. Tim Mandelbaum (Walter Schmidinger) confides to Katarina Egerman, left, that sinister external forces control his life. He is one in a series of homosexuals who appear in Bergman's later films.

Fanny and Alexander

(1983)

above, left: An anxious moment as Fanny (Pernilla Allwin) and Alexander (Bertil Guve) prepare to meet their new stepfather. The appearance of Bertil Guve is strikingly different from Bergman's initial description of Alexander in his screenplay. "Alexander," Bergman writes, "is ten years old, pale, thin, and nearsighted. His hair is rather sparse. He has a large nose, dark blue eyes, and a wide mouth."

above, right: Scene between Bishop Vergérus (Jan Malmajö) and Emilie Ekdahl (Ewa Fröling) just before their marriage. He tells her that when she and the children come to live at his home, he would like them to come without any of their possessions, making a complete break with the past. Now under his spell, Emilie agrees. "Hold me in your arms," she says, "as only you can."

right: Emilie with her sister-in-law Alma (Mona Malm) at the Christmas party. Bergman originally had Liv Ullmann in mind for the part of Emilie, but she was unavailable, as was Max von Sydow for the part of Bishop Vergérus. It is intriguing to try to visualize Ullmann and Von Sydow in these roles.

IT WOULD BE hard to find a transition in cinematic style as radical as that which occurs between the spare, modernist *From the Life of the Marionettes* and *Fanny and Alexander*, which has the texture and some of the narrative looseness of a nineteenth-century novel. Bergman refers to it as "the sum total of my life as a film-maker,"[11] but although it does contain many motifs belonging to the earlier movies, it has little of the tortured isolation and anxiety that are Bergman's hallmarks. Rather than being pessimistic, and limited to a small number of characters as in the chamber works, it employs a big cast, its spirit is cordial and tolerant, and it celebrates the life of a large, convivial family. *Fanny and Alexander* is a conscious farewell

in which Bergman looks back once again at his childhood, at his evolution from troubled boy to future artist.

Fanny and Alexander was made in two versions: a five-hour work in six installments for television and a three-hour, seventeen-minute feature film for international release. (The shooting of the movie has been recorded in Arne Carlsson's affectionate color documentary *The Making of Fanny and Alexander*, which provides a rare opportunity to observe Bergman directing one of his famous films.) A lavish undertaking,[12] it cost $6 million to produce, making it the most expensive film to be undertaken in Sweden up to that time. Financing proved difficult to find, but the Swedish Film Institute, together with Gaumont in Paris and West German television, eventually provided the necessary funding. When the movie was released in 1983 to an international audience that included thirty different countries, its reception was overwhelmingly favorable. It was honored as the year's best film in Sweden and France, and in America it was showered with prizes—both the New York Film Critics Award and the Golden Globe Award for Best Foreign Film of 1983, and the Academy Awards in 1984 for Best Foreign Film, Best Cinematography, Best Costumes, and Best Art Direction.

Set in 1910, the movie opens in Uppsala with a view of the life of the Ekdahls, a prominent family who live in a substantial house in the town square and own and operate the town's repertory theater. Helena Ekdahl (Gunn Wållgren), a noted actress who married a local grandee and is now his widow, is the matriarch of the family. She has several sons. Gustav Adolf (Jarl Kulle), a successful restaurateur, has a plump, attractive wife (Mona Malm) who adores him and displays a tolerant attitude toward his philandering. A lusty, middle-aged goat whom Kulle makes surprisingly ingratiating, Gustav Adolf is having a current affair with a lame, buxom servant Maj (Pernilla Wallgren), who allows Alexander, Gustav's nephew, to sleep with her at times and is suggested by the lame maid Lala in the household of Bergman's youth. Gustav Adolf's brother Carl (Börje Ahlstedt), a college professor of mediocre abilities who is heavily in debt and tied to a devoted but stolid German wife, is less well favored. In their bedroom, he despairs of his life and quarrels with his wife. Yet at other times he displays something of his brother's exuberance; during the Christmas festivities, the children gather wide-eyed on a staircase to watch him drop his pants and blow out the candles on a cake with an impressive breaking of wind.

Helena's third son, Oscar (Allan Edwall), the actor-manager of the theater, is kindly but dreamy and lost; his wife, Emilie (Ewa Fröling), is an actress in the local theater and a great beauty. In the printed text of the five-hour version, Oscar and Emilie have three children, but the eldest of them, Amanda, has been eliminated in the shorter feature film, leaving only Fanny (Pernilla Allwin), who is eight, and Alexander (Bertil Guve), who is ten. The youngsters who play Fanny and Alexander are a matched set of perfect beauty,

above: Bergman at left, with his cameraman, Sven Nykvist.

inset, above: Like Bergman as a child, Alexander is absorbed by his puppet theater in the opening shot of *Fanny and Alexander.*

inset, above right: Alexander
confronted by Bishop Vergérus.

Alexander's dark, sensuous features contrasting with the blonde hair
and serious blue eyes of Fanny. They belong not only to the Ekdahls'
social drama but also to fairy tale.

But Fanny, despite the film's title, is rather peripheral; Alexander,
modeled on Bergman as a child, is always the more important and
central figure. One sees him at the beginning as Bergman's surrogate,
lying under a table in his grandmother's large, quiet, and richly fur-

nished apartment as he takes in his surroundings as a theater of his imagination and operating his new gift of a "magic lantern" projector that enables him to be enthralled by screen images. This early section dealing with the Ekdahls at home, which runs close to an hour, has been directed by Bergman with the assurance of a great film artist. It contains radiant moments, like the Christmas festivities—the spirited handholding dance of the Ekdahls and their servants through the rooms of the house as they sing their yuletide song. Gunn Wåll-gren as Helena is a great presence, a little weary and detached from the boisterous occasion and most relaxed when she reminisces in a solitude of two with her old-time love Isak Jacobi (Erland Joseph-son), a Jewish antique dealer and moneylender. The section contains, too, a finely captured scene in which Oscar, after suffering a stroke in the theater during a rehearsal of *Hamlet*, is taken home—when no cab can be found—in a horse-drawn cart. Oscar's death is followed by an electrifying scene in which the children listen in an outer room as Emilie grieves; her mournful shrieks that come in a steady, undulating rhythm bring part one to a dramatic close.

Oddly, after Emilie marries Bishop Vergérus (Jan Malmsjö)—the passage of time is rather vague at this point—and goes with Fanny and Alexander to live in his fortresslike castle, the film loses all resemblance to the richly detailed social chronicle that Bergman had constructed in part one. In the text, Amanda reads a book by the brothers Grimm, and in truth the film at this point assumes the form of a fairy tale in which Emilie and the children are held under an evil enchantment. The bishop's retinue in the clammy castle with barred windows includes a grim-visaged mother and a rigid, unpleasant sister, both garbed in black, and a number of dour female servants. A

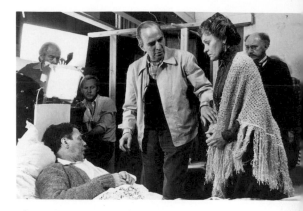

above: Bergman coaches Gunn Wållgren, who plays Helena Ekdahl, shown here with her dying son Oscar (Allan Edwall). At left, Sven Nykvist prepares to record the scene.

above: The Ekdahls, with friends and servants, pose for a Christmas photograph. The scene was cut in the film for theatrical release.

left: Fanny and Alexander arrive at the antique shop–home of Isak Jacobi (Erland Josephson) after he has spirited them away in a trunk from the bishop's residence. Standing between the children and Isak is Isak's son Aron (Mats Bergman).

top: Alexander has been caught by Bishop Vergérus in telling a lie, specifically about the death of the bishop's first wife and their two children. Alexander is now in for a caning. At right Fanny stands stiffly by.

top, right: As Alexander looks out of an upper-story window of his grandmother's house on the town square, he sees some of the guests arriving through the snow for their Christmas party.

Gothic touch is provided by the presence of the bishop's grotesquely bloated, bedridden aunt, who is unable to speak and has to be spoon-fed. In this austere and puritanical house where spontaneity and joy are banished in the name of Christianity, Alexander suffers acutely. When he tells Justina, a viperous house servant played wonderfully by Harriet Andersson ("Everyone 'hated' my character," Andersson told me), that the ghosts of the bishop's two drowned children hold him responsible for their deaths, she informs on him to the bishop and Alexander comes in for a caning. He is then compelled to ask forgiveness and to kiss the bishop's hand and is locked in the attic. Alexander's experience refracts Bergman's in two parts. The first centers on the Ekdahl house that fosters closeness and imagination and is presided over by sensuously evoked women; the other is dominated by a despotic father figure who intimidates and punishes Alexander—just as another ranking churchman, Erik Bergman, had punished his son. But although there are good things in this section, it is a falling off from the opening; there is less to hold it together, and it relies shamelessly on the emotions of melodrama.

Fanny and Alexander are rescued in melodramatic fashion by Isak, who hides them in a chest and through some kind of legerdemain (they are shown upstairs tucked in their beds at the same time as they are hidden in the chest) whisks them off to his antique shop–residence. Here magic rules. Awaking in the night and searching through the dim byways of the darkened shop for a place to relieve himself, Alexander hears a voice claiming to be God, to which Alexander gives defiant answers. Isak's nephew Aron (Bergman's son Mats) then appears to announce that he has been playing games with him. His namesake is Aaron of the Bible, the "artist" brother of

Moses whose rod possessed magical powers; but Aron, a puppeteer (like young Bergman), declares his disbelief in God, whose terrors he holds at bay through his art. Alexander next encounters a more disturbing figure in Isak's other nephew, Ismael, who is considered dangerous and has been locked away in a room that Alexander enters despite Isak's warning not to do so. Ismael (whose biblical name gives the idea of estrangement and exile) represents the destructive forces dwelling in imagination—and in Alexander himself. Through an extrasensory spell cast by Ismael but emanating from the boy's own thoughts, the bishop is burned to death horrifically in a fire at the castle; later the ghost of the bishop will pursue Alexander, who must live with guilt. But in the meantime the Ekdahl family is reunited, and the fairy tale has a happy ending as Gustav Adolf toasts the birth of two new daughters—Emilie's by the bishop and his own by the servant girl Maj—who offer a vision of hope for the future.

On a strictly realistic level, the Ekdahls, who mingle good-heartedly with the servants (Gustav Adolf's mistress and his daughter are to set up a milliner's shop together), are less than credible. In 1910 formal distinctions of class in Swedish society must have been more rather than less rigid than in later times. But the Ekdahls, too, belong to fable, to a golden age of lost innocence when human closeness and contact were possible, and Bergman lets them have their happy hour before darkness falls. That it will fall as the century unfolds is clearly indicated in Gustav Adolf's otherwise happy toast. The "poison," he remarks, "will strike at everyone, without exception." The theater, with which the Ekdahls' lives are so closely intertwined, offers only

Fanny and Alexander are fascinated by the images cast on a screen by Alexander's projector.

above: Emilie announces to the children that she is to marry the bishop, whose "comforting" hand can be seen behind her neck.

Isak Jacobi and Helena at the Ekdahl home. One-time lovers and oldtime friends, they have a relaxed mutual understanding.

the most fragile protection from time and the great outer world. Indeed, the theater itself is changing with the arrival of Strindberg, whose *Dream Play* Helena reads and quotes from to Emilie at the end: "Everything can happen; all is possible and probable. Time and space do not exist. On an insignificant realistic groundwork, the imagination spins and weaves new patterns." Strindberg's lines also sum up the continually evolving film "dreams" of Bergman, whose career has now reached its formal close in a fairy-tale form in which his imagination as a child was first set in motion.

A sumptuous, sometimes cockeyed film, *Fanny and Alexander* belongs especially to Bergman's late phase in which his imagination returns ever more frequently to themes of the past—of his parents' marriage and his childhood fixations that seem still strongly present for him. But they are present here with a disarming nostalgia and a kind of wide-eyed wonder at the human spectacle. The picture's cinematography, with its rich textures and formal compositions, is one of the finest achievements in Nykvist's long association with Bergman; it is also a handsome embellishment to Bergman's farewell, which has a warmth and generosity that do not quite conceal a vision of loneliness beneath the surface. The movie, too, seems an affectionate tribute to Bergman's life in the theater, for theater is at the heart of the Ekdahls' world. After *Fanny and Alexander*, Bergman will make one or two short films for Swedish television but primarily will devote himself to the theater, his old and great love. "They'll have to carry me out feet first," Bergman remarks saltily, "before I quit the stage."[13]

CONCLUSION:
Prolific Retirement

After the Rehearsal
(1984)

ALTHOUGH BERGMAN retired from making feature films with *Fanny and Alexander*, he has directed two fairly brief films for Swedish television. *After the Rehearsal*, which was written in 1980, set aside for several years, and then revised as a seventy-two-minute film, was aired on Swedish television in April 1984. When Jörn Donner, its producer, sold it to an American film distributor, Bergman attempted to prevent its release to theaters,[1] believing that it might give an impression that he had gone back on his decision to retire. But his attempts were unsuccessful, and the movie opened in New York in June 1984. *Rehearsal* is a single-set, one-act, three-character play that, despite the resourcefulness of cameraman Sven Nykvist, seems somewhat cramped when translated onto the large screen. The film centers upon a stage director in late middle age, Henrik Vogler (Erland Josephson), an obvious surrogate for Bergman; and two actresses—Rakel (Ingrid Thulin), who has been dead eight years but appears to Vogler in memory, and her daughter, Anna Egerman (Lena Olin), on the verge of her breakthrough role as Indra's daughter in the latest of Vogler's stagings of Strindberg's *A Dream Play*.

The film, which contains many echoes of *A Dream Play*, opens with Vogler's drowsing alone at his desk on a theater stage with his marked-up copy of the Strindberg work beside him; it is not entirely clear whether what follows may not, after all, be a dream. Vogler awakens as Anna enters the theater, ostensibly in search of a bracelet that she has left behind but actually to provoke an affair with Vogler—which will not only benefit her career but also spite her late mother, who had never loved her and had once, she believes, correctly, been Vogler's mistress. As they talk on the deserted stage, which for Vogler is filled with vibrant voices from the past, Rakel enters and an episode from the past is enacted while Anna, replaced by a thirteen-year-old version of herself (played by Nadja Palmstierna-Weiss, who resembles her and wears a similar red dress), remains seated in a frozen attitude on the center-stage couch. Rakel, too, attempts to use Vogler to advance her career, even offering to exchange sex with him for a larger role in place of the meager two

opposite: A scene from *Peer Gynt,* in the Dovre Mountains, with Hilde, played by Gunnel Fred, Great Grandfather Vaidur (Pierre Wilkner), and Great Grandmother (Agneta Ehrensvärd)

lines she has been given. But it is obvious that nothing can salvage her career; she is no longer reliable, having damaged her ability to act through her emotional problems and heavy drinking. As the sequence ends, in a magical moment of surprise, the camera moves upward from the bottom of the red dress, presumably of the young girl, to reveal the adult Anna holding hands with Vogler on the couch, and the action in the present resumes.

Anna informs Vogler that she is three months pregnant, which will make it impossible for her to appear five months hence when the play opens. Vogler is naturally disturbed that she has forfeited her chance for a part that would be the making of her. She could, she says, have an abortion, but Vogler opposes it; then it strikes him that she has already *had* the abortion and is merely acting. She is, in fact, acting, never having become pregnant at all—a way of making Vogler admire her and of opening the door to their affair. But just as Anna "acts" to attract Vogler's interest, Vogler "directs" as a way of declining her offer. As they pace about the stage, his arm over her shoulder, he improvises a script of what their affair would be like as it passes from its opening moves through its romantic delights to its inevitable ending. Although still feeling the tug of sex, the aging Vogler has become ascetic in his personal and professional life, giving his full attention to the discipline of his craft. "My rehearsal," he remarks, "is like an operation. Self-discipline, cleanliness, and stillness prevail. Then we approach the infinite, the enigmas, the darkness. Then we solve the riddles and learn the mechanism of repetition."

An autumnal meditation on the life of the theater, *Rehearsal* is remarkable for the accomplished acting Bergman elicits from Erland Josephson and Lena Olin, who turn small nuances into riches. Olin's ingenue about to make her breakthrough also proved prophetic. As Cordelia in Bergman's *King Lear*, a year after *Rehearsal* was shot, she was noticed by the Swedish-born producer Bertil Olson, who cast her in a starring role in *The Unbearable Lightness of Being*. The part, together with her starring ones in *Havana* and *Enemies, A Love Story*, made her internationally famous.

Karin's Face
(1986)

AFTER HIS father's death, Bergman came into possession of the family's photograph albums, and in 1983 he used them as the basis of his fourteen-minute 8-mm picture *Karin's Face*, which was screened in Gothenburg in January 1986 and released in the United States as a brief companion to another Bergman movie.[2] The film has a poignant piano accompaniment by Käbi Laretei and is itself musical in its fuguelike theme and variations. Karin's life is bracketed at the beginning by a photograph of her at the age of three and by a passport picture taken several months before her final heart attack. In the company of two older women, she is seen as a girl, a striking beauty with sensuous lips. The grandparents are shown by a large window in their home at Dalarna, and Erik Bergman appears as a young suitor. A marriage photograph focuses on Karin's hands and the wedding ring she wears. Erik next appears as a pastor, the camera moving in for a close-up of his eyes. The children begin to arrive, Karin with Dag and little Ingmar, seen together and with a close-up of their hands. Time passes, revealing Erik in a pulpit, and family scenes in which he and Karin are no longer young. The camera moves back and forth between Karin in the bloom of youth and in old age. To appreciate its impact, the film has to be seen. Finely felt and stunningly photographed, *Karin's Face* is an evocative miniature work of art.

The Magic Lantern

(1988)

IN THE SAME year that *After the Rehearsal* and *Karin's Face* were made, Bergman staged a new production of Molière's *Don Juan* in Salzburg, and in 1984 he returned to the Royal Dramatic Theater in Stockholm with a post-modernist, revisionist *King Lear,* which one reviewer described as being so powerful that it marked nothing less than the rebirth of Swedish theater.[3] In the following year Bergman staged Ibsen's *John Gabriel Borkman* in Munich, then returned to Stockholm to direct a made-for-television film, *The Blessed Ones*, about a middle-aged couple's unhappy marriage, that was written by Ulla Isaksson and starred Harriet Andersson and Per Myrberg. Since 1985, Bergman has directed at least one play a year at Dramaten, productions that have subsequently toured not only in Central and Eastern Europe but throughout other parts of the world as well. He also somehow found time to write his autobiography.

Bergman's autobiography, *The Magic Lantern*, published in America in 1988 after appearing in Sweden as *Laterna Magica* a year earlier, begins with his memories even of infancy and, at the age of four, of the birth of his sister Margareta, whom he attempts to suffocate when she steals attention from him. In danger of dying at birth, he was a sickly child with endless ailments who had to be dragged screaming to school. Sibling rivalry between Ingmar and his older brother, who oppressed and bullied him, was fierce, but Ingmar's ultimate anxiety stemmed from his witnessing the jarring marriage of his parents, with whom he would be locked in conflict throughout life. Bergman reveals a talent for concise portraiture, enlivened by earthy and at times—as in the case of his Uncle Carl, an inventor and childlike man with a compulsion to wet himself—baroque touches. Something of the grotesque enters into many aspects of the account, from Ingmar's awkward initiations into sex, graphically described, to his frequent psychosomatic illnesses. Worst of all was his "nervous stomach," which was related to his fear of failure; when his stomach attacks came on, he no longer had control over his bowels and thus had to be provided, humiliatingly, with his private lavatory while making his films.

Rather than advancing chronologically, the narrative is rendered impressionistically in a scrambled time sequence. Vivid vignettes follow one another as different aspects of his career and personal life are woven into a tapestry. But nothing is fully explored, and often more is left unsaid than revealed. The autobiography often has a novelistic quality, and never more so than at the end when Bergman revisits Hedvig Eleonora Church and after listening to Bach's *Christmas Oratorio* imagines himself entering his former home across the street to encounter his late mother writing her diary. In an imagined conversation with her, he asks why the foliage around the parsonage has thrived but not "*us*": "Why did everything become so miserable? . . . Were we given masks instead of faces? Were we given hysteria instead of feelings? Were we given shame and guilt instead of love and forgiveness? . . . Why did my brother become an invalid? Why was my sister crushed into a scream? . . . Why did I live with a never-healing infected sore that went through my body? . . . Why was I incapable of normal human relationships for so long?"[4] His weary mother does not answer; her image dissolves and Bergman, returned to the present, reads her diary entry written a few days before his birth, which reveals her misgivings about her marriage and Ingmar's imminent arrival into the world. Nothing in *The Magic Lantern* is as atmospheric or as finely felt as Bergman's rehearsal once again of this mother-son confrontation.

Hamlet

(1988)

BERGMAN'S production of *Hamlet*, staged at Dramaten in 1986 and performed at the Brooklyn Academy of Music's Majestic Theater in 1988 as part of the First New York International Festival of the Arts,[5] marks a high point in his recent work in the theater. In place of a poetic Hamlet, Bergman offers a Prince of Denmark who is at times as unattractive as the world from which he recoils. Attention is shifted from the eloquent soliloquies to continuous action, felt at such an intense physical level that one is forced to share Hamlet's pain. The play begins with an out-of-tune piano rendition of the "Merry Widow Waltz" as Claudius and Gertrude roll across the stage in unrestrained lust; as Claudius mounts the queen from behind, a row of state counselors in red robes and barristers' white wigs applauds rhythmically. Later, Claudius speaks his "O, my offense is rank" soliloquy while fondling a slut, whose red wig does

below: While Börje Ahlstedt as Claudius offers up an insincere prayer of contrition, Hamlet (Peter Stormare), standing behind him, is consumed with rage.

above: The second meeting of Hamlet with the Players, in which, with one arm around the shoulders of the Play King (Per Myrberg) and wielding a blunt dagger with the other, he speaks his "To be or not to be" soliloquy. Others in the troupe look on at left.

not quite conceal her white hair underneath and whose face wears a drunken smirk.

What is rotten in the state of Denmark is linked with sexuality, the catalyst of powerful emotions in Bergman's films—of humiliation, suffering, and violence. Gertrude dresses Ophelia up with red, spike-heeled shoes, smears her mouth with lipstick, and pulls a strap of her slip down over one shoulder. When she comes to Hamlet, the inner tension in him between sexual desire and revulsion is displayed powerfully: he spits in her face, then attempts to rape her, kissing her as in an ugly assault with his wide-opened mouth. Nor does Hamlet's violence end here. He stabs Polonius not through the arras but through one eye, then drags his body across the stage and hacks it with his sword—a scene that Bergman has Ophelia witness. In her mad scene, Ophelia appears with a pair of shears with which she chops off clumps of her hair and, instead of flowers, hands out nails. Bergman gives Ophelia greater prominence than in earlier *Hamlet*s, for when she is not a participant in the action she is an offstage witness. What drives her to distraction is not only Hamlet's treatment of her but also, and even more importantly, the inhumanity and hypocrisy of the court. In her innocence she is a primary victim and is not unlike the girl-waifs in Bergman's early films who are martyred by an irrational and morally insensitive world.

One of the most stunning features of this *Hamlet* is the manner in which Bergman has brought his cinematic imagination to bear on it. Although the stage is stripped of furnishing, the playing area marked only by a red circle, the production is full of startling visual ideas. Gertrude's announcement of Ophelia's suicide is followed by a vaudeville turn; the bowler-hatted Gravedigger plucks a long worm from Yorick's skull and sings a hearty music-hall song, accompanied by two masked jesters (queer, doll-like figures) placed symmetrically on each side of him, who play a trombone and saxophone. Ophelia then appears in the background as a witness to her own funeral, held in the rain and attended by a chorus of court officials in black mourning coats and black top hats, who dance away from her grave under their black umbrellas.

Costumes by Goran Wassberg scramble styles and periods. Hamlet, a perennial student-Bohemian, first appears in a long leather coat and dark glasses, while Horatio wears a bowler hat, spats, and pince-nez. Rosencrantz and Guildenstern, lacking identity à la Tom Stoppard, wear bright orange blazers and sport canes. Laertes is first seen in a crimson cadet's uniform but returns from Paris in a mod outfit and punk haircut. Polonius, a bureaucrat, constantly carries a briefcase and sidles up to the other characters in a sideways movement like that of a crab. In a *coup de théâtre* at the end, to the deafening sound of rock music from a ghetto blaster, Fortinbras (dressed in a guerilla leader's beret and fascistic jackboots) and his soldiers (wearing black riot helmets and flourishing submachine guns) arrive to take charge. After the bodies of Claudius, Gertrude, and Laertes are callously disposed of and Horatio is led out to be shot, Fortinbras speaks his lines over the dead Hamlet cynically before a video camera. Instead of order being restored, Bergman's ending initiates a new cycle of incoherence that will yield more suffering.

The production has a strong cast. Peter Stormare's Hamlet is restless, prancing, at times brutal, and extremely physical—whether dueling with Laertes or lying with homoerotic overtones in the lap of his school chum Horatio (Jan Waldekranz). Börje Ahlstedt's Claudius is as deeply soiled by his carnal indulgences as one would expect from a bloat king, while Gunnel Lindblom is an unhappy and more complex Gertrude. Pernilla Wallgren (the maid favored by Alexander in *Fanny and Alexander*) is less ethereal than is usual for Ophelia, although her spirit is finally broken. And Ulf Johanson is wonderfully comic both as Polonius and as the jaunty Gravedigger. Bergman's revisionist *Hamlet* touches closely on his own preoccupations in the hero's warring relationship with parental figures, his Oedipal relationship to his mother, and his anguished isolation. Early in the play, Hamlet lies on stage doubled up, his head tucked to his knees in a fetal position, an image reminiscent of Frost the clown's dream of a return to the womb and extinction of the pain of consciousness in *The Naked Night*. Bergman's concept sacrifices some of *Hamlet*'s reflectiveness and complexity but offers a fresh way of experiencing the play. In his review in *The New Republic*, Robert Brustein called the production "one of the most extraordinary theater events of our time";[6] it is, certainly, a staging filled with brilliant invention, surprise, and exhilaration.

above: Hamlet, right, hoists the skull of Yorick, while the gravedigger, played by Ulf Johanson, left, discourses humorously on death.

below: Long Day's Journey into

A Doll's House; Miss Julie; Long Day's Journey into Night

BERGMAN'S BOOK *Bilder* (*Images*), in which he discusses his work film by film, was published in Sweden in 1990. He had commented on the pictures in the interview collection *Bergman on Bergman* (1970), but in *Bilder* he elaborates on his earlier observations and in some cases revises his opinions. It was also a busy time for Bergman in the theater. In 1991 he staged his new production of *Peer Gynt* at Dramaten, and at Stockholm's Royal Opera he directed the opera *The Bacchantes*, a version of Euripides' *The Bacchae* with music by the Swedish composer Daniel Börtz. In that year, too, the Royal Dramatic Theater company traveled to New York to perform Bergman's recent productions of *A Doll's House*, *Miss Julie*, and *Long Day's Journey into Night* at the Brooklyn Academy of Music's Majestic Theater. All three drew rave reviews, the *New York Times* critic calling them the highlight not only of the New York International Festival of the Arts but also of the entire New York theater season.

In Bergman's staging of *A Doll's House*, the realistic framework

Night. At left, Thommy Berggren as a desolate Jamie, while Bibi Andersson, as Mary Tyrone, drops her wedding gown absentmindedly in the course of a closing monologue on the happiness of her marriage "for a time."

of Ibsen's play is dismantled, the action occurring on a simple raised platform backed by a large photograph of the interior of the Helmer house. When the actors are not involved in a scene, they sit on either side of the platform as mute witnesses. Through these characters who move in and out of Nora's consciousness and serve to define her life, Bergman focuses the drama on Nora's prison world from which she longs to escape. The hallmark of Bergman's production is its physicality. Nora, as played by Pernilla Östergren, is no longer the ingenuous doll figure of earlier stagings but a sensual woman with emerging resources. The tarantella she dances atop a table is a revelation of the powerful emotions that are stirring in her. Bergman's boldest stroke is to have altered the ending so that when Nora enters Torvald's bedroom to announce that she is leaving him, he is vulnerable and shorn of his authority as he lies naked in bed. The cast includes Erland Josephson as the doomed Dr. Rank, whose physical attraction to Nora is made unmistakably explicit. But it is Östergren who energizes the play in her determination to break free of a life of empty role playing.

Less fortunate than Nora is the title character in Strindberg's psychological drama *Miss Julie*. Strindberg thought of *Miss Julie* as a naturalistic play, and the principal characters—the valet Jean, enamored of the count's estate from childhood and now bent on rising in the world, and Julie, the count's daughter who has inherited a troubled family past—are, indeed, defined by their social backgrounds. But Strindberg's interest in the characters' psychic drives gives the work its peculiar power. Their compulsions are projected in the dreams both have—Julie atop a pillar and longing to get down, "to go down deep into the earth," and Jean struggling to climb the slippery trunk of a tree to plunder a bird's nest containing "golden eggs." Bergman's conception of the play is that of a psychic landscape circumscribed by the spotlessly clean manor-house kitchen where the action unfolds. Here aristocrat and servant engage in a strenuous duel culminating in sexual intercourse and Julie's suicide.

In earlier productions, Kristin, the cook (and Jean's fiancée) who drowses while Jean and Julie reveal their deepest natures, is a drab, peripheral figure, but Bergman has given her fuller dimension as a woman of peasant strength who senses that she and Jean will inherit the future. The play takes place on Sweden's festive Midsummer Night's Eve when the servants dance together outside the kitchen window. As they stumble about drunkenly, they add a hint of nightmare to Julie's dream state. Lena Olin was widely praised for her emotionally charged performance as Julie, and Peter Stormare (Bergman's Hamlet) is appropriately brutish as the servant who dreams of opening his own hotel in Switzerland but is reduced to cringing at the sight of his master's boots. Julie, wearing a scarlet dress against a gray-white background, is given the play's final ironic triumph. Her suicide is an aristocratic gesture for which Jean and Kristin would never have the nerve.

Bergman's production of *Long Day's Journey into Night* is a kinsman's tribute to O'Neill's vision of a close yet disunited family in ruins. O'Neill's play has been abridged by Bergman to run four hours and has a spare but effective set designed by Gunilla Palmstierna-Weiss that consists of some mismatching parlor chairs and a table. A photograph of the exterior of the Connecticut seashore house is projected onto a screen at the rear of the stage, the outer world made dreamlike by heavy mist and a mournful foghorn. The play's small cast includes James Tyrone, the actor-patriarch who has mortgaged his talent for financial security; Mary, his wife, reared in a convent and soiled by life; Jamie, the elder son, given to drink and whores and consumed by a very Irish sense of doom; and Edmund, the family's youngest, aspiring to be a writer but already racked by consumption. In alternating confrontations, they all ask the same question: what went wrong?

There have been notable James Tyrones in the past—Laurence Olivier's, in a London production, as a nervy, mercurial Irishman, is the oddest; Ralph Richardson's in the film version is, I think, indisputably the greatest. Jarl Kulle's patriarch, a ham actor at home as well as on the stage, struck me as being more European than American, but in his bluster he can hold the stage against anyone. Thommy Berggren as Jamie has the hand-me-down flash of his father, and Peter Stormare's Edmund is a touching, passionate victim. One of the most striking features of Bergman's production is the emphasis he gives to the Tyrone mother (Bibi Andersson), around whom the male characters all gravitate in a mixture of love and concern with her drug addiction. In one of her appearances she expresses her lost, longed-for closeness to the Virgin Mary with outstretched arms reminiscent of the crucified attitude characters strike in Bergman's films. She comes down from her room at the end carrying her carefully preserved bridal gown, which could stand for her marriage to the worldly life; and at this climactic moment she crystallizes not only the frustration of her own ideals but also those of the other family members. In Bergman's envisioning of *Long Day's Journey* the characters are like ghosts locked into the prison of their isolation, and they have a stunning power.

Den goda viljan/ The Best Intentions

(1991)

BERGMAN'S BOOK *Den goda viljan*, about his parents' courtship and marriage between the years 1909 and 1918, was published in Sweden in 1991 and evolves from *Karin's Face* and *The Magic Lantern*. Bergman makes it clear from the outset that the book is not a factual recording of the past but a freely imagined

reconstruction, much more a novel than a biography. He even goes so far as to call it a fairy tale. "Its unreliability with regard to facts, dates, names, and situations," he remarks, "is total."[7]

When Bergman wrote *Den goda viljan*, he envisioned it as a film, even commenting in the book that he could see Pernilla Östergren and Samuel Fröler in the roles of his mother and father. But he did not intend to direct the film himself; instead he contacted the young Danish director Bille August to ask if he would be interested in making the movie. August, whose episodic, visually stunning *Pelle the Conqueror* won an Academy Award as Best Picture in 1988, read *Den goda viljan*, liked it, and agreed to direct it. Bergman and August then worked together on the shooting script of the film for which, as Bergman had hoped, Pernilla Östergren and Samuel Fröler were cast in the starring roles. *The Best Intentions*, as the film is titled for English-language audiences, was made both as a six-hour television miniseries to be shown in four ninety-minute segments and as a two-hour, forty-five-minute feature film for international release. August spent nine months making the movie, and by its finish Miss Östergren had become Mrs. August. *The Best Intentions* was shown at Christmastime of 1991 on Scandinavian television and won the Palm d'Or at the 1992 Cannes Film Festival, with an additional award to Östergren as Best Actress.

A notable feature of *The Best Intentions* is that Bergman explores his parents' relationship not only more fully than ever before but also with unusual understanding of their tragic partnership. *The Best Intentions* begins in 1909, the same period as *Fanny and Alexander*, but the mythic Ekdahl family has been replaced by the realistic Åkerbloms, whose affluence and sociability contrast sharply with Henrik's status as a poor student who harbors grudges against his better-off relatives' neglect of his family and is at odds with himself. The picture's handsome settings have been photographed by Jørgen Persson with a sensuous richness, but an ominous melancholy is felt throughout. It is a long film, and during its middle section it loses momentum before it quickens again as it moves toward the conclusion, in which Anna and Henrik are reunited after an unhappy separation. In a park near the Åkerblom apartment, Anna and Henrik sit at opposite ends of a public bench, near and yet distant from each other—a chilly tableau in which they seem frozen in the ambivalence of their marriage.

At times the film seems foreshortened in editing. Some of the characters in the small factory town in the snowy Swedish hinterlands where Henrik has his first pastorate seem a little blurred, as if a portion of their stories had been left on the cutting-room floor; and Anna's brother Ernst (Björn Kjellman), although he makes a confident contrast to the socially insecure Henrik, appears too briefly to have any distinct interest in his own right. But the principal characters are fully intact. Ghita Nørby as Anna's mother, who interferes with the couple's plans when she foresees that their temperaments are too different to make a successful marriage, is a matriarch of size and believability. Max von Sydow as Anna's father Johan, white haired and spectacled, does not have a large part but as soon as he appears he has such fullness of life that he takes over the film. Striking, too, is the abused waif Petrus, who is taken in by Anna and Henrik until, in a fit of jealousy, he nearly succeeds in drowning their infant son Dag. With his straggling hair, drooping eyes, leprous complexion, and gnarled emotions, he provides a Gothic touch and focuses for the well-bred, strong-willed Anna everything she hates in the mean life Henrik has charted for them.

above: Anna and Henrik in a romantic scene at the Åkerblom residence while the parents are away.

Östergren as Anna and Fröler as Henrik—who have a strong resemblance to Bergman's parents in their youth—give extremely sensitive performances. Östergren's intensity beneath a quiet surface makes her a formidable antagonist to Fröler's stubborn pastor, whose limitations also make him sympathetic. Neither Anna nor Henrik is blamed for the marital misfortune that unfolds with tremendous inevitability. The sense of Bergman's forgiveness of his parents is implied in his earlier films, but never before has he been able to put himself in their place so fully, to set aside his grievances as totally as in *The Best Intentions*, one of the most quietly moving of his marriage scenarios.

The publication in April 1993 of *Den goda viljan* in an English-language edition enables one to see *The Best Intentions* in a fuller dimension. Entitled *The Best Intentions: A Novel*, it alternates narrative passages with blocks of dialogue and has the quality both of a detailed, evocative novel and a strongly visualized drama or film. The book contains characters and scenes not included in the movie and fills out other characters more fully. At times, in Bergman's depiction of the large Åkerblom family, it is even reminiscent of *Fanny and Alexander*. Rather strikingly, Henrik's mother, Alma, plays a more prominent role in the book and is a decisive influence on Henrik. Their bonding has obvious Oedipal overtones that are apparent in a scene in which the mother and son swim in the nude. Bound to her and her grievances, Henrik is never fully able to trust or enter totally into the world. Alma Bergman and Karin Åkerblom have a parallel relationship as interfering mothers implicated in the frustration of their children, a frustration that in Henrik's case involves a strong, Bergmanesque sense of guilt.

above: Anna with her father, Johan Åkerblom (Max von Sydow), who is thirty years older than his wife. Johan becomes a great cameo role for Von Sydow.

What is also striking in Bergman's novel is that the frustration of Anna and Henrik is frequently reflected in the other characters. Karin had married Johan Åkerblom, thirty years her senior, because she felt he was lonely and they could "alleviate each other's loneliness." With his death after Anna's marriage to Henrik, and her recognition that her interference in their lives has made them both hate her, she lives with a loneliness she has sought to escape. Alma Bergman's bleak life is barely sustained by her obsessive love for her son, whom she has lost through his marriage to Anna; after her death, Henrik remarks that "she was always alone." Alone, too, is Petrus Farg, who seems a

grotesque, peripheral figure in the film but belongs very much to the moral landscape of Bergman's novel. The displaced child of a broken marriage, he lives in self-enclosed torment. Nordenson, head of the Iron Works in Forsboda, is also enclosed upon himself in his painful isolation from his wife and daughters, the townspeople who work for him, and from God, in whose existence he does not believe. Before blowing his brains out with a shotgun, he leaves a note declaring that it "will be a great relief to go into final, and as I see it total, loneliness." At one point he taunts Henrik, remarking, "God is love and love is God, isn't that so, Pastor?," words that remind the reader immediately of *Winter Light*. Henrik, in fact, is reminiscent of the forsaken minister in that film in his conversation with the theologian Nathan Soderblom. When Soderblom speaks of God's presence, Henrik replies: "For me it's absence, silence. I speak, and God says nothing." Bille August's film has the nature of an episodic domestic chronicle of a marriage destined to fail, but Bergman's novel is focused more insistently on existential anguish. Had Bergman directed the film, this dimension of his parents' experience would surely have been more sharply felt.

above: The Best Intentions: Anna Åkerblom and Henrik Bergman have an ominously difficult courtship. They are played to perfection by Pernilla Östergren and Samuel Fröler.

opposite: Wisely or not, Anna Åkerblom is determined to have Henrik.

Sunday's Children

(1992)

T HE SPRING OF 1993 saw not only the publication in English of Bergman's book *The Best Intentions*, but also the public screening of a new film, *Sunday's Children*, written by Bergman and directed by his youngest son, Daniel. In addition, Bergman's productions of Henrik Ibsen's *Peer Gynt* and Yukio Mishima's *Madame de Sade* were staged at the Brooklyn Academy of Music.

Sunday's Children was shown in two screenings at the Museum of Modern Art as part of its 1993 New Directors/New Films series. At this writing, it has as yet not gone into theatrical release. In his review in the *New York Times*, Vincent Canby wrote admiringly of the film, calling it a "richly poignant memoir" of a "high and exciting caliber."[8] The movie is set in the late 1920s in the Swedish countryside, where a boy about nine years old named Pu (Henrik Linnros) spends the summer with his family. Like the Ekdahls in *Fanny and Alexander*, Pu's family includes not only the parents and children but also aunts, uncles, and cousins who live on the most relaxed and cordial terms with the servants. At the beginning Pu idolizes his father, Henrik (Thommy Berggren, who played Jamie Tyrone in Bergman's production of *Long Day's Journey into Night* and was the young officer in Bo Widerberg's film *Elvira Madigan*). Henrik is pastor to the royal family, and his arrival at the local train station after performing his duties in Stockholm provides a dramatic opening.

But beneath outward appearances, all is not well. At night Pu overhears arguments between his father and mother (Lena Endre), who says that she is going to take the children and go back to her parents in Uppsala. The summer brings disturbing recognitions in other respects as well. One day in August, Pu accompanies his father on a trip—by train, ferry, and bicycle—to a distant parish. In the course of the day the future is foreseen in flashforwards. In one of these, set in 1968, Pu as an adult visits his elderly, widowed father, who has lost his faith and is afraid of death. He asks Pu's forgiveness, but whereas such forgiveness seems obviously granted in *The Best Intentions*, in *Sunday's Children* it is obstinately withheld. Bergman's darkly shaded tale of the relations of father and son has magical moments and, as with so much of Bergman's work, a sense of mystery.

Peer Gynt

BERGMAN'S production of *Peer Gynt* toured in European capitals for two years before being presented for a limited engagement at the Brooklyn Academy of Music in May 1993. Unlike Bergman's lavish staging of the play at Malmö in 1957, the new staging creates epic spectacle, fantasy, and fairy tale through an economy of means. A center-stage rectangular platform that can be raised, lowered, or tilted at one side provides the essential acting space for the performers, supplemented by a ramp into the orchestra that brings the actors in close proximity to the audience. Bergman has shaped the play concisely into three acts that mark the stages of Peer's journey through life, or rather his life as it is dreamed by him. It begins with the cottage sequence with Peer's mother, Åse (Bibi Andersson), whom he leaves to pursue his megalomaniac dream adventures. He steals away a bride at a wedding feast, meets Solveig (Lena Endre), whom he idealizes yet leaves, and dallies in lechery with the Woman in Green, daughter of the Troll King. Nothing in the production is more lively or more comic yet grotesque than the sequence with the green-faced, tail-wagging trolls, whose goatish appetites reflect Peer's own undeveloped self.

In the succeeding acts, "A Foreign Land" and "The Return Home," Peer becomes a wealthy capitalist in the slave trade, loses his fortune, wanders in the Moroccan desert, and visits a Cairo madhouse, an experience that is like a descent into hell. In the end, he returns to the cottage he left at the opening to confront his wasted life. The Button Molder prepares to melt him down in his vat as worthless material, but the now-blind Solveig, who has waited patiently for his return, shields him in her embrace, providing Peer with an eleventh-hour discovery of his true self. After an elaborate

above: Scene at the Cairo madhouse in *Peer Gynt*. Börje Ahlstedt as Peer Gynt stands at left foreground while behind him, in white costumes, are the mad people.

below: Opening scene of *Madame de Sade*, using an open space to represent

184

an eighteenth-century drawing room, with a drawing of a Japanese cherry tree on a green panel in the background. Second from left is Stina Ekblad as Renée, or Madame de Sade, who looks across stage to her mother, Madame de Montreuil (Anita Björk), right.

fantasia of self-evasion, he is seen in a fetal position preparing, as it were, to return to the womb.

Bergman's envisioning of *Peer Gynt*, while dark, is constantly witty. Johan Rabaeus as the Troll King is splendidly comic, but it is Börje Ahlstedt (Uncle Carl in *Fanny and Alexander*) who provides the constant focus of the work. Ahlstedt may seem at first to be oddly miscast as Peer, since rather than being young, lusty, and consumed by preposterous illusions, he is a figure of sagging middle age even at the beginning. But if something is lost, something is also gained. Ahlstedt's Peer is closer to death than a boy would be, underscoring his desperate effort to stave off life's encroaching darkness. More-over, his Peer is a shabby anti-hero, a lonely and pathetic clown who might have come from Samuel Beckett. With his baggy pants and bowler hat, he is also reminiscent of Charlie Chaplin,[9] and in a strik-ing sequence with the Boig, he is encircled by fifteen Chaplinesque figures wearing similar baggy pants and bowler hats who hold mir-rors up to him as reflections of dazzling light play fantastically across the ceiling and walls of the theater. In the Cairo madhouse, white-clad figures trapped within their own tormented egos evoke horror and isolation. One of them, The Pen, hacks off one hand with a sharp knife, which he then uses to slash his throat from ear to ear—as blood flows plentifully and air-raid sirens sound deafeningly through the theater. This is a production of *Peer Gynt* one would not have wanted to miss.

Madame de Sade

YUKIO MISHIMA'S *Madame de Sade* was first staged in Japan in 1965, five years before the author's spectacular ritual sui-cide. Although the production made a striking impression, it attracted little interest in the West, largely because of its absence of overt action. When Bergman presented the work in Stockholm in 1989, however, it drew rave reviews, and its staging at the Brooklyn Academy of Music in May 1993 evoked a similar response. Influ-enced by the classicism of Racine, *Madame de Sade* makes use of a single set and involves only six characters, all of whom are women. The Marquis de Sade casts his fascination throughout but he never appears, his strange life being seen wholly through the eyes of the women. Renée, or Madame de Sade, the central figure, has remained doggedly faithful to her husband, who has become notorious as a monster of vice during his long imprisonment. Her mother, the con-trolling and manipulative Madame de Montreuil, on the other hand, is a pillar of respectability and the marquis's fiercest critic. Others include Renée's cynical sister Anne; Baroness de Simiane, who is piously religious; and Countess de Saint-Fond, who cultivates the perversities of the marquis. These characters, on whom a precisely choreographed decorum is imposed, set in motion a drama of restraint and freedom in which even a glance may have shattering implications.

The play begins in an eighteenth-century drawing room—an open space with arches set against the background of an imposing green panel with the delicate drawing of a Japanese cherry tree. The time is 1772, when the marquis has been sentenced to death, and Renée with members of her circle discuss his life in an atmosphere of reserve and formality. By act two, six years later, however, the backdrop has become a flaming tree seen against a ·fiery red sky. Here reserve falls away as Madame de Montreuil denounces the marquis' infamous orgies in which Renée had shared. "You never attempted," Renée cries, "even in your wildest dreams, to imagine what it would be like to unlock the strange door that opens on a sky full of stars." In act three, a dozen years later, the French Revolution has erupted, and the backdrop now is a darkened sky filled with storm clouds. The marquis has been freed from prison and is at Renée's door, but she has her servant turn him away. Having devoted her life to winning his release, she at last recognizes that in writing his book *Justine* in prison he had freed himself while revealing the prison in which humanity lives. In the brilliant play of Mishima's ideas, in which the marquis is allied with holiness as well as destruction, *Madame de Sade* has the texture of urgent romantic poetry, and it has been staged by Bergman with unfailing tact and resourcefulness. Anita Björk as Madame de Montreuil and Stina Ekblad as Renée give compelling performances, but as always with Bergman the stars are but part of an accomplished ensemble. At the end of his admiring review, the critic for the *New York Times* concluded: "From his films, this play and his other productions at the Brooklyn Academy, it is evident that no other director has achieved such brilliance both on screen and on stage."[10]

The recent productions at the Brooklyn Academy of Music, however, represent only part of Bergman's new work in the theater. Also during the spring of 1993, at the Royal Dramatic Theater in Stockholm, he staged *Die Zeit und das Zimmer* (*Time and the Room*) by Botho Strauss, the German author whose writing has been compared both to that of Peter Handke and to the Theater of the Absurd. The spring of 1994 will see the publication of Bergman's *Images: My Life in Film*, a translation into English of his book *Bilder*, and two new Bergman productions at the Royal Dramatic Theater—*Goldberg Variations*, by Georg Tabori, the Hungarian novelist and playwright who has lived and worked in the United States and Germany, and *The Winter's Tale*, Shakespeare's drama of sin and forgiveness in the ripeness of time. It is curious that Bergman—a sickly, neurasthenic child—should have proved to have such stamina, his creative energy still vigorous even in his seventies. In 1994, astonishingly, he will have worked in films and the theater for fifty years.

above: Madame de Sade centers on the confrontations of women, typified by this scene in which the gown worn by the central figure incorporates Japanese motifs into the formalized world of the French aristocracy.

186

The Bergman Legacy

ALTHOUGH HE neglected his children in his early career, Bergman—who turned seventy-five on July 14, 1993—has now become something of a patriarch, his name having devolved to a second generation in Swedish theater and film.[11] His son Daniel, by Käbi Laretei, is also a film director. Daniel has made a number of children's films and directed the recent, previously discussed *Sunday's Children*. Bergman's marriage to Ellen Lundström has produced a whole flock of stagestruck offspring. Eva, the eldest, is head of the Gothenburg City Theater, where her father was director in the 1940s, and in 1993 will direct a production of *Faust* at Dramaten. Jan, who has worked at Dramaten and for Swedish television, heads the Swedish National Theater, a touring group, and is also a stage director. When *Miss Julie*, *A Doll's House*, and *Long Day's Journey Into Night* were performed in New York, Jan came with the company in his father's place. Both of the twins, Anna and Mats, have also been active in the theater. Anna, who is married and lives in England, is an actress—and the author of a book about her relationship with her father. Mats, who played Aron in *Fanny and Alexander*, has been a director at several theaters in Sweden and at present is a tenured actor with the company at Dramaten, where he will soon direct a production of Pierre Beaumarchais's play *The Marriage of Figaro*.

Those belonging to Bergman's extended professional family also remain close to him, and after his retirement have continued to have significant careers. Sven Nykvist is one of the most renowned cinematographers in the world. After filming *Autumn Sonata*, Nykvist began working in Hollywood, where he was the cinematographer for Louis Malle's *Pretty Baby* (1978) and for Bob Rafelson's remake of *The Postman Always Rings Twice* (1981) and his *Cannery Row* (1982). Following his return to Sweden to film *Fanny and Alexander*, he photographed other American and European films, including *Swann in Love* (1984), *The Unbearable Lightness of Being* (1988), Woody Allen's portion of *New York Stories* and his *Crimes and Misdemeanors* (both in 1989), and Nora Ephron's *Sleepless in Seattle* (1993). He is quick to point out, however, that Bergman remains the greatest director with whom he has worked. "Ingmar Bergman," he comments, "has meant more to me than almost anyone else in my whole life because of what he taught me. He got me interested in what I think is the most important thing in photography—using light to create the right mood."[12]

Actors and actresses whom Bergman made famous also continue to add to their reputations. Harriet Andersson and Bibi Andersson (who made her debut as a stage director at Dramaten in 1991 with a production of Sam Shepard's *True West*) perform regularly in the Swedish theater as well as in the movies. Apart from her roles for Bergman, Ingrid Thulin has given compelling performances in Mai

Bergman with Sven Nykvist preparing to shoot the scene between Tomas and Märta in the schoolroom in *Winter Light*.

Zetterling's *Night Games*, Luchino Visconti's *The Damned*, and Alain Resnais's *La Guerre est finie*, and like another of Bergman's actresses, Gunnel Lindblom, has also become a film director. Erland Josephson, a close friend of Bergman's, has appeared in over a hundred Swedish stage productions and continues to be active in the international theater as well as in European cinema. Of Bergman's actors, Max von Sydow and Liv Ullmann have enjoyed the largest international recognition. Even while working with Bergman, Von Sydow was called to Hollywood (Bergman advised him not to go), where he has made a great number of films, including *The Quiller Memorandum* and *The Exorcist*, in which he has become convincingly a score of different characters. He has also co-starred notably with Ullmann in *The Emigrants* (1972) and its sequel, *The New Land* (1973), by the highly regarded Swedish director Jan Troell; appeared in Woody Allen's *Hannah and Her Sisters* (1986); and given one of his most memorable performances in Bille August's *Pelle the Conqueror* (1988).

Liv Ullmann has become one of the most admired actresses on the international scene. In the 1970s while working with Bergman, she was named Best Actress by either the New York Film Critics or the National Society of Film Critics for six years in a row. Working apart from him, she has appeared in a variety of films ranging from *The Abdication* (1974) to *The Wild Duck* (1985) and has enjoyed notable successes on the stage. She has starred in *A Doll's House* (1975), *Anna Christie* (1977), *I Remember Mama* (1979), and *Ghosts* (1982) in New York, in addition to her stage appearances in London and Oslo. She has also published a best-selling memoir, *Changing* (1978), and its sequel, *Choices* (1984), and devoted a large amount of her time working for UNICEF, for which she was honored with the Dag Hammarskjöld award in 1986.

Most recently Ullmann made her debut as a film director with the movie *Sofie*, which opened in New York in May 1993. In turning to directing, she joins others from Bergman's inner circle, including Sven Nykvist, whose film *The Ox* (1992) starred Ullmann and Von Sydow. Ullmann's *Sofie*, richly photographed by *The Best Intention*'s cinematographer Jørgen Persson, is necessarily reminiscent of Bergman in its cast, which includes Ghita Nørby, who played Karin Åkerblom in *The Best Intentions*, and Erland Josephson, giving one of his most winning performances as a Jewish patriarch, even as he had in *Fanny and Alexander*. With the company of talented actors that he gathered around him—Liv Ullmann, Max von Sydow, Erland Josephson, the late Gunnar Björnstrand, Eva Dahlbeck, Birger Malmsten, Ingrid Thulin, Gunnel Lindblom, Bibi Andersson, Harriet Andersson, and Lena Olin, to name only some—Bergman has enriched Sweden's film heritage immeasurably.

But his influence extends well beyond Sweden. When *The Seventh Seal* and *Wild Strawberries* made their impact in America in the late 1950s, the art film had as yet no sizable following. The films of

Ingrid Thulin laughing at something Bergman has just said, but the prevailing mood on the set of *Winter Light* was tense. Bergman would waken at two in the morning with "snakes" in his stomach.

Bergman, along with those of Fellini and Kurosawa, excited and enlarged the consciousness of the American film-going public. An alternative to the movies produced in Hollywood was suddenly discovered, with far-reaching consequences for the emerging film market of the 1960s and for a new generation of American independent filmmakers. Part of the literacy and seriousness of Bergman's 1950s films, deriving from his deep immersion in the theater, is that they have the nature of skillfully constructed plays. Later Bergman was to make fuller use of the resources of cinema; in *The Silence* and *Cries and Whispers*, for example, buildings and their interiors become an integral part of their emotional texture. The effect of light is carefully studied to underscore the exact shading of the characters' inner states; and Bergman gives ever-increasing attention to his actors' faces, which the medium of film makes possible but a stage play precludes. But one still has a sense of Bergman the dramatist: as he discovers the progression of emotion played out in the human face, it is as if the face itself were a stage.

Even in the earlier films, Bergman tends to draw the viewer into his characters' inner states; as they peer into mirrors, for instance, they become more subjective representations of who it is they are. But this tendency as the films progress is given enlarged attention. In *The Silence*, Bergman observes Ester and Anna with the most patient attention. Often in close-ups and sometimes in strange, sustained intervals of complete silence, he seems to enter into what is happening inside them, and this probe of their inner experience becomes the dramatic center of the film. This subjective tendency reaches its apogee in *Persona*, in its psychic duel between Alma and Elisabet, who retreats into muteness, and it persists in such internalized films as *The Passion of Anna*.

Critics sometimes hold strong views about the earlier and later films, preferring one period to another. But, in fact, Bergman has produced remarkable movies in both phases of his career. If some of the pictures had to be sacrificed, I would not want to lose *The Seventh Seal* or *Wild Strawberries* (although neither is perfect), or the still earlier films that begin with *Summer Interlude* and include *Secrets of Women*, *Summer with Monika*, *The Naked Night*, *A Lesson in Love*, and *Smiles of a Summer Night*, all of which have a startling purity and freshness. But neither would I be willing to give up, for instance, *The Magician*, *Through a Glass Darkly*, *The Silence*, *Persona*, *Cries and Whispers*, *The Magic Flute*, *Scenes from a Marriage*, or *Fanny and Alexander*. Dividing the works by period alone also obscures the unpredictable variation in conception and style from film to film, from beginning to end, that reveal the workings of Bergman's imagination. The worldly understanding of *Secrets of Woman* is followed by the controlled naïveté of *Summer with Monika*, which is followed by the jarring, expressionist pessimism of *The Naked Night*, which is followed by the high-spirited, farcical comedy of *A Lesson in Love*. *Brink of Life* and *Hour of the Wolf* were made by the same director, as were

The Serpent's Egg and *Autumn Sonata*; *The Virgin Spring* and *The Devil's Eye*; *Fårö Document* and *Now About These Women*; *Shame* and *After the Rehearsal*; *Persona* and *Scenes from a Marriage*; *From the Life of the Marionettes* and *Fanny and Alexander*. In the ever-varying stylization of his films, Bergman is prodigious.

Although Bergman, the son of a pastor, and Henry James, the son of a theologian, would seem to have nothing otherwise in common, they have in at least one respect. As they move out of a theological background into the world, they place extraordinary emphasis upon art—James in his tales of artists and writers, and Bergman in his films involving the performing arts. One notes this propensity in Bergman in the ballet backgrounds of *Three Strange Loves* and *Summer Interlude*; the musicians in *Eva*, *Night is My Future*, *To Joy*, *Now About These Women*, *Shame*, and *Autumn Sonata*; the painter in *Hour of the Wolf*; the circus performers in *The Naked Night*; the spiritualist performers in *The Magician*; the troupe of dwarfs in *The Silence*; the film director and his crew in *Prison*; and above all the actors in *Smiles of a Summer Night*, *The Seventh Seal*, *Persona*, *The Ritual*, *After the Rehearsal*, and *Fanny and Alexander*. In *Smiles of a Summer Night,* Desirée is an appropriately central figure since her theatrical world reflects the actual one in its transience and vanity. In *The Naked Night,* when the circus performers and the company at the theater converge, like intersecting planes of illusion, Albert is forced to the terrifying recognition of his absolute helplessness and loneliness in the world. And in *Fanny and Alexander*, Bergman harmonizes bourgeois society with the ongoing life of the theater in the Ekdahls.

Bergman's concern with the sexual and marital relations of men and women runs through almost all of the films; but here, too, one is conscious at times of the idea of theater. In the early, rather stagy films of the 1940s, Bergman typically regards young couples as fugitives escaping, or attempting to escape, from the oppressiveness of the world around them. This is true, for example, of Johannes and Sally in *Ship to India* and Berit and Gösta in *Port of Call*. *Three Strange Loves* marks a turning point, for in this film the couple, Rut and Bertil, have discovered that their marriage is hell, and that the only thing that could possibly be worse would be to be alone. The same point is made, although more brutally, in *The Naked Night*. *The Naked Night* was such strong medicine that it almost cost Bergman his career; and in the time ahead, anticipated by *Secrets of Women*, he made a series of witty movies about the disillusionment of marriage and the need for compromise that culminates in *Smiles of a Summer Night*—a work notable for its stagelike sets, the role playing of its characters, and its theatricality.

In *Wild Strawberries* warring couples appear again—the bitterly unhappy Alman and his wife, to whom Isak Borg gives a lift on the highway, and Isak's estranged son, Evald, and his wife, Marianne. But they are not quite at the center of the film. As his vision darkens in the 1960s, Bergman refocuses his theme again in his Fårö films— "chamber films" that are also "chamber plays"—that involve disinte-

Bergman during the shooting of *Face to Face,* in which characters struggle with the phantom of their own authenticity. "Reality," says Dr. Tomas Jacobi, "is perhaps not at all what I imagine. Perhaps it doesn't exist, in fact. Perhaps it only exists as a longing."

grating marriages or liaisons. The abstract psychic landscape of the couple's conflict in *The Passion of Anna* then begins to yield to films dealing with couples placed within the context of everyday Swedish society. Swedish audiences recognized themselves in Johan and Marianne when the enormously popular *Scenes from a Marriage* was presented on television in installments, each like an act of a play.

Scenes from a Marriage, with its marital tensions, shifting of partners, and underlying loneliness, touches rather closely on the films of Bergman's American admirer Woody Allen, who reflects in some degree his generation's response to Bergman. As an independent filmmaker making modestly budgeted films that reach out to a literate, sophisticated audience, Allen has found his inspiration partly in Sweden's most famous director. As in the case of Bergman, he works with a loyal group of actors who appear and reappear in his films like members of a repertory company. Moreover, although Allen comes out of American popular culture—including silent and talking pictures, vaudeville, and stand-up comedy—he frequently alludes to Bergman in his work. In some films, these enriching echoes of Bergman are enlarged upon considerably. *A Midsummer Night's Sex Comedy*—which is set at a turn-of-the-century country house where three couples trade partners, and which involves a professor who prides himself on his rationalism yet is about to marry an attractive, much younger woman—is a variation on the theme of *Smiles of a Summer Night*. In *Love and Death*, Boris, seeking answers to the riddle of existence, encounters the white-sheeted figure of Death three times, and at the end in a takeoff of *The Seventh Seal* goes off with him in a dance of death. Allen's gloomy *Interiors* is fashioned so closely on a Bergman model that it is like a parody of one of his chamber films about the disintegration of a family.

Allen's temperamental affinity with Bergman can be noticed in his depressed view of life, despite his humor; his anxiety and obsession with loneliness, sex, and death; his guilt. Still, these features of Allen's imagination also belong to Jewish tragicomedy in which man is a clown performing in an arena of life's meaninglessness and suffering. In certain respects Allen is not as close to Bergman as he might seem. His softly filtered nostalgia, for Manhattan among much else, is unimaginable in Bergman. There are passages of nostalgia in *Wild Strawberries* and at the end of *Cries and Whispers*, but what surrounds and encloses them is a confirmation of tragic isolation. Allen's celebration of city life, with its sparkling textures and promise of what can happen there, also contrasts with Bergman's closeness to the natural world, which occasions very moving moments of insight and reverie. It is as if Bergman and Allen carry their different childhood environments with them in their adult visions. Although Allen raises serious questions about the nature of existence, his comedy tends to refine them through a tender pathos, replacing the need, as in Bergman, to probe them more searchingly. They are different, too, in that Allen enjoys life more than Bergman, relishing contemporary sophistication and the adventure of falling in love, which for Bergman means an exposure of the self to intense pain. Sexual guilt is evident enough in Allen, but in Bergman it is cold Swedish guilt.

In its *Festschrift* issue devoted to Bergman in the Swedish film journal *Chaplin*, Woody Allen calls him "probably the greatest film artist, all things considered, since the invention of the motion picture camera."[13] Like O'Neill, Bergman is concerned with revealing the human experience in its relation to ultimate things, to God or at least to the ethical foundations of being, shaking audiences out of their complacency into a recognition of the lonely and anxious terms of existence. He is "literary" in the special sense that he confronts issues more usually found on the printed page than in films. His themes are modernist ones—the loss of faith, the barriers that circumvent communication between individuals, the deep core of isolation in the experience of men and women.

Bergman's accomplishment as a director can be described in various ways. He is the great *auteur*, having after his early period written almost all of the films he has directed, and he has as much distinction as a writer as he has as a director. The continually self-referential nature of his films also makes him unique, giving shape to the large body of his work as if it were a single, evolving entity. But it would be risky to try to pin him down with a single, all-embracing label. He has a strong sense of the worldly life, as the relations of his couples demonstrate, yet is disposed to refract their experience through a lens of subjectivity. Contradictions can be noticed in his very sense of life, which at times is depicted as being mysteriously devoid of meaning, while at other times it seems to affirm positive values, such as the nurturing power of love and human closeness. It might be wiser to speak of certain attributes that affect his work. One is integrity. His concern with emotional authenticity is enormous—as can be seen in his ability to create mood and the exactly felt psychological states of his characters; to find a fully realized expressive image; and to elicit performances that have hypnotic power and that can be compared to perfect pitch in music. Another of Bergman's distinguishing traits is passion. Bergman is a master at depicting suffering, which is, one might say, a vessel of passion. Whether in their suffering or in heightened states akin to pure joy, Bergman's characters spring from a passionate intensity. They have about them a peculiar quality of nakedness, are emotionally exposed, and are thus always at risk in the bold thrust of their creation on screen. In the seriousness of his commitment—in his fidelity to craftsmanship and in the intensity of his passion that can be electrifying— Bergman is surely one of our few great contemporary filmmakers.

Notes

CHAPTER I
1 Cowie, 1–19; Gado, 1–19.
2 Quoted in Gado, 12.
3 Bergman, *Magic Lantern*, 3.
4 Bergman, *Magic Lantern*, 8.
5 Quoted in Gado, 10.
6 Quoted in Cowie, 7.
7 Bergman, *Magic Lantern*, 23.
8 Quoted in Cowie, 14.
9 Quoted in Cowie, 17.
10 Quoted in Bergman profile in Charles Moritz, ed., *Current Biography Yearbook 1981* (New York, 1981), 20.
11 Quoted in Cowie, 21.
12 Quoted in Cowie, 21–22.
13 Gado, 98.
14 Gado, 99.
15 Gado, 99–103.

CHAPTER II
1 Quoted in Cowie, 34.
2 Bergman, *Bergman on Bergman*, 28.
3 Cowie, 50.
4 Cowie, 55.
5 Steene, *Ingmar Bergman*, 42.
6 Cowie, 60.
7 Quoted in Gado, 43.
8 Bergman, *Bergman on Bergman*, 33.
9 Bergman, *Bergman on Bergman*, 32–33.
10 Donner, 64.
11 Cowie, 73.

CHAPTER III
1 Cowie, 79.
2 Bergman, *Bergman on Bergman*, 45.
3 Bergman, *Bergman on Bergman*, 47.
4 Gado, 47.
5 Gado, 139.
6 Bergman, *Bergman on Bergman*, 51.
7 Bergman, *Bergman on Bergman*, 51.
8 Bergman, *Bergman on Bergman*, 63.
9 Gado, 146–47.
10 Bergman, *Bergman on Bergman*, 72.
11 Cowie, 100.
12 Cowie, 160.
13 Quoted in Gado, 161.
14 Gado, 161.
15 Cowie, 112.
16 Cowie, 112–13.
17 Gado, 103.
18 Samuels interview in Kaminsky, 118.

CHAPTER IV
1 Jones, 6.
2 Bergman, *Bergman on Bergman*, 66–67.
3 Young, 142.
4 Quoted in Young, 142.
5 Mosley, 58.
6 Bergman, *Bergman on Bergman*, 103.
7 Bergman, *Bergman on Bergman*, 113.
8 Cowie, 136.

9 Cowie, 136.
10 Cyrus Harvey, in conversation.
11 Bergman, *Bergman on Bergman*, 132–33.
12 Bergman, *Bergman on Bergman*, 133.
13 Bergman, *Bergman on Bergman*, 133.
14 Quoted in Cowie, 157.
15 Gado, 224–25.
16 Gado, 227.
17 Quoted in Cowie, 172.

CHAPTER V
1 Cowie, 180.
2 Quoted in Gado, 242.
3 Gado, 241.
4 Bergman, *Bergman on Bergman*, 149.
5 Bergman, *Bergman on Bergman*, 151.
6 Bergman, *Bergman on Bergman*, 168.
7 Cowie, 196–97.
8 Bergman, *Bergman on Bergman*, 163.
9 Bergman, *Bergman on Bergman*, 163.
10 Bergman, text, *Through a Glass Darkly*, in *A Film Trilogy*, 51.
11 Bergman, *Bergman on Bergman*, 151.
12 Bergman, *Bergman on Bergman*, 173–74.
13 Bergman, *Bergman on Bergman*, 174.
14 Bergman, *Bergman on Bergman*, 175.
15 Bergman, epigraph, *A Film Trilogy*, n.p.
16 Cowie, 215–16.

CHAPTER VI
1 Bergman, *Bergman on Bergman*, 157.
2 Gado, 320–21.
3 Cowie, 228; Bergman, *Bergman on Bergman*, 195–96.
4 Gado, 321–22.
5 Bergman, *Bergman on Bergman*, 196.
6 Bergman, "The Snakeskin," in *Persona and Shame*, 13.
7 Cowie, 228–31.
8 Cowie, 241.
9 Bergman, *Hour of the Wolf*, in *Four Stories by Ingmar Bergman*, 104.
10 *Four Stories*, 105.
11 *Four Stories*, 105.
12 Bergman, *Bergman on Bergman*, 218.
13 Wood, 159.
14 Bergman, *Bergman on Bergman*, 237.
15 Bergman, *Bergman on Bergman*, 238.
16 Samuels interview in Kaminsky, 102.

CHAPTER VII
1 Cowie, 266.
2 Gado, 395.
3 Gado, 396; Cowie, 270–72.
4 Samuels interview in Kaminsky, 127.
5 Gado, 397–99.
6 Bergman, *Cries and Whispers*, in *Four Stories by Ingmar Bergman*, 61.
7 Bergman, *Cries and Whispers*, 61.

8 Cowie, 275–76.
9 Bergman, preface, *Scenes from a Marriage*, in *The Marriage Scenarios*, 4.
10 Cowie, 295–97.

CHAPTER VIII
1 Quoted in Gado, 441.
2 Jones, 23.
3 Gado, 463–71; Cowie, 305–12; Bergman, *Magic Lantern*, 86–106.
4 Gado, 466.
5 Cowie, 313–16.
6 Bergman, *Magic Lantern*, 183–85; Ingrid Bergman, *Ingrid Bergman: My Story* (New York: Delacorte, 1980), 464–76.
7 Bergman, *Magic Lantern*, 183.
8 Ingrid Bergman, 476.
9 Cowie, 330–31.
10 Jones, 65.
11 Quoted in Richard Grenier, review of *Fanny and Alexander*, Commentary, Sept. 1983, 65.
12 Cowie, 338.
13 Quoted in Pauline Kael, review of *Fanny and Alexander*, *New Yorker*, June 13, 1983, 117.

CHAPTER IX
1 Gado, 507.
2 Gado, 512, and in conversation.
3 Gado, 508.
4 Bergman, *Magic Lantern*, 284–85.
5 By special permission of the Brooklyn Academy of Music and the Billy Rose Theater Collection at Lincoln Center, I was able to view a rare tape of a filmed performance of Bergman's *Hamlet* at the Majestic Theater in 1988.
6 Robert Brustein, "Twenty-First Century Hamlet," *The New Republic*, July 18–25, 1988, 28.
7 Quoted in Rochelle Wright's unpublished conference paper, "The Imagined Past in Ingmar Bergman's *Den goda viljan*," 4.
8 Vincent Canby, "A Bergman Memoir by Son and Father," *New York Times*, Apr. 3, 1993, sec. C, 17.
9 Marker, 283–84.
10 Mel Gussow, "De Sade, via Many Filters But Clear," *New York Times*, May 22, 1993, sec. C, 11, 14.
11 Interview with Ann-Christine Jernberg, Royal Dramatic Theater, Stockholm.
12 Quoted in Sven Nykvist profile in Charles Moritz, ed., *Current Biography Yearbook 1989* (New York, 1989), 430.
13 Woody Allen, *Chaplin*, special issue, 1988, 35.

Selected Bibliography

Bergman, Ingmar. *Autumn Sonata: A Film.* Screenplay, translated by Alan Blair. New York: Pantheon, 1978.

————. *Bergman on Bergman: Interviews with Ingmar Bergman by Stig Björkman, Torsten Manns, and Jonas Sima.* Translated by Paul Britten Austin. New York: Simon and Schuster, 1973.

————. *The Best Intentions.* A novel, translated by Joan Tate. New York: Arcade, 1993.

————. *Bilder.* Stockholm: Norstedts, 1990.

————. *Den goda viljan.* Stockholm: Norstedts, 1991.

————. *Face to Face: A Film.* Screenplay, translated by Alan Blair. New York: Pantheon, 1976.

————. *Fanny and Alexander.* Screenplay, translated by Alan Blair. New York: Pantheon, 1982.

————. *A Film Trilogy.* Translated by Paul Britten Austin. London: Marion Boyars, 1967. (Screenplays of *Through a Glass Darkly, Winter Light,* and *The Silence.*)

————. *Four Screenplays of Ingmar Bergman.* Translated by Lars Malmström and David Kushner. New York: Simon and Schuster, 1960. (Screenplays of *Smiles of a Summer Night, The Seventh Seal, Wild Strawberries,* and *The Magician.*)

————. *Four Stories by Ingmar Bergman.* Translated by Alan Blair. New York: Doubleday, 1977. (Screenplays of *The Touch, Cries and Whispers, Hour of the Wolf,* and *The Passion of Anna.*)

————. *From the Life of the Marionettes.* Translated by Alan Blair. New York: Pantheon, 1980.

————. *The Magic Lantern: An Autobiography.* Translated by Joan Tate. New York: Viking, 1988.

————. *The Marriage Scenarios.* Translated by Alan Blair. New York: Pantheon, 1978. (Screenplays of *Scenes from a Marriage, Face to Face,* and *Autumn Sonata.*)

————. *Moraliteter (Morality Plays).* Stockholm: Bonniers, 1948.

————. *Persona and Shame.* Screenplays, translated by Keith Bradfield. New York: Grossman, 1972.

————. *A Project for the Theatre.* Edited and introduced by Frederick J. Marker and Lise-Lone Marker. New York: Frederick Ungar, 1983. (Scripts of Bergman's stage productions of *A Doll's House, Miss Julie,* and *Scenes from a Marriage.*)

————. *Scenes from a Marriage.* Screenplay, translated by Alan Blair. New York: Pantheon, 1974.

————. *The Serpent's Egg: A Film by Ingmar Bergman.* Screenplay, translated by Alan Blair. New York: Pantheon, 1977.

————. *The Seventh Seal: A Film by Ingmar Bergman.* Screenplay, translated by Lars Malmström and David Kushner. New York: Simon and Schuster, 1960.

————. *Three Films by Ingmar Bergman.* Translated by Paul Britten Austin. New York: Grove Press, 1970. (Screenplays of *Through a Glass Darkly, Winter Light,* and *The Silence.*)

————. *The Virgin Spring.* Screenplay by Ulla Isaksson, translated by Lars Malmström and David Kushner. New York: Ballantine Books, 1960.

————. *Wild Strawberries, a Film.* Screenplay, translated by Lars Malström and David Kushner. New York: Simon and Schuster, 1969.

————. *Wood Painting: A Morality Play.* Translated by Rudolph Goodman and Leif Sjöberg. *Tulane Drama Review,* 1961.

Bergom-Larsson, Maria. *Ingmar Bergman and Society.* South Brunswick, N.J.: A. S. Barnes, in collaboration with the Swedish Film Institute, 1978.

Blake, Richard A. *The Lutheran Milieu of the Films of Ingmar Bergman.* New York: Arno Press, 1978.

Cowie, Peter. *Ingmar Bergman: A Critical Biography.* 2nd ed. New York: Scribner's, 1992.

Donner, Jörn. *The Films of Ingmar Bergman.* Translated by Holger Lundbergh. New York: Dover, 1972. (Originally published as *The Personal Vision of Ingmar Bergman,* Indiana University Press, 1964.)

Gado, Frank. *The Passion of Ingmar Bergman.* Durham: Duke University Press, 1986.

Gibson, Arthur. *The Silence of God: Creative Response to the Films of Ingmar Bergman.* New York: Harper & Row, 1969.

Gill, Jerry H. *Ingmar Bergman and the Search for Meaning.* Grand Rapids: Eerdmans, 1969.

Höök, Marianne. *Ingmar Bergman.* Stockholm: Wahlström och Widstrand, 1962.

Jones, G. William, ed. *Talking with Ingmar Bergman.* Dallas: Southern Methodist University Press, 1983.

Kaminsky, Stuart M., ed. *Ingmar Bergman: Essays in Criticism.* London: Oxford University Press, 1975.

Kawin, Bruce P. *Mindscreen: Bergman, Godard, and First-Person Film.* Princeton: Princeton University Press, 1978.

Ketcham, Charles B. *The Influence of Existentialism on Ingmar Bergman: An Analysis of the Theological Ideas Shaping a Filmmaker's Art.* Lewiston, N.Y.: E. Mellen Press, 1986.

Lauder, Robert E. *God, Death, Art, and Love: The Philosophical Vision of Ingmar Bergman.* Prologue by Liv Ullmann. New York: Paulist Press, 1989.

Linton-Malmfors, Birgit, ed. *Den dubbla verkligheten: Karin och Erik Bergman i dagböcker och brev 1907–1936 (A Double Reality: Diaries and Letters of Karin and Erik Bergman, 1907–1936).* Stockholm: Carlssons, 1992.

Livingston, Paisley. *Ingmar Bergman and the Rituals of Art.* Ithaca: Cornell University Press, 1982.

Marker, Lise-Lone. *Ingmar Bergman: A Life in the Theater.* Cambridge and New York: Cambridge University Press, 1992. Updated edition of *Ingmar Bergman: Four Decades in the Theater,* 1982.

Mosley, Philip. *Ingmar Bergman: The Cinema as Mistress.* Boston: Marion Boyers, 1981.

Simon, John. *Ingmar Bergman Directs.* New York: Harcourt Brace Jovanovich, 1972.

Sjöman, Vilgot. *L. 136, Diary with Ingmar Bergman.* Translated by Alan Blair. Ann Arbor, Mich.: Karoma, 1978.

Steene, Birgitta. *Ingmar Bergman.* New York: Twayne, 1968.

————. *Ingmar Bergman: A Guide to References and Resources.* Boston: G. K. Hall, 1987.

————, ed. *Focus on "The Seventh Seal."* Englewood Cliffs, N.J.: Prentice-Hall, 1972.

Strindberg, August. *A Dream Play,* adapted by Ingmar Bergman. New York: Dial Press, 1973.

Wood, Robin. *Ingmar Bergman.* New York: Praeger, 1969.

Young, Vernon. *Cinema Borealis: Ingmar Bergman and the Swedish Ethos.* New York: Avon, 1975.

Filmography

An asterisk (*) indicates a film written but not directed by Bergman.

*Hets(Torment/Frenzy)
Svensk Filmindustri. *Director*: Alf Sjöberg. *Executive producer*: Harald Molander. *Screenplay*: Ingmar Bergman. *Photography*: Martin Bodin. *Artistic adviser*: Victor Sjöström. *Art direction*: Arne Åkermark. *Music*: Hilding Rosenberg. *Production manager*: Gösta Ström. *Assistant director*: Ingmar Bergman. *Editor*: Oscar Rosander.
Cast: Stig Järrel (Caligula), Alf Kjellin (Jan-Erik Widgren), Mai Zetterling (Bertha Olsson), Olof Winnerstrand (school principal), Gösta Cederlund (the teacher, Pippi), Stig Olin (Jan-Erik's friend, Sandman), Jan Molander (a student, Pettersson), Olav Riego (Jan-Erik's father), Märta Arbiin (Jan-Erik's mother), Anders Nyström (Jan-Erik's brother), Hugo Björne (physician), Gunnar Björnstrand (teacher in opening sequence), Curt Edgard, Birger Malmsten (students).
Running time: 101 minutes. Black and white. *Shot on location*: Norra Latin School, Stockholm, and Råsunda Studios, February 21–May 25, 1944. *Swedish premiere*: October 2, 1944. *U.S. opening*: April 21, 1946. *U.S. distribution*: Oxford Films.

Kris (Crisis)
Svensk Filmindustri. *Director*: Ingmar Bergman. *Executive producer*: Harald Molander. *Screenplay*: Ingmar Bergman, from the radio play *Moderhjertet*, by Leck Fischer. *Photography*: Gösta Roosling. *Artistic adviser*: Victor Sjöström. *Art direction*: Arne Åkermark. *Music*: Erland von Koch. *Sound*: Lennart Svensson. *Assistant director*: Lars-Eric Kjellgren. *Unit managers*: Harry Malmstedt, Ragnar Carlberg. *Editor*: Oscar Rosander. *Continuity*: Seivie Ewerstein.
Cast: Dagny Lind (Ingeborg Johnson), Inga Landgré (Nelly), Marianne Löfgren (Jenny), Stig Olin (Jack), Allan Bohlin (Ulf), Ernst Eklund (Uncle Edvard), Signe Wirff (Aunt Jessie), Svea Holst (Malin), Arne Lindblad (mayor), Julia Caesar (mayor's wife), Dagmar Olsson (singer at ball), Siv Thulin (assistant in beauty salon), Anna-Lisa Baude, M. Carelick (customers in beauty salon), Karl Erik Flens (Nelly's friend at ball), Erik Forslund (gentleman at party).
Running Time: 93 minutes. Black and white. *Shot on location*: Hedemora in central Sweden and Råsunda Studios, July 4–August 31, 1945. *Swedish premiere*: February 25, 1946.

Det Regnar På Vår Kärlek (It Rains on Our Love)
Sveriges Folkbiografer. *Director*: Ingmar Bergman. *Executive producer*: Lorens Marmstedt. *Screenplay*: Ingmar Bergman and Herbert Grevenius, from the play, *Bra Mennesker*, by Oskar Braathen. *Photography*: Göran Strindberg, Hilding Bladh. *Art direction*: P. A. Lundgren. *Music*: Erland von Koch, with excerpts from Richard Wagner and Bernhard Flies. *Sound*: Lars Nordberg. *Editor*: Tage Holmberg. *Continuity*: Gun Holmgren.
Cast: Barbro Kollberg (Maggi), Birger Malmsten (David Lindell), Gösta Cederlund (man with umbrella), Ludde Gentzel (Håkansson), Douglas Håge (Andersson), Hjördis Pettersson (Mrs. Andersson), Julia Caesar (Hanna Ledin), Sture Ericsson and Ulf Johansson (peddlers), Gunnar Björnstrand (Mr. Purman), Åke Fridell (assistant vicar), Torsten Hillberg (vicar), Benkt-Åke Benktsson (prosecutor), Erik Rosén (judge), Magnus Kesster (Folke Törnberg, bicycle repairman), Sif Ruud (Gerti, his wife), Erland Josephson (clerk in vicar's office).
Running time: 95 minutes. Black and white. *Shot on location*: Koloniträdgård, outside Stockholm, and Novilla Studios in Stockholm's Deer Garden, late spring–early summer 1946. *Swedish premiere*: November 9, 1946.

*Kvinna Utan Ansikte (Woman Without a Face)
Svensk Filmindustri. *Director*: Gustaf Molander. *Screenplay*: Ingmar Bergman. *Photography*: Åke Dahlqvist. *Art direction*: Arne Åkermark, Nils Svenwall. *Music*: Erik Nordgren, Julius Jacobsen. *Sound*: Sven Hansen. *Editor*: Oscar Rosander. *Continuity*: Lucie Kjellberg.
Cast: Alf Kjellin (Martin Grandé), Gunn Wållgren (Rut Köhler), Anita Björk (Frida Grandé), Stig Olin (Ragnar Ekberg), Olof Winnerstrand (Martin's father), Marianne Löfgren (Charlotte, Rut's mother), Georg Funkquist (Victor), Åke Grönberg (Sam Svensson), Linnea Hillberg (Martin's mother).
Running time: 100 minutes. Black and white. *Shot on location*: Råsunda Studios and Märsta Station, February 3–spring 1947. *Swedish premiere*: September 16, 1947.

Skepp till Indialand (Ship to India/Frustration)
Sveriges Folkbiografer. *Director*: Ingmar Bergman. *Executive producer*: Lorens Marmstedt. *Screenplay*: Ingmar Bergman, after Martin Söderhjelm's play *Skepp till Indialand*, first produced at the Swedish Theater in Helsinki, October 23, 1946. *Photography*: Göran Strindberg. *Art direction*: P. A. Lundgren. *Music*: Erland von Koch. *Sound*: Lars Nordberg, Sven Josephson. *Editor*: Tage Holmberg. *Continuity*: Gerda Osten.
Cast: Holger Löwenadler (Captain Alexander Blom), Birger Malmsten (Johannes Blom), Gertrud Fridh (Sally), Anna Lindahl (Alice Blom), Lasse Krantz (Hans, a crewman), Jan Molander (Bertil, a crewman), Erik Hell (Pekka, a crewman), Naemi Briese (Selma), Hjördis Pettersson (Sofie), Åke Fridell (manager of music hall), Kiki (dwarf).

Running time: 102 minutes. Black and white. *Shot on location*: Stockholm and Novilla Studios in Stockholm's Deer Park, May 28–July 16, 1947. *Swedish premiere*: September 22, 1947. *U.S. opening*: August 29, 1949, Rialto, New York City. *U.S. distribution*: Film Classics, Janus Films.

Musik i Mörker (Night is My Future/Music in Darkness)
Terrafilm. *Director*: Ingmar Bergman. *Executive producer*: Lorens Marmstedt. *Screenplay*: Dagmar Edqvist, after her novel of the same name. *Photography*: Göran Strindberg. *Art direction*: P. A. Lundgren. *Music*: Erland von Koch, with excerpts from Chopin, Beethoven, Badarczewska-Baranowska, Schumann, Handel, Wagner, and Tom Andy (pseudonym for Thomas Andersen). *Sound*: Olle Jakobsson. *Editor*: Lennart Wallén. *Production manager*: Allan Ekelund. *Continuity*: Ulla Kihlberg.
Cast: Mai Zetterling (Ingrid Olofsdotter), Birger Malmsten (Bengt Vyldeke), Bibi Skoglund (Agneta Vyldeke, his sister), Olof Winnerstrand (Kerrman, the vicar), Naima Wifstrand (Beatrice Schröder), Åke Claesson (Augustin Schröder), Hilda Borgström (Lovis), Douglas Håge (Kruge, restaurant owner), Gunnar Björnstrand (Klasson, violinist), Bengt Eklund (Ebbe Larsson), Segol Mann (Anton Nord), Bengt Logardt (Einar Born), Marianne Gyllenhammar (Blanche), John Elfström (Otto Klemens, blind worker), Rune Andreasson (Evert), Barbro Flodquist (Hjördis, his mother), Ulla Andreasson (Sylvia), Sven Lindberg (Hedström, music director).
Running time: 85 minutes. Black and white. *Shot on location*: Sandrews Studios, Stockholm, November 1–December 30, 1947. *Swedish premiere*: January 17, 1948. *U.S. opening*: January 8, 1963, Eighth Street Playhouse, New York City. *U.S. distribution*: Embassy Pictures/Janus Films.

Hamnstad (Port of Call)
Svensk Filmindustri. *Director*: Ingmar Bergman. *Executive producer*: Harald Molander. *Screenplay*: Ingmar Bergman, from Olle Länsberg's *Guldet och murarna*. *Photography*: Gunnar Fischer. *Art direction*: Nils Svenwall. *Unit manager*: Gösta Ström. *Music*: Erland von Koch, Adolphe Adam, Sven Sjöholm. *Sound*: Sven Hansen. *Production manager*: Lars-Eric Kjellgren. *Assistant director*: Stig Ossian Ericsson. *Editor*: Oscar Rosander. *Continuity*: Ingegerd Ericsson.
Cast: Nine-Christine Jönsson (Berit Holm), Bengt Eklund (Gösta Andersson), Erik Hell (Berit's father), Berta Hall (Berit's mother), Mimi Nelson (Gertrud), Sture Ericsson (her father), Birgitta Valberg (Agnes Vilander, social worker), Hans Strååt (Vilander), Harry Ahlin (man from Skåne), Nils Hallberg (Gustav), Sven-Eric Gamble ("Eken," the Stockholm kid), Sif Ruud (Mrs. Krona), Kolbjörn Knudsen (seaman), Yngve Nord-

wall (factory foreman), Torsten Lilliecrona, Hans Sundberg (his friends), Bengt Blomgren (Gunnar), Helge Karlsson (his father), Hanny Schedin (his mother).
Running time: 99 minutes. Black and white. *Shot on location*: Gothenburg and Hindås, and on the Södertälje-Stockholm train, May 27–July 17, 1948. *Swedish premiere*: October 18, 1948. *U.S. opening*: November 1959.

*Eva
Svensk Filmindustri. *Director*: Gustaf Molander. *Screenplay*: Ingmar Bergman and Gustaf Molander, from a synopsis by Ingmar Bergman. *Photography*: Åke Dahlqvist. *Art direction*: Nils Svenwall. *Music*: Erik Nordgren. *Sound*: Sven Hansen. *Editor*: Oscar Rosander.
Cast: Birger Malmsten (Bo Fredriksson), Eva Stiberg (Eva), Eva Dahlbeck (Susanne), Stig Olin (Göran), Åke Claesson (Fredriksson), Wanda Rothgardt (Mrs. Fredriksson), Inga Landgré (Frida), Hilda Borgström (Mrs. Berglund), Axel Hogel (Johansson), Lasse Sarri (Bo at twelve).
Running time: 97 minutes. Black and white. *Shot on location*: Tylösand, Nynäshamn, Hudiksvall, Tveteberg, Handen, Tumba, Bogesund, and Norrköping, and Råsunda Studios, May 27–June 28, 1948. *Swedish premiere*: December 26, 1948.

Fängelse (Prison/The Devil's Wanton)
Terrafilm. *Director*: Ingmar Bergman. *Executive producer*: Lorens Marmstedt. *Screenplay*: Ingmar Bergman. *Photography*: Göran Strindberg. *Art direction*: P. A. Lundgren. *Music*: Erland von Koch. *Sound*: Olle Jakobsson. *Production manager*: Allan Ekelund. *Editor*: Lennart Wallén. *Continuity*: Chris Poijes.
Cast: Doris Svedlund (Birgitta-Carolina Söderberg), Birger Malmsten (Tomas), Eva Henning (Sofi, his wife), Hasse Ekman (Martin Grandé), Stig Olin (Peter), Irma Christensson (Linnéa), Birgitta-Carolina's sister), Anders Henrikson (Paul, professor of mathematics), Marianne Löfgren (Signe Bohlin), Curt Masreliez (Alf, the pimp), Birgit "Bibi" Lindqvist (Anna Bohlin), Arne Ragneborn (postman), Carl-Henrik Fant (Arne, an actor), Inger Juel (Greta, an actress), Torsten Lilliecrona (cinematographer).
Running time: 80 minutes. Black and white. *Shot on location*: Stockholm's "Old Town" and Sandrews Studios, Stockholm, November 16, 1948–March 4, 1949. *Swedish premiere*: March 19, 1949. *U.S. opening*: July 4, 1962, 55th Street Playhouse, New York City. *U.S. distribution*: Embassy Pictures/Janus Films.

Törst (Three Strange Loves/Thirst)
Svensk Filmindustri. *Director*: Ingmar Bergman. *Screenplay*: Herbert Grevenius, from Birgit Tengroth's short story collection, *Törst. Photography*: Gunnar Fischer. *Art direction*: Nils Svenwall. *Music*: Erik Nordgren. *Sound*: Lennart Unnerstad. *Orchestration*: Eskil Eckert-Lundin. *Choreography*: Ellen Bergman. *Costumes*: Gösta Ström. *Production manager*: Helge Hagerman. *Stu-

dio manager*: Hugo Bolander. *Unit managers*: Gösta Ström, Hilmer Peters. *Editor*: Oscar Rosander. *Continuity*: Ingegerd Ericsson.
Cast: Eva Henning (Rut), Birger Malmsten (Bertil, her husband), Birgit Tengroth (Viola), Mimi Nelson (Valborg), Hasse Ekman (psychiatrist), Bengt Eklund (Raoul), Gaby Stenberg (Astrid, his wife), Naima Wifstrand (Miss Henriksson, ballet teacher), Sven-Eric Gamble (worker in glass factory), Gunnar Nielsen (Rosengren's assistant), Estrid Hesse (patient), Helge Hagerman (Swedish priest), Calle Flygare (Danish priest), Monica Weinzierl (small girl on train), Verner Arpe (German conductor), Else-Merete Heiberg (Norwegian lady on train), Ingmar Bergman (passenger on train).
Running time: 88 minutes. Black and white. *Shot on location*: Stockholm and Basel, Switzerland, and Råsunda Studios, March 15–July 5, 1949. *Swedish premiere*: October 17, 1949. *U.S. opening*: July 11, 1961. *U.S. distribution*: Janus Films.

Till Glädje (To Joy)
Svensk Filmindustri. *Director*: Ingmar Bergman. *Screenplay*: Ingmar Bergman. *Photography*: Gunnar Fischer. *Art direction*: Nils Svenwall. *Music*: Beethoven ("Egmont Overture," First and Ninth Symphonies), Mozart, Mendelssohn, Smetana, Sam Samson, and Erik Johnsson. *Sound*: Sven Hansen. *Orchestration*: Eskil Eckert-Lundin. *Production manager*: Allan Ekelund. *Unit manager*: Tor Borong. *Editor*: Oscar Rosander. *Continuity*: Ingegerd Ericsson.
Cast: Maj-Britt Nilsson (Martha), Stig Olin (Stig Eriksson), Victor Sjöström (Sönderby), Birger Malmsten (Marcel), John Ekman (Mikael Bro), Margit Carlqvist (Nelly Bro), Sif Ruud (Stina), Erland Josephson (Bertil), Ernst Brunman (janitor at concert house), Allan Ekelund (vicar at wedding), Maud Hyttenberg (toyshop assistant), Berit Holmström (Lisa), Eva Fritz-Nilsson (Lisa as a baby), Björn Montin (Lasse), Staffan Axelsson (Lasse as a baby), Ingmar Bergman (himself).
Running time: 98 minutes. Black and white. *Shot on location*: Hälsingborg and Arild, southern Sweden, and Råsunda Studios, July 11–September 2, 1949. *Swedish premiere*: February 20, 1950.

*Medan Staden Sover (While the City Sleeps)
Svensk Filmindustri. *Diretor*: Lars-Eric Kjellgren. *Screenplay*: Lars-Eric Kjellgren and P. A. Fogelström from the latter's novel *Ligister*, synopsis by Ingmar Bergman. *Photography*: Martin Bodin. *Art direction*: Nils Svenwall. *Location manager*: Gustaf Roger. *Music*: Erik Nordgren. *Sound*: Sven Hansen. *Editor*: Oscar Rosander.
Cast: Sven-Eric Gamble (Jompa), Inga Landgré (Iris), Adolph Jahr (her father), Elof Ahrle (the boss), Ulf Palme (Kalle Lund), Hilding Gavle (a heel), John Elfström (Jompa's father), Barbro Hiort af Ornäs (Rut), Carl Ström (doorman), Märta Dorff (Iris's mother), Harriet Andersson, et al.
Running time: 101 minutes. Black and

white. *Shot on location*: southern Stockholm and Råsunda Studios, January–February, 1950. *Swedish premiere*: September 8, 1950.

Sånt Händer Inte Här (This Doesn't Happen Here/High Tension)
Svensk Filmindustri. *Director*: Ingmar Bergman. *Screenplay*: Herbert Grevenius, from the novel *I løpet av tölv timer*, by Waldemar Brøgger. *Photography*: Gunnar Fischer. *Art direction*: Nils Svenwall. *Sound*: Sven Hansen. *Music*: Erik Nordgren (music in export version by Herbert Stéen-Östling). *Orchestration*: Eskil Eckert-Lundin. *Production manager*: Helge Hagerman. *Assistant director*: Hugo Bolander. *Editor*: Lennart Wallén. *Continuity*: Sol-Britt Norlander. *Speaker*: Stig Olin.
Cast: Signe Hasso (Vera), Alf Kjellin (Björn Almkvist), Ulf Palme (Atkä Natas), Gösta Cederlund (doctor), Yngve Nordwall (Lindell), Hanno Kompus (priest), Els Vaarman (female refugee), Rudolph Lipp ("the shadow"), Segol Mann, Willy Koblanck, Gregor Dahlman, Gösta Holmström, Ivan Bousé (Liquidatzia agents), Stig Olin (young man), Magnus Kesster (houseowner), Alexander von Baumgarten (ship's captain), Ragnar Klange (motorist), Lillie Wästfeldt (his wife).
Running time: 84 minutes. Black and white. *Shot on location*: Stadsgården and Ängby, Stockholm, and Råsunda Studios, July 6–August 19, 1950. *Swedish premiere*: October 23, 1950.

Sommarlek (Summer Interlude/Illicit Interlude)
Svensk Filmindustri. *Director*: Ingmar Bergman. *Screenplay*: Ingmar Bergman and Herbert Grevenius from an unpublished story by Bergman entitled "Mari." *Photography*: Gunnar Fischer. *Art direction*: Nils Svenwall. *Music*: Erik Nordgren, Delibes, Chopin, and Tchaikovsky. *Orchestration*: Eskil Eckert-Lundin. *Production manager*: Allan Ekelund. *Unit manager*: Gösta Ström. *Editor*: Oscar Rosander. *Continuity*: Ingegerd Ericsson.
Cast: Maj-Britt Nilsson (Marie), Birger Malmsten (Henrik), Alf Kjellin (David Nyström), Georg Funkquist (Uncle Erland), Renée Björling (Aunt Elizabeth), Mimi Pollak (Henrik's aunt), Annalisa Ericson (Kaj, a ballerina), Stig Olin (ballet master), Gunnar Olsson (pastor), John Botvid (Karl, a janitor), Carl Ström (Sandell, stage manager), Torsten Lilliecrona (lighting man), Marianne Schuler (Kerstin), Ernst Brunman (boat's captain), Gun Skogberg (Marie as ballerina), and the ballet at the Royal Opera, Stockholm.
Running time: 96 minutes. Black and white. *Shot on location*: Stockholm archipelago and Råsunda Studios, April 3–June 18, 1950. *Swedish premiere*: October 1, 1951. *U.S. opening*: October 26, 1954, Plaza Theater, New York City. *U.S. distribution*: Gaston Hakim Productions.

*Frånskild (Divorced)
Svensk Filmindustri. *Director*: Gustaf Molander. *Screenplay*: Ingmar Bergman and

Herbert Grevenius, from a synopsis by Bergman. *Photography*: Åke Dahlqvist. *Art direction*: Nils Svenwall. *Music*: Erik Nordgren. *Editor*: Oscar Rosander.
Cast: Inga Tidblad (Gertrud Holmgren), Alf Kjellin (Dr. Bertil Nordelius), Doris Svedlund (Marianne Berg), Hjördis Pettersson (Mrs. Nordelius), Håkan Westergren (man on the train), Holger Löwenadler (Tore Holmgren), Irma Christensson (Dr. Cecilia Lindeman, Tore's new wife), Marianne Löfgren (Ingeborg), Stig Olin (Hans).
Running time: 103 minutes. Black and white. *Shot on location*: Stockholm and Uppsala, and Råsunda Studios, November 15–December 30, 1950. *Swedish premiere*: December 26, 1951.

Kvinnors Väntan (Secrets of Women/Waiting Women)
Svensk Filmindustri. *Director*: Ingmar Bergman. *Screenplay*: Ingmar Bergman. *Photography*: Gunnar Fischer. *Art direction*: Nils Svenwall. *Music*: Erik Nordgren. *Sound*: Sven Hansen. *Orchestration*: Eskil Eckert-Lundin. *Production manager*: Allan Ekelund. *Studio manager*: Gustaf Roger. *Editor*: Oscar Rosander. *Continuity*: Bente Munk.
Cast: Anita Björk (Rakel), Jarl Kulle (Kaj, her lover), Karl-Arne Holmsten (Eugen, her husband), Maj-Britt Nilsson (Marta Lobelius), Birger Malmsten (Martin, her husband), Eva Dahlbeck (Karin Lobelius), Gunnar Björnstrand (Fredrik, her husband), Gerd Andersson (Maj, Marta's younger sister), Björn Bjelvenstam (her boyfriend), Aino Taube (Annette), Håkan Westergren (Paul, her husband), Märta Arbiin (nurse), Kjell Nordensköld (American pilot), Carl Ström (doctor), Torsten Lilliecrona (nightclub headwaiter), Naima Wifstrand (old Mrs. Lobelius).
Running time: 107 minutes. Black and white. *Shot on location*: Siarö in the Stockholm archipelago, Paris, and Råsunda Studios, April 3–June 20, 1952. *Swedish premiere*: November 3, 1952. *U.S. opening*: July 11, 1961, Fifth Avenue Cinema, New York City. *U.S. distribution*: Janus Films.

Sommaren med Monika (Summer with Monika)
Svensk Filmindustri. *Director*: Ingmar Bergman. *Screenplay*: Ingmar Bergman and P. A. Fogelström, from a novel of the same title by Fogelström. *Photography*: Gunnar Fischer. *Art direction*: P. A. Lundgren and Nils Svenwall. *Music*: Erik Nordgren, with waltz "Karlekens hamn," by Filip Olsson. *Sound*: Sven Hansen. *Orchestration*: Eskil Eckert-Lundin. *Production manager*: Allan Ekelund. *Editors*: Tage Holmberg, Gösta Lewin. *Continuity*: Birgit Nordlindh.
Cast: Harriet Andersson (Monika), Lars Ekborg (Harry), John Harryson (Lelle), Georg Skarstedt (Harry's father), Gösta Eriksson (Harry's boss), Åke Fridell (Monika's father), Åke Grönberg (Harry's construction boss), Gösta Gustafsson, Sigge Fürst, Gösta Prüzelius (employees in glass shop), Arthur Fischer (Monika's boss), Torsten Lilliecrona (driver), Bengt Eklund, Gustaf Färingborg (Monika's male colleagues at work), Ivar Wahlgren (owner of summer house), Renée

Björling (his wife), Catrin Westerlund (his daughter).
Running time: 96 minutes. Black and white. *Shot on location*: near the island of Ornö in the Stockholm archipelago and Råsunda Studios, July 22–October 6, 1952. *Swedish premiere*: February 9, 1953. *U.S. opening*: February 3, 1956, Orpheum Theater, Los Angeles. *U.S. distribution*: Janus Films/Gaston Hakim.

Gycklarnas Afton (The Naked Night/Sawdust and Tinsel)
Sandrews. *Director*: Ingmar Bergman. *Executive producer*: Rune Waldekranz. *Screenplay*: Ingmar Bergman. *Photography*: Hilding Bladh, Göran Strindberg, and Sven Nykvist. *Music*: Karl-Birger Blomdahl. *Sound*: Olle Jakobsson. *Costumes*: Mago (Max Goldstein). *Production manager*: Lars-Owe Carlberg. *Editor*: Carl-Olov Skeppstedt. *Continuity*: Marianne Axelsson.
Cast: Harriet Andersson (Anne), Åke Grönberg (Albert Johansson), Hasse Ekman (Frans), Anders Ek (Frost), Gudrun Brost (Alma), Annika Tretow (Agda, Albert's wife), Gunnar Björnstrand (Mr. Sjuberg), Erik Strandmark (Jens), Kiki (dwarf), Åke Fridell (officer), Curt Löwgren (Blom), Lissi Ahland, Karl-Axel Forsberg, Olva Riego, John Starck, Erna Groth, Agda Hilin (theater actors), Julie Bernby (tightrope dancer).
Running time: 92 minutes. Black and white. *Shot on location*: in Arild, southern Sweden, and Sandrews Studios, Stockholm, spring–summer 1953. *Swedish premiere*: September 14, 1953. *U.S. opening*: April 9, 1956, Little Carnegie, New York City. *U.S. distribution*: Times Films Corp./Janus Films.

En Lektion i Kärlek (A Lesson in Love)
Svensk Filmindustri. *Director*: Ingmar Bergman. *Screenplay*: Ingmar Bergman. *Photography*: Martin Bodin. *Art direction*: P. A. Lundgren. *Music*: Dag Wirén. *Sound*: Sven Hansen. *Orchestration*: Eskil Eckert-Lundin. *Production manager*: Allan Ekelund. *Studio manager*: Gustaf Roger. *Assistant director*: Rolf Carlsten. *Editor*: Oscar Rosander. *Continuity*: Birgit Nordlindh, Bente Munk.
Cast: Eva Dahlbeck (Marianne Erneman), Gunnar Björnstrand (David Erneman), Yvonne Lombard (Suzanne), Harriet Andersson (Nix), Åke Grönberg (Carl-Adam), Olof Winnerstrand (David's father), Renée Björling (David's mother), Birgitte Reimar (Lise, maid), John Elfström (Sam, chauffeur), Dagmar Ebbesen (nurse), Helge Hagerman (traveling salesman), Sigge Fürst (pastor), Gösta Prüzelius (train conductor), Carl Ström (Uncle Axel), Arne Lindblad (hotel manager), Torsten Lilliecrona (hotel clerk), George Adelly (bartender).
Running time: 94 minutes. Black and white. *Shot on location*: Filmstaden (Råsunda), in Copenhagen, on the Malmö-Copenhagen ferry, in Hälsingborg, Arild, Ramlösa, Pålsjöskog, the Mjölby train station, Beatelund, and Saltsjöbaden, July 30–September 16, 1953. *Swedish premiere*: October 4, 1954. *U.S. opening*: March 14, 1960, Murray Hill Theater, New York City. *U.S. distribution*: Janus Films.

Kvinnodröm (Dreams/Journey into Autumn)
Sandrews. *Director*: Ingmar Bergman. *Executive producer*: Rune Waldekranz. *Screenplay*: Ingmar Bergman. *Photography*: Hilding Bladh. *Art direction*: Gittan Gustafsson. *Sound*: Olle Jakobsson. *Production manager*: Lars-Owe Carlberg. *Assistant director*: Hans Abramson. *Editor*: Carl-Olov Skeppstedt. *Continuity*: Katherina Faragó.
Cast: Eva Dahlbeck (Susanne), Harriet Andersson (Doris), Gunnar Björnstrand (Consul Sönderby), Ulf Palme (Henrik Lobelius), Inga Landgré (Mrs. Lobelius), Sven Lindberg (Palle), Naima Wifstrand (Mrs. Arén), Git Gay (lady in fashion studio), Ludde Gentzel (Sundström, photographer in Gothenburg), Kerstin Hedeby (Marianne), Jessie Flaws (makeup artist), Marianne Nielsen (Fanny), Siv Ericks (Katja), Bengt Schütt (fashion designer), Axel Düberg (photographer in Stockholm), Renée Björling (Mrs. Berger).
Running time: 86 minutes. Black and white. *Shot on location*: Sandrews Studios, Stockholm, June 15–August 4, 1954. *Swedish premiere*: August 22, 1955. *U.S. opening*: May 31, 1960, Fifth Avenue Cinema, New York City. *U.S. distribution*: Janus Films.

Sommarnattens Leende (Smiles of a Summer Night)
Svensk Filmindustri. *Director*: Ingmar Bergman. *Screenplay*: Ingmar Bergman. *Photography*: Gunnar Fischer. *Art direction*: P. A. Lundgren. *Music*: Erik Nordgren. *Sound*: P. O. Pettersson. *Orchestration*: Eskil Eckert-Lundin. *Costumes*: Mago (Max Goldstein). *Production manager*: Allen Ekelund. *Location manager*: Gustaf Roger. *Assistant director*: Lennart Olsson. *Editor*: Oscar Rosander. *Continuity*: Katherina Faragó.
Cast: Eva Dahlbeck (Desirée Armfeldt), Gunnar Björnstrand (Fredrik Egerman), Ulla Jacobsson (Anne Egerman), Björn Bjelvenstam (Henrik Egerman), Naima Wifstrand (old Mrs. Armfeldt), Harriet Andersson (Petra), Margit Carlquist (Charlotte Malcolm), Jarl Kulle (Count Malcolm), Åke Fridell (Frid), Jullan Kindahl (Beata, the cook), Gull Natorp (Malla, Desirée's maid), Birgitta Valberg, Bibi Andersson (actresses), Anders Wulff (Desirée's son), Gunnar Nielsen (Malcolm's aide).
Running time: 108 minutes. Black and white. *Shot on location*: Skåne (southern Sweden), and Råsunda Studios, June 28–August 29, 1955, plus two days in November 1955. *Swedish premiere*: December 26, 1955. *U.S. opening*: December 23, 1957, Sutton Theater, New York City. *U.S. distribution*: Bank Film Distributors of America.

*Sista Paret Ut (Last Couple Out)
Svensk Filmindustri. *Director*: Alf Sjöberg. *Screenplay*: Ingmar Bergman and Alf Sjöberg from a story by Ingmar Bergman. *Photography*: Martin Bodin.
Cast: Björn Bjelvenstam (Bo), Bibi Andersson (Kerstin), Harriet Andersson (Anita), Olof Widgren (Bo's father), Eva Dahlbeck (Bo's mother), Märta Arbin (Bo's grandmother), Aino Taube (Kerstin's mother), Jarl Kulle (Dr. Fårell), Hugo Björne

(teacher).
Running time: 98 minutes. Black and white. *Swedish premiere*: November 12, 1956.

Det Sjunde Inseglet (The Seventh Seal)

Svensk Filmindustri. *Director*: Ingmar Bergman. *Screenplay*: Ingmar Bergman, from his play "Painting on Wood." *Photography*: Gunnar Fischer. *Art direction*: P. A. Lundgren. *Music*: Erik Nordgren. *Sound*: Aaby Wedin. *Special sound effects*: Evald Andersson. *Orchestration*: Sixten Ehrling. *Choreography*: Else Fisher. *Costumes*: Manne Lindholm. *Production manager*: Allan Ekelund. *Assistant director*: Lennart Olsson. *Editor*: Lennart Wallén. *Continuity*: Katherina Faragó.
Cast: Max von Sydow (Antonius Block), Gunnar Björnstrand (Squire Jöns), Bengt Ekerot (Death), Nils Poppe (Jof), Bibi Andersson (Mia), Åke Fridell (Plog, the smith), Inga Gill (Plog's wife, Lisa), Maud Hansson (the accused witch), Inga Landgré (knight's wife), Gunnel Lindblom (mute girl), Bertil Anderberg (Raval), Anders Ek (doomsday monk), Gunnar Olsson (church painter), Erik Strandmark (Skat), Lars Lind (monk outside church), Bengt-Åke Benktsson (merchant in tavern), Gudrun Brost (tavern hostess).
Running time: 95 minutes. Black and white. *Shot on location*: Östanå, Viby, Skevik, Gustafsberg, and Skytteholm outside Stockholm; Hovs hallar in southern Sweden; and Råsunda Studios, July 2–August 24, 1956. *Swedish premiere*: February 16, 1957. *U.S. opening*: October 13, 1958, Paris Theater, New York City. *U.S. distribution*: Janus Films.

Smultronstallet (Wild Strawberries)

Svensk Filmindustri. *Director*: Ingmar Bergman. *Screenplay*: Ingmar Bergman. *Photography*: Gunnar Fischer. *Art direction*: Gittan Gustafsson. *Music*: Erik Nordgren. *Sound*: Aaby Wedin. *Costumes*: Millie Ström. *Production manager*: Allan Ekelund. *Location manager*: Sven Sjönell. *Assistant director*: Gösta Ekman. *Editor*: Oscar Rosander. *Continuity*: Katherina Faragó.
Cast: Victor Sjöström (Isak Borg), Bibi Andersson (Sara), Ingrid Thulin (Marianne), Gunnar Björnstrand (Evald), Folke Sundquist (Anders), Björn Bjelvenstam (Viktor), Naima Wifstrand (Isak's mother), Jullan Kindahl (Agda, Isak's housekeeper), Gunnar Sjöberg (Alman), Gunnel Broström (his wife), Gertrud Fridh (Isak's wife), Åke Fridell (her lover), Max von Sydow (Åkerman), Anne-Marie Wiman (his wife), Sif Ruud (aunt at breakfast table), Yngve Nordwall (Uncle Aron), Per Sjöstrand (Sigfrid), Gio Petré (Sigbritt), Gunnel Lindblom (Charlotta), Maud Hansson (Angelica), Eva Norée (Anna), Lena Bergman, Monica Ehrling (the twins), Per Skogsberg (Hagbart), Göran Lundquist (Benjamin), Professor Helge Wulff (rector, University of Lund).
Running time: 90 minutes. Black and white. *Shot on location*: Lake Vättern, the university town of Lund, and Dalarö and Ängö in the Stockholm archipelago, and Råsunda Studios, July 2–August 27, 1957. *Swedish*

premiere: December 26, 1957. *U.S. opening*: June 22, 1959, Beekman Theater, New York City. *U.S. distribution*: Janus Films.

Nära Livet (Brink of Life/So Close to Life)

Nordisk Tonefilm. *Director*: Ingmar Bergman. *Screenplay*: Ingmar Bergman and Ulla Isaksson, from a short story, "Det vänliga, det värdiga," in her book, *Dödens faster*. *Photography*: Max Wilén. *Art direction*: Bibi Lindström. *Sound*: Lennart Svensson. *Production manager*: Gösta Hammarbäck. *Editor*: Carl-Olov Skeppstedt. *Continuity*: Ingrid Wallin.
Cast: Eva Dahlbeck (Stina Andersson), Ingrid Thulin (Cecilia Ellius), Bibi Andersson (Hjördis), Barbro Hiort af Ornäs (Sister Brita), Erland Josephson (Anders Ellius), Inga Landgré (Greta Ellius), Max von Sydow (Harry Andersson), Gunnar Sjöberg (Dr. Nordlander), Anne-Marie Gyllenspetz (welfare worker), Sissi Kaiser (Sister Marit), Margareta Krook (Dr. Larsson), Lars Lind (Dr. Thylenius), Monica Ekberg (Hjördis's friend), Gun Jönsson (night nurse).
Running time: 84 minutes. Black and white. *Shot on location*: South Hospital, Stockholm, and Nordisk Tonefilm Studios, Stockholm, in 1957. *Swedish premiere*: March 31, 1958. *U.S. opening*: November 8, 1959, Little Carnegie, New York City. *U.S. distribution*: Ajay Film Co./Janus Films.

Ansiktet (The Magician/The Face)

Svensk Filmindustri. *Director*: Ingmar Bergman. *Screenplay*: Ingmar Bergman. *Photography*: Gunnar Fischer. *Art direction*: P. A. Lundgren. *Music*: Erik Nordgren. *Sound*: Aaby Wedin. *Orchestration*: Eskil Eckert-Lundin. *Costumes*: Manne Lindholm and Greta Johansson. *Production manager*: Allan Ekelund. *Studio manager*: Carl Henry Cagarp. *Assistant director*: Gösta Ekman. *Editor*: Oscar Rosander. *Continuity*: Katherina Faragó.
Cast: Max von Sydow (Albert Emanuel Vogler), Ingrid Thulin (Manda Vogler), Åke Fridell (Tubal), Naima Wifstrand (Vogler's grandmother), Gunnar Björnstrand (Dr. Vergérus), Bengt Ekerot (Spegel), Bibi Andersson (Sara Lindqvist), Gertrud Fridh (Ottilia Egerman), Erland Josephson (Consul Abraham Egerman), Lars Ekborg (Simson, the coachman), Toivo Pawlo (Starbeck), Ulla Sjöblom (Henrietta), Axel Düberg (Rustan, the butler), Birgitta Pettersson (Sanna, the maid), Oscar Ljung (Antonsson), Sif Ruud (Sofia Garp).
Running time: 100 minutes. Black and white. *Shot on location*: Råsunda Studios, June 30–August 27, 1958. *Swedish premiere*: December 27, 1958. *U.S. opening*: August 27, 1959, Fifth Avenue Theater, New York City. *U.S. distribution*: Janus Films.

Jungfrukallan (The Virgin Spring)

Svensk Filmindustri. *Director*: Ingmar Bergman. *Screenplay*: Ulla Isaksson, based on a fourteenth-century legend, "Töres dotter i Vänge." *Photography*: Sven Nykvist. *Art direction*: P. A. Lundgren. *Music*: Erik Nordgren. *Sound*: Aaby Wedin. *Costumes*: Marik

Vos. *Production manager*: Allan Ekelund. *Unit manager*: Carl Henry Cagarp. *Assistant director*: Lenn Hjortzberg. *Editor*: Oscar Rosander. *Continuity*: Ulla Furås.
Cast: Birgitta Pettersson (Karin), Gunnel Lindblom (Ingeri), Max von Sydow (Töre), Birgitta Valberg (Märeta), Axel Düberg (herdsman/rapist), Tor Isedal (mute herdsman), Ove Porath (boy), Allan Edwall (beggar), Axel Slangus (bridge keeper), Oscar Ljung, Tor Borong, Leif Forstenberg (farmhands).
Running time: 88 minutes. Black and white. *Shot on location*: Styggeforsen and Skattungsbyn, Dalarna, and Råsunda Studios, May 14–late August 1959. *Swedish premiere*: February 8, 1960. *U.S. opening*: November 14, 1960, Beekman Theater, New York City. *U.S. distribution*: Janus Films.

Djävulens Öga (The Devil's Eye)

Svensk Filmindustri. *Director*: Ingmar Bergman. *Screenplay*: Ingmar Bergman, based on the radio play, *Don Juan vender tilbage*, by Oluf Bang. *Photography*: Gunnar Fischer. *Art direction*: P. A. Lundgren. *Music*: Erik Nordgren, with excerpts from Domenico Scarlatti, played by Käbi Laretei. *Sound*: Stig Flodin. *Costumes*: Mago (Max Goldstein). *Production manager*: Allan Ekelund. *Unit manager*: Lars-Owe Carlberg. *Assistant director*: Lenn Hjortzberg. *Editor*: Oscar Rosander. *Continuity*: Ulla Furås.
Cast: Jarl Kulle (Don Juan), Bibi Andersson (Britt-Marie), Stig Järrel (Satan), Nils Poppe (pastor), Gertrud Fridh (Renata, the pastor's wife), Sture Lagerwall (Pablo, Don Juan's servant), Georg Funkquist (Count Armand de Rochefoucauld), Gunnar Sjöberg (Marquis Giuseppe Maria de Maccopazza), Torsten Winge (old man), Axel Düberg (Jonas), Kristina Adolphson (veiled woman), Allan Edwall (Ear Devil), Ragnar Arvedson (Devil in Attendance), Gunnar Björnstrand (narrator).
Running time: 86 minutes. Black and white. *Shot on location*: Råsunda Studios, October 19, 1959–January 1, 1960. *Swedish premiere*: October 17, 1960. *U.S. opening*: October 30, 1961, Beekman Theater, New York City. *U.S. distribution*: Janus Films.

Såsom i en Spegel (Through a Glass Darkly)

Svensk Filmindustri. *Director*: Ingmar Bergman. *Screenplay*: Ingmar Bergman. *Photography*: Sven Nykvist. *Art direction*: P. A. Lundgren. *Music*: Erik Nordgren, with excerpts from Bach's Suite No. 2 in D Minor for Cello, played by Erling Bengtsson. *Sound*: Stig Flodin. *Sound effects*: Evald Andersson. *Costumes*: Mago (Max Goldstein). *Production manager*: Allan Ekelund. *Unit manager*: Lars-Owe Carlberg. *Assistant director*: Lenn Hjortzberg. *Editor*: Ulla Ryghe. *Continuity*: Ulla Furås.
Cast: Harriet Andersson (Karin), Max von Sydow (Martin), Gunnar Björnstrand (David), Lars Passgärd (Minus).
Running time: 89 minutes. Black and white. *Shot on location*: Fårö and Råsunda Studios, July 12–September 16, 1960. *Swedish premiere*: October 17, 1961. *U.S. opening*:

March 13, 1962, Beekman Theater, New York City. *U.S. distribution*: Janus Films.

*Lustgarden (The Pleasure Garden)
Svensk Filmindustri. *Director*: Alf Kjellin. *Screenplay*: Buntel Eriksson (joint pseudonym for Ingmar Bergman and Erland Josephson). *Photography*: Gunnar Fischer. *Artistic adviser*: Ingmar Bergman. *Art direction*: P. A. Lundgren. *Editor*: Ulla Ryghe.
Cast: Gunnar Björnstrand (David Franzén), Sickan Carlsson (Fanny), Bibi Andersson (Anna, her daughter), Stig Järrel (Lundberg), Kristina Adolphson (Astrid), Per Myrberg (young pastor), Gösta Cederlund, Torsten Winge, Hjördis Pettersson.
Running time: 93 minutes. Eastmancolor.
Shot on location: Vadstena, Arboga, Skänninge, and Råsunda Studios, early–late summer 1961. *Swedish premiere*: December 26, 1961.

Nattvardsgästerna (Winter Light/The Communicants)
Svensk Filmindustri. *Director*: Ingmar Bergman. *Screenplay*: Ingmar Bergman. *Photography*: Sven Nykvist. *Art direction*: P. A. Lundgren. *Music*: excerpts from Swedish psalms. *Sound*: Stig Flodin. *Sound effects*: Evald Andersson. *Costumes*: Mago. *Production manager*: Allan Ekelund. *Unit manager*: Lars-Owe Carlberg. *Assistant directors*: Lenn Hjortzberg, Vilgot Sjöman. *Editor*: Ulla Ryghe. *Continuity*: Katherina Faragó.
Cast: Ingrid Thulin (Märta Lundberg), Gunnar Björnstrand (Tomas Ericsson), Gunnel Lindblom (Karin Persson), Max von Sydow (Jonas Persson), Allan Edwall (Algot Frövik), Kolbjörn Knudsen (Knut Aronsson), Olof Thunberg (Fredrik Blom, organist), Elsa Ebbesen-Thornblad (Magdalena Ledfors), Tor Borong (Johan Åkerblom), Bertha Sånnell (Hanna Appelblad), Helena Palmgren (Doris), Eddie Axberg (Johan Strand), Lars-Owe Carlberg (local police officer), Ingmarie Hjort (Persson's daughter), Stefan Larsson (Persson's son).
Running time: 80 minutes. Black and white.
Shot on location: Dalarna, Sweden, and Råsunda Studios, October 4, 1961–January 14, 1962. *Swedish premiere*: December 11, 1962. *U.S. opening*: May 13, 1963, Beekman Theater, New York City. *U.S. distribution*: Janus Films.

Tystnaden (The Silence)
Svensk Filmindustri. *Director*: Ingmar Bergman. *Screenplay*: Ingmar Bergman. *Photography*: Sven Nykvist. *Art direction*: P. A. Lundgren. *Music*: Excerpts from Johann Sebastian Bach's "Goldberg Variations" and R. Mersey's "Mayfair Waltz." *Sound*: Stig Flodin. *Sound effects*: Ivan Renliden. *Costumes*: Marik Vos Lundh. *Production manager*: Allan Ekelund. *Unit manager*: Lars-Owe Carlberg. *Assistant directors*: Lars-Erik Liedholm, Lenn Hjortzberg. *Editor*: Ulla Ryghe. *Continuity*: Katherina Faragó.
Cast: Ingrid Thulin (Ester), Gunnel Lindblom (Anna), Jörgen Lindström (Johan, her son), Håkan Jahnberg (waiter in hotel), Birger Malmsten (waiter in bar), the Eduar-

dinis (seven dwarfs), Eduardo Gutierrez (their impresario), Lissi Alandh (woman in cabaret), Leif Forstenberg (man in cabaret), Nils Waldt (cinema cashier), Birger Lensander (cinema doorman), Eskil Kalling (man in bar), Karl-Arne Bergman (newspaper seller in bar), Olof Widgren (old man in hotel corridor).
Running time: 96 minutes. Black and white.
Shot on location: Råsunda Studios, July 9–September 19, 1962. *Swedish premiere*: September 23, 1963. *U.S. opening*: February 3, 1964, Rialto and Translux East, New York City. *U.S. distribution*: Janus Films.

För Att Inte Tala Om Alla Dessa Kvinnor (Now About These Women/All These Women)
Svensk Filmindustri. *Director*: Ingmar Bergman. *Screenplay*: Buntel Eriksson (joint pseudonym for Ingmar Bergman and Erland Josephson). *Photography*: Sven Nykvist. *Art direction*: P. A. Lundgren. *Music*: Erik Nordgren, with excerpts from Bach's Suite No. 3 in C Major and Suite No. 3 in D Minor. *Sound*: P. O. Pettersson. *Sound effects*: Evald Andersson. *Orchestration*: Charles Redland. *Costumes*: Mago (Max Goldstein). *Production manager*: Allan Ekelund. *Unit manager*: Lars-Owe Carlberg. *Assistant directors*: Lenn Hjortzberg and Lars-Erik Liedholm. *Editor*: Ulla Ryghe. *Continuity*: Katherina Faragó.
Cast: Jarl Kulle (Cornelius), Bibi Andersson (Bumble Bee, Felix's mistress), Harriet Andersson (Isolde, Felix's chambermaid), Eva Dahlbeck (Adelaide, Felix's wife), Karin Kavli (Madame Tussaud), Gertrud Fridh (Traviata), Mona Malm (Cecilia), Barbro Hiort af Ornäs (Beatrice, Felix's accompanist), Allan Edwall (Jilker, Felix's impresario), Georg Funkquist (Tristan).
Running time: 80 minutes. Eastmancolor.
Shot on location: Norrviken's Gardens, Båstad, Sweden, and Råsunda Studios, May 21–July 24, 1963. *Swedish premiere*: June 15, 1964. *U.S. opening*: October 5, 1964, Cinema Village, New York City. *U.S. distribution*: Janus Films.

Persona
Svensk Filmindustri. *Director*: Ingmar Bergman. *Screenplay*: Ingmar Bergman. *Photography*: Sven Nykvist. *Art direction*: Bibi Lindström. *Music*: Lars Johan Werle, with excerpts from Bach's Violin Concerto in E Major. *Sound*: P. O. Pettersson. *Sound effects*: Evald Andersson. *Mixing*: Olle Jakobsson. *Costumes*: Mago (Max Goldstein). *Production manager*: Lars-Owe Carlberg. *Unit manager*: Bo Vibenius. *Assistant director*: Lenn Hjortzberg. *Editor*: Ulla Ryghe. *Continuity*: Kerstin Berg.
Cast: Bibi Andersson (Sister Alma), Liv Ullmann (Elisabet Vogler), Margaretha Krook (doctor), Gunnar Björnstrand (Mr. Vogler), Jörgen Lindström (Elisabet's young son).
Running time: 84 minutes. Black and white.
Shot on location: island of Fårö and Råsunda Studios, July 19–September 15, 1965. *Swedish premiere*: October 18, 1966. *U.S. opening*: March 6, 1967. *U.S. distribution*: Lopert Pictures.

Stimulantia (segment entitled "Daniel")
Svensk Filmindustri. *Director*: Ingmar Bergman. *Script*: Ingmar Bergman. *Photography*: Ingmar Bergman. *Speaker*: Ingmar Bergman. *Music*: Käbi Laretei plays "Ah, vous dis-je, Madame," by Mozart. *Production manager*: Olle Nordemar. *Editor*: Ulla Ryghe. Other episodes directed by Hans Abramson, Jörn Donner, Lars Görling, Arne Arnbom, Hans Alfredson and Tage Danielsson, Gustaf Molander, and Vilgot Sjöman.
Cast: Daniel Sebastian Bergman, Käbi Laretei (themselves).
Running time: 16 minutes. Eastmancolor. Shot in and around Bergman's home, at that time in Djursholm, Sweden, 1963–65. *Swedish premiere*: March 28, 1967.

Vargtimmen (Hour of the Wolf)
Svensk Filmindustri. *Director*: Ingmar Bergman. *Screenplay*: Ingmar Bergman. *Photography*: Sven Nykvist. *Art direction*: Marik Vos-Lundh. *Music*: Lars Johan Werle, with excerpts from Bach's Sarabande in Partita No. 3 in A Minor and Mozart's *The Magic Flute*. *Sound*: P. O. Pettersson. *Sound effects*: Evald Andersson. *Mixing*: Olle Jakobsson. *Costumes*: Mago (Max Gordon). *Production manager*: Lars-Owe Carlberg. *Unit manager*: Bo Vibenius. *Assistant director*: Lenn Hjortzberg. *Editor and continuity*: Ulla Ryghe.
Cast: Liv Ullmann (Alma), Max von Sydow (Johan), Erland Josephson (Baron von Merkens), Gertrud Fridh (his wife), Gudrun Brost (old Mrs. von Merkens), Ingrid Thulin (Veronica Vogler), Bertil Anderberg (Ernst von Merkens), Georg Rydeberg (Lindhorst), Ulf Johanson (Heerbrand), Naima Wifstrand (old lady in Alma's "vision"/old woman with rubber face), Mikael Rundqvist (boy in fishing sequence), Lenn Hjortzberg (Kreisler), Agda Helin (maid), Folke Sundquist (Tamino), Mona Seilitz.
Running time: 89 minutes. Black and white.
Shot on location: Hovs hallar in southern Sweden and Råsunda Studios, May 23–November 23, 1966. *Swedish premiere*: February 19, 1968. *U.S. opening*: April 9, 1968, 34th Street East Theater, New York City. *U.S. distribution*: Lopert Pictures Corp.

Skammen (Shame/The Shame)
Svensk Filmindustri. *Director*: Ingmar Bergman. *Screenplay*: Ingmar Bergman. *Photography*: Sven Nykvist. *Art direction*: P. A. Lundgren. *Music*: Excerpts from Bach. *Sound*: Lennart Engholm. *Sound effects*: Evald Andersson. *Mixing*: Olle Jakobsson. *Costumes*: Mago (Max Goldstein), Eivor Kullberg. *Production manager*: Lars-Owe Carlberg. *Assistant director*: Raymond Lundberg. *Editor*: Ulla Ryghe. *Continuity*: Katherina Faragó. *Military advisers*: Lennart Bergqvist and Stig Lindberg.
Cast: Liv Ullmann (Eva Rosenberg), Max von Sydow (Jan Rosenberg), Gunnar Björnstrand (Jacobi), Birgitta Valberg (Mrs. Jacobi), Sigge Fürst (Philip), Hans Alfredson (Lobelius), Ingvar Kjellson (Oswald), Frank Sundström (interrogator), Ulf Johansson (doctor), Frej Lindqvist (stooped man),

Rune Lindström (stout gentleman), Willy Peters (older officer), Bengt Eklund (orderly), Åke Jörnfalk (condemned man), Vilgot Sjöman (interviewer).
Running time: 102 minutes. Black and white. *Shot on location*: island of Fårö, September 12–November 23, 1967. *Swedish premiere*: September 29, 1968. *U.S. opening*: December 23, 1968, Fine Arts, New York City. *U.S. distribution*: Lopert Pictures.

Riten (The Ritual/The Rite)
Svensk Filmindustri/Sveriges TV/Cinematograph. *Director*: Ingmar Bergman. *Screenplay*: Ingmar Bergman. *Photography*: Sven Nykvist. *Art direction*: Lennart Blomkvist. *Sound*: Lennart Engholm, Berndt Frithiof. *Special effects*: Nils Skeppstedt. *Mixing*: Olle Jakobsson. *Costumes*: Mago (Max Goldstein). *Production manager*: Lars-Owe Carlberg. *Assistant director*: Christer Dahl. *Editor*: Siv Kanälv. *Continuity*: Birgitta Särnö.
Cast: Ingrid Thulin (Thea Winkelmann), Anders Ek (Albert Emmanuel Sebastian Fischer), Gunnar Björnstrand (Hans Winkelmann), Erik Hell (Judge Abramsson), Ingmar Bergman (priest in confessional).
Running time: 72 minutes. Black and white. *Shot on location*: Studios at Filmstaden, Stockholm, May 13–June 20, 1967. *Swedish premiere*: March 25, 1969 (Swedish TV). *U.S. opening*: September 18, 1969, New York Film Festival, Tully Hall, Lincoln Center. *U.S. distribution*: Janus Films.

En Passion (The Passion of Anna/A Passion)
Svensk Filmindustri/Cinematograph. *Director*: Ingmar Bergman. *Screenplay*: Ingmar Bergman. *Photography*: Sven Nykvist. *Art direction*: P. A. Lundgren. *Set decoration*: Lennart Blomkvist. *Music*: Excerpts from Bach's Partita No. 3 in A Minor and from Allan Gray's song "Always Romantic." *Sound*: Lennart Engholm. *Sound effects*: Ulf Nordholm. *Mixing*: Olle Jakobsson. *Costumes*: Mago (Max Goldstein). *Production manager*: Lars-Owe Carlberg. *Unit manager*: Brian Wikström. *Editor*: Siv Kanälv. *Continuity*: Katherina Faragó.
Cast: Max von Sydow (Andreas Winkelmann), Liv Ullmann (Anna Fromm), Bibi Andersson (Eva Vergérus), Erland Josephson (Elis Vergérus), Erik Hell (Johan Andersson), Sigge Fürst (Verner), Svea Holst (his wife), Annika Kronberg (Katarina), Hjördis Pettersson (Johan's sister), Lars-Owe Carlberg and Brian Wikström (two policemen), Barbro Hiort af Ornäs, Malin Ek, Brita Brunius, Brita Öberg, Marianne Karlbeck (women in nightmare sequence).
Running time: 101 minutes. Eastmancolor. *Shot on location*: Fårö, September–December 1968. *Swedish premiere*: November 10, 1969. *U.S. distribution*: United Artists.

Fårö-Dokument (Fårö Document)
Cinematograph. *Director*: Ingmar Bergman. *Photography*: Sven Nykvist. *Sound*: Arne Carlsson. *Production manager*: Lars-Owe Carlberg. *Editor*: Siv Kanälv-Lundgren.
Cast: Ingmar Bergman (reporter), local people on the island of Fårö.
Running time: 78 minutes. Partly in Eastmancolor. *Shot on location*: island of Fårö, spring, 1969. *Premiere*: January 1, 1970, SR/TV (Swedish TV). Never shown commercially in the U.S.

Beröringen (The Touch)
Cinematograph/ABC Pictures. *Director*: Ingmar Bergman. *Screenplay*: Ingmar Bergman. *Photography*: Sven Nykvist. *Art direction*: P. A. Lundgren. *Music*: Jan Johansson. *Sound*: Lennart Engholm. *Costumes*: Mago (Max Goldstein). *Production manager*: Lars-Owe Carlberg. *Location manager*: Lotti Ekberg. *Assistant director*: Arne Carlsson. *Editor*: Siv Kanälv-Lundgren. *Continuity*: Katherina Faragó.
Cast: Elliott Gould (David Kovac), Bibi Andersson (Karin Vergérus), Max von Sydow (Dr. Andreas Vergérus), Sheila Reid (Sara Kovac), Barbro Hiort af Ornäs (Karin's mother), Staffan Hallerstam (Anders Vergérus), Maria Nolgård (Agnes Vergérus), Åke Lindström (doctor), Mimmi Wahlander (nurse), Else Ebbesen (matron), Anna von Rosen, Karin Nilsson (neighbors), Erik Nyhlen (archeologist), Margareta Byström (Dr. Vergérus's secretary), Alan Simon (museum curator), Harry Schein, Stig Björkman (guests at party).
Running time: 114 minutes. Eastmancolor. *Shot on location*: Gotland, London, Film Teknik Studios, Stockholm, September 14–November 13, 1970. *Swedish premiere*: August 30, 1971. *U.S. opening*: July 14, 1971, The Baronet, New York City. *U.S. distribution*: ABC/Cinerama.

Viskningar Och Rop (Cries and Whispers)
Cinematograph/Swedish Film Institute. *Director*: Ingmar Bergman. *Screenplay*: Ingmar Bergman. *Photography*: Sven Nykvist. *Art direction*: Marik Vos. *Music*: Chopin's Mazurka in A Minor, Op. 17, no. 4, played by Käbi Laretei; Bach's Sarabande No. 5 in D Minor, played by Pierre Fournier. *Sound*: Owe Svensson. *Mixing*: Sven Fahlén, Owe Svensson. *Costumes*: Greta Johansson. *Production manager*: Lars-Owe Carlberg. *Location manager*: Hans Rehnberg. *Editor*: Siv Lundgren. *Continuity*: Katherina Faragó.
Cast: Harriet Andersson (Agnes), Kari Sylwan (Anna), Ingrid Thulin (Karin), Liv Ullmann (Maria and the mother), Erland Josephson (the doctor), Henning Moritzen (Joakim, Maria's husband), Georg Årlin (Fredrik, Karin's husband), Anders Ek (the pastor), Linn Ullmann (Maria's daughter), Rosanna Mariano (Agnes as a child), Lena Bergman (Maria as a child), Monika Priede (Karin as a child), Greta Johansson and Karin Johansson (women dressing Agnes's body).
Running time: 90 minutes. Eastmancolor. *Shot on location*: Taxinge-Näsby estate, Mariefred, Sweden, September 7–October 29, 1971. *World premiere*: December 21, 1972, Cinema I Theater, New York City. *Swedish opening*: March 5, 1973. *U.S. distribution*: New World Films.

Scener Ur Ett Äktenskap (Scenes from a Marriage)
Cinematograph. *Director*: Ingmar Bergman. *Screenplay*: Ingmar Bergman. *Photography*: Sven Nykvist. *Art direction*: Björn Thulin. *Sound and mixing*: Owe Svensson. *Costumes*: Inger Pehrsson. *Production manager/Executive producer*: Lars-Owe Carlberg. *Editor*: Siv Lundgren. *Continuity*: Ulla Stattin.
Cast: Liv Ullmann (Marianne), Erland Josephson (Johan), Bibi Andersson (Katarina), Jan Malmsjö (Peter), Anita Wall (interviewer), Gunnel Lindblom (Eva), Barbro Hiort af Ornäs (Mrs. Jacobi), Bertil Nordström (Arne), Arne Carlsson.
Running time: TV version: 282 minutes; American film version: 155 minutes. Eastmancolor. *Shot on location*: Stockholm and Fårö, July 24–October 3, 1972. *Swedish TV premiere*: April 11, 1973. *U.S. opening*: September 21, 1974, Cinema I Theater, New York City. *U.S. distribution*: Donald Rugoff.

Trollflöjten (The Magic Flute)
Cinematograph/Sveriges TV 2. *Director*: Ingmar Bergman. *Screenplay*: Ingmar Bergman, based on the opera by Mozart, libretto by Schikaneder. *Photography*: Sven Nykvist. *Art direction*: Henny Noremark. *Music*: Mozart's *Die Zauberflöte*. *Sound*: Helmut Mühle (music), Peter Hennix (dialogue). *Mixing*: Bengt Törncrantz. *Orchestration*: Eric Ericsson and SR Symphony/Choir. *Choreography*: Donya Feyer. *Costumes*: Karin Erskine, Henny Noremark. *Production manager*: Måns Reuterswärd. *Location manager*: Ann-Marie Jartelius. *Assistant director*: Kerstin Forsmark. *Editor*: Siv Lundgren. *Continuity*: Katherina Faragó.
Cast: Josef Köstlinger (Tamino), Irma Urrila (Pamina), Håkan Hagegård (Papageno), Elizabeth Erikson (Papagena), Britt-Marie Aruhn (first lady), Kirsten Vaupel (second lady), Birgitta Smiding (third lady), Ulrik Cold (Sarastro), Birgit Nordin (Queen of the Night), Ragnar Ulfung (Monostatos), Erik Saedén (the speaker), Gösta Prüzelius (first priest), Ulf Johanson (second priest), Hans Johansson, Jerker Arvidson (two guards), Helene Friberg (girl in the audience).
Running time: 135 minutes. Eastmancolor. Recorded at the Cirkus Theatre, Stockholm, April 6, 1974, and filmed at Filmhuset, Stockholm, April 16–July 1974. *Swedish premiere*: October 4, 1975. *U.S. opening*: November 11, 1975, Coronet, New York City. *U.S. distribution*: Surrogate Co./Carmen F. Zollo.

Ansikte Mot Ansikte (Face to Face)
Cinematograph AB. *Director*: Ingmar Bergman. *Screenplay*: Ingmar Bergman. *Photography*: Sven Nykvist. *Art direction*: Anne Hagegård, Peter Krupenin. *Music*: Mozart's Fantasy in C Minor, K. 475, played by Käbi Laretei. *Sound*: Owe Svensson. *Costumes*: Maggie Strindberg. *Production manager*: Lars-Owe Carlberg. *Location manager*: Katherina Faragó. *Assistant director*: Peder Langenskiöld. *Editor*: Siv Lundgren. *Continuity*: Kerstin Eriksdotter.
Cast: Liv Ullmann (Dr. Jenny Isaksson),

Erland Josephson (Dr. Tomas Jacobi), Gunnar Björnstrand (grandpa), Aino Taube (grandma), Kari Sylwan (Maria), Sif Ruud (Mrs. Wankel, psychiatrist's wife), Sven Lindberg (Jenny's husband), Tore Segelcke (woman specter), Ulf Johanson (Dr. Wankel), Kristina Adolphson (nurse), Gösta Ekman (actor), Marianne Aminoff (Jenny's mother), Gösta Prüzelius (Jenny's father), Birger Malmsten, Göran Stangertz (rapists), Rebecca Pawlo, Lena Olin (boutique girls). *Running time*: English-language version: 136 minutes. Eastmancolor. *Shot on location*: SFI Studios, Filmhuset, Stockholm, April–June 30, 1975. *U.S. premiere*: April 5, 1976. *Swedish TV premiere*: Broadcast in four weekly parts on SR/TV 2, April 28–May 19, 1976. *U.S. distribution*: Dino De Laurentiis, Paramount.

Das Schlangenei (The Serpent's Egg; Swedish title, Örmens ägg)
Rialto Film (West Berlin)/Dino De Laurentiis Corp. (Los Angeles). *Director*: Ingmar Bergman. *Producer*: Dino De Laurentiis. *Executive producer*: Horst Wendlant. *Screenplay*: Ingmar Bergman. *Photography*: Sven Nykvist. *Additional photography*: Peter Rohe, Dieter Lohmann. *Art direction*: Erner Achmann, Herbert Strabel. *Music*: Rolf Wilhelm. *Sound*: Karsten Ullrich. *Production designer*: Rolf Zehetbauer. *Scenic artist*: Friedrich Thaler. *Choreography*: Heino Hallhuber. *Costumes*: Charlotte Flemming. *Assistant director*: Wieland Liebske. *Production manager*: Georg Föcking. *Production executive*: Harold Nebenzal. *Editor*: Jutta Hering, Petra von Oelffen.
Cast: Liv Ullmann (Manuela Rosenberg), David Carradine (Abel Rosenberg), Gert Fröbe (Inspector Bauer), Heinz Bennent (Hans Vergérus), James Whitmore (priest), Glynn Turman (Monroe), Georg Hartmann (Hollinger), Edith Heerdegen (Mrs. Holle), Kyra Mladeck (Miss Dorst), Fritz Strassner (Dr. Soltermann), Hans Quest (Dr. Silbermann), Wolfgang Weiser (civil servant), Paula Braend (Mrs. Hemse), Walter Schmidinger (Solomon), Lisi Mangold (Mikaela), Grischa Huber (Stella), Paul Bürks (cabaret comedian).
Running time: 119 minutes. Eastmancolor. *Shot on location*: Bavaria Studios, Munich, October–December 1976. *Swedish premiere*: October 28, 1977. *U.S. opening*: February 1978. *U.S. distribution*: Dino De Laurentiis.

Höstsonaten (Autumn Sonata)
Personafilm. *Director*: Ingmar Bergman. *Screenplay*: Ingmar Bergman. *Photography*: Sven Nykvist. *Art direction*: Anna Asp. *Music*: Excerpts from Chopin's Preludium No. 2 in A Minor, played by Käbi Laretei; Bach's Suite No. 4 in E Flat Major, performed by Claude Genetay; and Handel's Sonata in F Major, op. 1, performed by Frans Brüggen, Gustave Leonhardt, and Anne Bylsmå. *Sound and mixing*: Owe Svensson. *Costumes*: Inger Pehrsson. *Production manager*: Katherina Faragó. *Unit manager*: Hans Lindgren. *Assistant director*: Peder Langenskiöld. *Production assistant*: Lena Hansson. *Editor*: Sylvia Ingemarsson. *Continuity*: Kerstin Eriksdotter.

Cast: Ingrid Bergman (Charlotte), Liv Ullmann (Eva), Lena Nyman (Helena), Halvar Björk (Eva's husband), Georg Lökkeberg (Leonardo), Linn Ullmann (Eva as a child), Erland Josephson (Josef), Gunnar Björnstrand (Paul, Charlotte's agent), Marianne Aminoff (Charlotte's secretary), Mimi Pollak (piano teacher), Arne Bang-Hansen (Uncle Otto).
Running time: 93 minutes. Eastmancolor. *Shot on location*: Molde, Norway, and Norsk Film Studios, Oslo, September 20–October 30, 1977. *Swedish premiere*: October 8, 1978. *U.S. opening*: October 8, 1978, The Baronet, New York City. *U.S. distribution*: New World Films.

Fårö-Dokument 1979 (Fårö Document 79/ Fårö 79)
Cinematograph AB/SR/TV 2. *Director*: Ingmar Bergman. *Photography*: Arne Carlsson. *Music*: Svante Pettersson, Sigvard Huldt, Dag and Lena, Ingmar Nordströms, Strix Q, Rock de Luxe, Ola and the Janglers. *Sound*: Thomas Samuelsson, Lars Persson. *Sound recording*: Owe Svensson, Conrad Weyns. *Production manager*: Lars-Owe Carlberg. *Production assistants*: Peder Langenskiöld, Robert Herlitz, Siv Lundgren, Daniel Bergman. *Editor*: Sylvia Ingemarsson. *Narrator*: Ingmar Bergman.
Cast: Themselves—Richard Östman, Ulla Silvergren, Annelie Nyström, Per Broman, Irena Broman, Inge Nordström, Annika Liljegren, Arne Eriksson, Adolf Ekström, Victoria Ekström, Anton Ekström, Valter Broman, Erik Ekström, Ingrid Ekman, Per Nordberg, Gunilla Johannsson, Herbert Olsson, Rune Nilsson, Joe Nordenberg, Jan Nordberg.
Running time: 103 minutes. Color. *Shot on location*: Fårö. *Swedish premiere*: Swedish TV 2, December 24, 1979. *U.S. opening*: October 30, 1980, Coronet Theater, New York City.

Aus Dem Leben Der Marionetten (From the Life of the Marionettes)
Personafilm. *Director*: Ingmar Bergman. *Producers*: Horst Wendlandt, Ingmar Bergman. *Screenplay*: Ingmar Bergman. *Photography*: Sven Nykvist. *Art direction*: Herbert Strabel. *Music*: Rolf Wilhelm; song, "Touch Me, Take Me" (in English, singer uncredited). *Sound*: Peter Beil, Norbert Lill. *Sound rerecording*: Milan Bor. *Production design*: Rolf Zehetbauer. *Set decoration*: Rolf Zehetbauer. *Costumes*: Charlotte Flemming, Egon Strasser. *Production managers*: Paulette Hufnagel, Irmgard Kelpinski. *Unit managers*: Michael Juncker, Franz Achter. *Assistant directors*: Trudy von Trotha, Johannes Kaetzler. *Editor*: Petra von Oelffen (English-language version: Geri Ashur). *Continuity*: Helma Flacksmeire.
Cast: Robert Atzorn (Peter Egerman), Christine Buchegger (Katarina Egerman), Martin Benrath (Mogens Jensen), Rita Russek (Katarina), Lola Müthel (Peter's mother), Walter Schmidinger (Tim Mandelbaum), Heinz Bennent (psychiatrist), Ruth Olafs (nurse), Gaby Dohm (secretary), Karl Heintz Pelser (interrogator), Toni Berger (guard).

Running time: 104 minutes. Partly in Eastmancolor. *Shot on location*: Tobis Film Studios, Munich, beginning in October 1979 (completion date unavailable). *Premiere*: October 8, 1980, in Paris. Shown on West German TV November 3, 1980, and began West German commercial run three days later. *Swedish opening*: January 24, 1981. *U.S. opening*: November 7, 1981, Mann's Fine Arts, Los Angeles. *U.S. distribution*: Swank Motion Pictures.

Fanny Och Alexander (Fanny and Alexander)
Svensk Filmindustri/Sveriges TV 1/Personafilm (Munich)/Gaumont (Paris). *Director*: Ingmar Bergman. *Executive producer*: Jörn Donner. *Screenplay*: Ingmar Bergman. *Photography*: Sven Nykvist. *Art direction*: Anna Asp. *Stills*: Arne Carlsson. *Music*: Daniel Bell. *Sound*: Owe Svensson, Bo Persson. *Set decoration*: Kaj Larsen. *Wardrobe*: Marik Vos-Lundh. *Makeup*: Leif Quiström, Anna-Lena Melin, Barbro Holmberg-Haugen. *Production manager*: Katherina Faragó. *Assistant director*: Peter Schildt. *Unit manager*: Eva Ivarsson, Brita Werkmäster. *Editor*: Sylvia Ingemarsson. *Continuity*: Kerstin Eriksdotter.
Cast: Gunn Wållgren (Helena Ekdahl), Allan Edwall (Oscar Ekdahl), Ewa Fröling (Emilie Ekdahl), Bertil Guve (Alexander), Pernilla Allwin (Fanny), Börje Ahlstedt (Carl Ekdahl), Christina Schollin (Lydia Ekdahl), Jarl Kulle (Gustav Adolf Ekdahl), Mona Malm (Alma Ekdahl), Maria Granlund (Petra), Emelie Werkö (Jenny), Kristian Almgren (Putte), Angelica Wallgren (Eva), Majlis Granlund (Miss Vega), Svea Holst-Widén (Miss Ester), Siv Ericks (Alida), Inga Ålenius (Lisen), Kristina Adolphson (Siri), Eva von Hanno (Berta), Pernilla Wallgren (Maj), Käbi Laretei (Aunt Anna), Sonya Hedebratt (Aunt Emma), Erland Josephson (Isak Jacobi), Mats Bergman (Aron), Stina Ekblad (Ismael), Gunnar Björnstrand (Filip Landahl), Anna Bergman (Hanna Schwartz), Per Mattson (Mikael Bergman), Nils Brandt (Harald Morsing), Heinz Hopf (Tomas Graal), Åke Lagergren (Johan Armfeldt), Lickå Sjöman (Grete Holm), Sune Mangs (Mr. Salenius), Maud Hyttenberg (Mrs. Sinclair), Kerstin Karte (prompter), Tore Karte (administrative director), Marianne Karlbeck (Mrs. Palmgren), Gus Dahlström (set decorator), Gösta Prüzelius (Dr. Fürstenberg), Georg Årlin (colonel), Ernst Günther (dean of the university), Jan Malmsjö (Bishop Edvard Vergérus), Kerstin Tidelius (Henrietta Vergérus), Marianne Aminoff (Blenda Vergérus), Marrit Olsson (Malla Tander), Brita Billsten (Karna), Harriet Andersson (Justina).
Running time: 197 minutes. TV version: 300 minutes. Eastmancolor. *Shot on location*: Uppsala and Svensk Filmindustri Studios, Filmhuset, Stockholm, early September 1981–March 27, 1982. *Swedish premiere*: December 19, 1982. TV version: December 26, 1984 (first of four segments). *U.S. opening*: June 16, 1983, Cinema 1 and Cinema 2, New York City. *U.S. distribution*: Embassy Pictures.

Efter Repetitionem *(After the Rehearsal)*
Cinematograph (Stockholm), for Persona–film (Munich). *Director*: Ingmar Bergman. *Producer*: Jörn Donner. *Screenplay*: Ingmar Bergman. *Photography*: Sven Nykvist. *Production design*: Anna Asp. *Unit manager*: Eva Bergman. *Editor*: Sylvia Ingemarsson.
Cast: Erland Josephson (Henrik Vogler), Lena Olin (Anna Egerman), Ingrid Thulin (Rakel), Nadja Palmstierna-Weiss (Anna at age twelve), Bertil Guve (Henrik at age twelve).
Running time: 72 minutes. Color. Broadcast on Swedish Radio/TV Channel 1, April 9, 1984, after which shown theatrically abroad. *U.S. premiere*: Lincoln Plaza Cinema 1, New York City, June 21, 1984. *U.S. distribution*: Triumph Films, a Columbia/Gaumont company.

De två saliga *(The Blessed Ones)*
Swedish Television TV 2, in association with Channel 4. *Director*: Ingmar Bergman. *Screenplay*: Ulla Isaksson, from her own novel. *Photography*: Per Norén, Per-Olof Runa, Jan Wictorinus. *Sound*: Alvar Piehl. *Production managers*: Pia Ehrnvall, Katinka Faragó. *Costumes*: Inger Pehrsson. *Editor*: Sylvia Ingemarsson.
Cast: Harriet Andersson (Viveka), Per Myrberg (Sune), Christina Schollin (Anneka), Lasse Pöysti (Dr. Dettow), Irma Christensson (Mrs. Storm), Björn Gustafson (Olsson), Kristina Adolphson, Lars-Owe Carlberg.
Running time: 89 minutes. Color. Broadcast on Swedish Television/TV Channel 2, 1986. No theatrical release.

Index

Credits

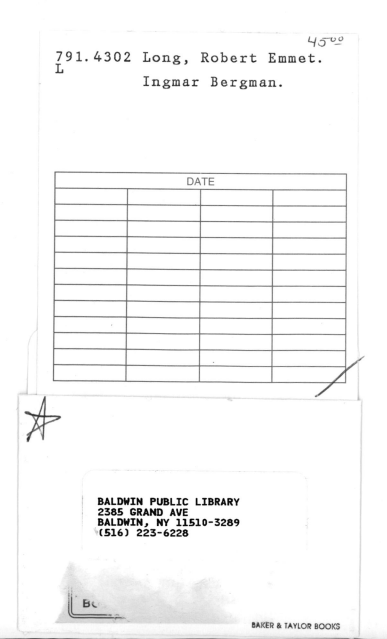